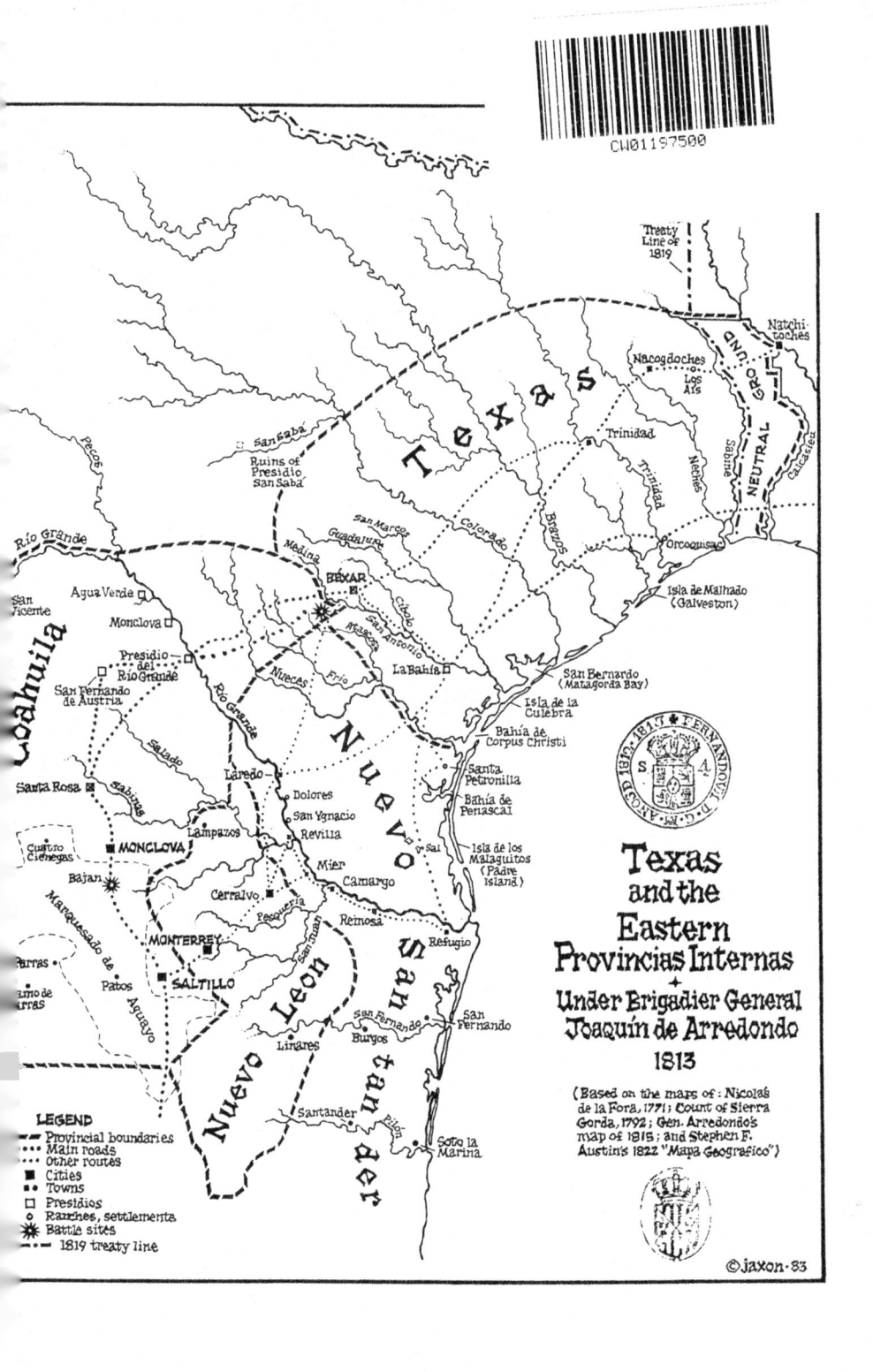

Texas and the Eastern Provincias Internas
Under Brigadier General Joaquín de Arredondo
1813

(Based on the maps of: Nicolás de la Fora, 1771; Count of Sierra Gorda, 1792; Gen. Arredondo's map of 1815; and Stephen F. Austin's 1822 "Mapa Geográfico")

LEGEND
- Provincial boundaries
- Main roads
- Other routes
- ■ Cities
- •• Towns
- ☐ Presidios
- ○ Ranches, settlements
- ✹ Battle sites
- — · — 1819 treaty line

© jaxon · 83

Author Ted Schwarz

FORGOTTEN BATTLEFIELD
OF THE
FIRST TEXAS REVOLUTION
The Battle of Medina, August 18, 1813

TED SCHWARZ

Robert H. Thonhoff, Editor and Annotator
Illustrated by
Jack Jackson

EAKIN PRESS ⚜ Fort Worth, Texas
www.EakinPress.com

Copyright © 1985
ByRobert H. Thonhoff
Published By Eakin Press
An Imprint of Wild Horse Media Group
P.O. Box 331779
Fort Worth, Texas 76163
1-817-344-7036
www.EakinPress.com
ALL RIGHTS RESERVED
1 2 3 4 5 6 7 8 9
ISBN-10: 1-94013-003-4
ISBN-13: 978-1-940130-99-6

Library of Congress Cataloging-in-Publication Data

Schwarz, Ted, 1911–1977.
  Forgotten Battlefield of the First Texas Revolution.

  Bibliography: p.
  Includes index.
  1. Gutierrez–Magee Expedition, 1812–1813. 2. Texas — History — 1810–1821. I. Thonhoff, Robert H., 1929–. II. Title.
F389.S39   1985   976.4′02   85–15954
ISBN 0–89015–519–4

Dedicated to the memory
of the
Unknown Soldiers
who died in
la batalla del encinal de Medina
18 de Agosto de 1813

*A foggy mist had covered all
the land; and underneath their
feet, all scattered, lay dead
skulls and bones of men
whose life had gone astray.*
— Edmund Spenser

Contents

Picture of Ted Schwarz (1911–1977)	frontispiece
Editor's Foreword	vii
Author's Preface	xi
Acknowledgments	xv
PART ONE The Gutiérrez–Magee Expedition: American-Provoked Filibuster	
1. The Prologue	3
2. Revolution Sweeps Texas	17
PART TWO The First Republic of Texas	
3. Texas an Independent State	37
4. Spain Strikes Back	45
5. Shaler Switches Commanders	57
PART THREE Defeat in *El Encinal De Medina*	
6. Arredondo Probes for Advantage	69
7. Toledo Moves to Set a Trap	77
8. Discovery, Pursuit, Mutiny	83
9. Disaster in the *Encinal*	97
10. Swift Vengeance	107
PART FOUR Unknown, Unhonored, Unsung	
11. Epilogue	119
12. Battleground Revisited	133
Editor's Postscript	145
Illustrations	155
Endnotes	169
Bibliography	183
Index	193

Illustrations

Author Ted Schwarz (1911–1977)   Frontispiece
MAPS
Artist's Map of the Battle Area   155
General Austin's Map of 1840   156
General Highway Map, Atascosa County, Texas, 1964   157
United States Department of the Interior Geological
    Survey Map, Poteet Quadrangle, 1968   158
USDA-ASCS Aerial Photograph of the
    Battlefield Area   159
General Land Office Map of Atascosa County,
    circa 1896   160
PHOTOGRAPHS
Robert H. Thonhoff and Jerome Korus standing in the
    rut of the *camino que cortaba*   161
Panorama of the cleared land portion of the battlefield
    site on the James Engleman Farm   161
Battle of the Medina Marker at the Intersection of US
    281 and FM 2537 near Losoya, Texas   162
Crypt site at El Carmen Church   163
Camino Real Marker on Old Pleasanton Road between
    Lehr and Thelma in southern Bexar County   164
Camino Real Marker on Old Pleasanton Road at
    Bexar–Atascosa County Line   164
Camino Real Marker on Old Pleasanton Road near
    entrance to Maurice Weynand farm in northern
    Atascosa County   165
Copy of Arredondo's Report *Número 1*   166
Copy of Arredondo's Report *Número 2*   167
¿Quien Sabe? Tree   168

Foreword by the Editor and Annotator

Ted Schwarz was my good friend and history colleague. He even came by to visit me at my home in Fashing, Texas — and not many people have even heard of, much less seen, Fashing, Texas. This was back in the early 1970s, and we had a number of occasions after that time to visit and talk about the so-called "Battle of Medina." We both agreed that this epochal battle occurred in the northern part of Atascosa County and *not* on the Medina River in Bexar County as is generally acknowledged. (Fashing, by the way, is in eastern Atascosa County.)

Ted and I continued to see each other at the annual meetings of the Texas State Historical Association until 1977. In the meantime, he had taken a special interest in my book with Robert S. Weddle, *Drama & Conflict: The Texas Saga of 1776* (Madrona Press, 1976). He especially liked its information on the Rancho del Atascoso, its descriptions of *el camino real* and the Laredo Road, and its references to the Pastias Indians, who were Atascosa County's first cowboys. I missed seeing Ted and his dear wife, Illene, for the next couple years. At the 1980 annual meeting I was saddened to learn that Ted had died on March 17, 1977, and that Illene had died exactly one year later. Ted had finished his manuscript on *Forgotten Battlefield,* but he did not get to live to see it published.

Through our connections with the Texas State Historical Association, Ted's stepson, Captain Ed L. Kimbrell, then living in Seattle, Washington, learned of me, my friendship with Ted, my interest in his book, and my knowledge of its subject. Captain Ed, a retired Alaskan ship captain, contacted me and asked if I would consider guiding Ted's manuscript to publication. After a thorough study of the manuscript and research materials, and after many on-site inspections of the battlefield area, myself armed with maps and diary accounts that Ted didn't have, I agreed to edit the work and to seek a publisher. Happily, Ed Eakin of Eakin Press consented to publish the book.

The forthcoming Texas Sesquicentennial that will be observed in 1985–1986 seems like an appropriate time for the publication of *Forgotten Battlefield of the First Texas Revolution*. The Medina battle of 1813 served as a prelude for the military operations of the 1835–1836 period. Many of the officers and soldiers on both sides, including Santa Anna, received an important part of their training on the Medina Battleground.

It has been a pleasure and an honor to edit this work. I thank Captain Ed Kimbrell for entrusting the manuscript and research materials of Ted Schwarz to me. I hope that the publication of this work will give Ted the recognition he deserves as the historian who rescued the battlefield of *la batalla del encinal de Medina, 18 de Agosto de 1813,* from oblivion.

Once having delved into Ted's manuscript, I soon discerned the precarious position of the *vecinos* (residents) of Texas, whom I shall call *Tejanos* in this book, during the turbulent times of the 1810s. Many of them descended from the founding families of Texas, which had been settled as a Spanish province for nearly one hundred years. The *Tejanos* were forced to take a side, Republican or Royalist, and they suffered greatly for whichever choice they made. One should empathize with them and not be quick or harsh in any kind of judgment.

Probably the toughest problem I encountered in the editing process was that of proper identification of the participants in the story told by the book. The over-used and ofttimes misused terms of "Mexican" or "Anglo-American" simply do not categorically fit all the people involved. Like Americans of today, they came from a variety of ancestral backgrounds. Therefore I have used the terms "Mexican" and "Anglo-American" as sparingly as possible, opting instead for the words "royalists," "republicans," "North Americans," and "Tejanos," I hope that the reader will try to understand me on this point.

I am indebted to many people who have helped me in the search of the battlefield. Outstanding in this regard is Jerome Korus, who has spent many a weekend with me scouting the *camino que cortaba* and searching for battlefield artifacts. I am grateful, also, to Jerome's dear wife, Mary, who has offered me the hospitality of her home many, many times during my historical sojourns in northern Atascosa County. Thanks, also, are extended to Jerome's daughter, Sandra, and her fiancé, Marvin Wiatrek, for their help.

I am greatly indebted to the landowners of the battlefield area who have allowed me access to their property in my search for evidence of the battlefield. For this favor, I say *muchas gracias* not only to Jerome Korus but also to Dr. George B. Jaggy, James E. Engleman, Mrs. Gertrude Korus, H. T. Sauter, Calvin Bruce, Arthur Weynand, Maurice Weynand, Floyd Kindla, Alois Rakowitz, Alfred Sotelo, and Curtis Mahula.

To Miss Sadie Bruce, longtime resident of the area, I give special thanks for pointing out the track of the Laredo Road that ran within a stone's throw from her home. This proved to be the clue that solved the road puzzle of the area. Special thanks, also, go to my friend Roger Williams of Poteet, Texas. Roger was raised near the battlefield area, and he helped me greatly in my search for the tracks of the Lower Presidio Road and for the watering spots known to him as Haiduk Pond and Horton's Pond, all of which proved to be invaluable to me in piecing the road puzzle together.

I owe very special thanks to several *amigos mios* who have stuck by me weekend after weekend, combing the battlefield area with their sophisticated metal-detecting equipment in search of battlefield artifacts. These gentlemen were George T. Williams, David O. Pearson, Robert M. Benavides, and Clarence C. Belzung, all CPS personnel in San Antonio. Although our search for cannonballs and musketballs has been thus far disappointing in its results, we are far from discouraged. We all plan to continue our probe for "hard evidence" of the battlefield even after this book is published and to report our findings in subsequent printings.

Greatly appreciated are Edwin Espey, Jr., his son Justin, and his employee Dan Rodriguez, who donated a day of their time and equipment to help me search for the mass burial site of about seven hundred men killed in the Medina Battle. We didn't find their bones that day, but we plan to continue the search.

Others who have helped me search for battlefield artifacts and to whom I owe thanks include A. H. (Petie) Hierholzer, Ernie Sauceda, Stephen Spencer, Elo Henke, Joe Lisk, Bill Yates, Frank Haeglin, Raymond Falke, J. F. Andrews, and Victor Gaenzel, Sr.

To Jack Jackson I wish to extend special thanks not only for the fine job in illustrating this book but also for furnishing me with information from his research on his own manuscript for *Los Mesteños* plus other materials I needed from the archives in Austin.

Muchas gracias go to Bexar County Clerk Robert D. Green and to Bexar County Archivist John O. Leal for all their assistance in providing me with maps, survey records, and Bexar Archives materials that relate to the battlefield site.

Muchas gracias, also, go to Henry Guerra, known to many South Texans as *la voz de San Antonio* ("the Voice of San Antonio"), for his interest in this writing project and for his special telephone call to tell me about the José María Sánchez diary account of 1828, which further corroborated my findings.

I wish, also, to acknowledge the friendly help accorded to me by Sharon Crutchfield and Bernice Strong of the DRT Alamo Library, by Tom Shelton of the Institute of Texan Cultures Library, and by Bill Richter and Ralph Elder of The University of Texas Archives.

To Frank Repka, of Pleasanton, Texas, I am indebted not only for his interest, help, and encouragement in this writing task but also for the use of his Center Pharmacy in Pleasanton as headquarters central for my many on-site visits to the battlefield in northern Atascosa County.

I am deeply grateful to my publisher, Ed Eakin, for all the patience, trust, and confidence he has accorded me in my writing efforts. Many thanks, also, are extended to Eakin Publications editor Shirley Ratisseau for her good advice, epigraph, the line editing, and helpful suggestions in readying this book for publication.

Finally, much love and appreciation are bestowed upon my dear wife, Victoria Balser Thonhoff, for the support and encouragement she has given me in all my historical endeavors these past thirty-four years.

ROBERT H. THONHOFF

Fashing, Texas
June 1, 1985

Author's Preface

Less than three decades after George Washington had turned the British world upside down at Yorktown, the brash young nation whose independence he had thus ensured was not only once again engaged in war with England, but was actively promoting a wanton filibuster into Spanish dominion in the Southwest. That invasion ended in one of the most disastrous battles ever fought in the country. In marking the eighty-seventh anniversary of that fight, an article in the August 19, 1900, edition of *The Galveston Daily News* remarked that,

> It was the bloodiest battle ever fought in Texas, but ninety Americans escaping death, ... More lives were lost than in all the battles and sieges of the war of the second republic [of Texas] on both sides put together.

This grim encounter, which eclipsed the Alamo, Goliad, and San Jacinto together in its death toll, was the battle of *el encinal de Medina,* fought August 18, 1813, some ten to twelve miles below the Medina River in Southwest Texas. With the most gruesome finality it halted and destroyed the American filibustering expedition which had crossed into Texas from Louisiana a year earlier and had swept the Spanish King's troops completely out of the Province of Texas. The badly whipped sons of the revolutionaries who had founded the United States fled back to their homeland, leaving the bones of hundreds of their comrades to bleach on the sands of the *encinal.* In Texas, liberty awaited yet the coming of another generation of Americans.

The so-called battle of Medina is little remembered, its battleground is forgotten, yet the outcome of that grisly fight influenced the destinies of no less than five sovereign nations.

It decisively delayed for eight more years Mexico's own bid for independence from the confused and disintegrating Spanish empire. It wiped out Texas's first independent, republican government which for a single hot summer held absolute sway over the vast leagues from the Rio Grande to the Louisiana border. It also brought to an abrupt end the clandestine efforts of James Monroe to annex Texas to the United States, and it rebuffed Napoleonic agents who had busily intrigued to stir up trouble between Spain and the United States. Of the European powers with North American interests or ambitions, only England escaped its impact; she was busy fighting the United States in the War of 1812.

No historical event of the Southwest has suffered more distortion of fact, more fabrication of incident from the whole cloth, nor more promotion of emotional bias than has the Battle of Medina. Private narrators and renowned historians alike have contributed generously to this *mélange* of misinformation, the latter compounding each other's errors to the point where the most improbable alleged occurrences have found their way into history books as accepted facts. The battle has been served little better by the modern writers. Those who have given it their attention have either dismissed the fight with a few lines while concentrating on other aspects of the Gutiérrez–Magee Expedition or, too often, their research has been so superficial that the published results have been a hodgepodge of fact, halftruth, misinformation, and error.

For a half century the author has nurtured a keen interest in those events relating to the First Republican State of Texas and, from time to time, has searched for the Medina battlefield. In recent years he has examined in depth source documents ranging from originals in the National Archives in Washington to collections in the Bancroft Library in Berkeley, as well as archival transcripts from Spain and Mexico. In this work he will attempt to set history aright.

So that the reader may be briefed concerning the impact of Mexican and Texan independence movements on early nineteenth century American history, and to provide him with a background of the events leading up to the Medina fight, the early chapters will summarize the advance of the Gutiérrez–Magee filibustering expedition into Spanish Texas and will trace the story of its chief protagonist, José Bernardo Gutiérrez de Lara. The Medina engagement and the events immediately following take up most of the second half of the work, with the concluding chapters bringing into focus data that were uncovered concerning the people involved and that reveal the location of the lost battle site.

TED SCHWARZ

Coupeville, Washington
August 18, 1976

Author's Acknowledgments

For a book that was almost a half century in gestation, it becomes difficult to recall the many, many wonderful people who have lent their encouragement and who have contributed bits and pieces to the final whole. The seed probably was planted by Mrs. Annie McDonald, my first teacher who made Texas history so interesting as she taught it to older students from Mrs. Pennybacker's red-backed text — in the one-room Dobrowolski board-and-batten schoolhouse — that I assimilated a lifetime interest in the subject. My mother was an inveterate reader and encouraged me in the "vice." My father made up for his lack of much formal schooling with an ardent interest in people and excursions with him always exposed me to interesting stories told by interesting people, many of them old-timers. After living the first six years of my life on the old Erasmo Seguin rancho in Karnes County, my parents had the providential sagacity to move to Atascosa County and settle on a farm in a section rich with Indian and colonial lore. The old Spanish roads ran nearby and at the back of our place, a hill yielded relics by the handful. My horse, old Fanny, and I explored the surrounding countryside at every opportunity, questioning the "signs" that we found and wondering, always wondering about the nature of the people who had passed there.

In our 1920 Chevrolet touring car, our family made frequent trips to San Antonio, negotiating the deep sands through the *encinal* and eagerly looking for the first pavement which then began at the bat tower at Mitchell Lake. Even then the mysterious post oak thicket held a fascination, and , perhaps subconsciously, I looked for the spirits of the patriots who had fallen in the battle of Medina. Somehow, I always knew that the battleground was in the woods and not at the Medina River.

The passage of time has dimmed memories of stories heard in my earlier years and the names of many of the narrators now escape me. Among those remembered are Uncle Bob Lauderdale, Trail Driver, who claimed he recalled men who had fought in the battle; Mrs. Viola Gibson, Jourdanton druggist and historian; Judge James Waltom, who tramped the fields with me to point out "signs" of earlier occupation; publisher Nelson Potter of the *Atascosa Monitor*, who published several of my pieces in the early thirties; John Becker, Confederate veteran; a grandson of José Antonio Navarro; and several descendants of Mexican and Spanish families who had settled in the area long before. The consensus was always that the so-called Medina battle took place in Atascosa County and NOT on the Medina River.

Came the Texas Centennial in 1936, promoting a veritable orgy of commemorative observances and placing of monuments, and Bexar County claimed for the Medina River the granite slab provided by the State to mark the battle of Medina. Shortly thereafter, the pursuit of several careers (and two wars) removed me from the State for almost thirty years.

When I got back to the project, the old-timers had passed on, farms had given way to cattle ranches (completing the circle that had begun with the Spanish and Mexican pioneers), and Pleasanton was billing itself as "Birthplace of the Cowboy." However, with shortened hindsight, it traced the birthdate to the cattle drives of the 1870s instead of to the *ranchos* of the mid-eighteenth century! Locating the battleground then became a task of tedious research and of dogging library people from Texas to California, probing and prying out bits of information which might help pinpoint the site. In the early stages, Mrs. Raymond Ullman of the Clayton Memorial Library and Mrs. Marion M. Branon of the Texas Room, both of the Houston Library system, were of inestimable help. Later, personnel of the Gates Memorial Library, Port Arthur, The University of Texas El Paso Library Microfilm Room, the Los Angeles Public Library History Room, and the great Bancroft Library in Berkeley moved the project forward with their generous help. Lizbeth Smith of St. Mary's University Academic Library, San Antonio, contributed photocopies of Spanish documents which were most useful since access to the originals cleared up questions raised by the published translations. The Reverend Maynard Geiger, Archivist of the Santa Barbara Mission Archive-Library (and custodian of 70,000 pages of original documents, not one of which proved pertinent to Medina) was a prince in pointing me to relevant printed materials on his shelves. Doctor Chester V. Kielman, Librarian-Archivist, Barker Texas History Center, opened many useful doors including access to a rare file of *The Western Stock Journal,* published in Pleasanton in the seventies. Bob Tissing was most helpful in finding transcripts of original Spanish documents in The University of Texas Archives, while Doctor Nettie Lee Benson, custodian of the Latin American Collection, gave much of her time to locating data concerning Gutiérrez and to taking rubbings of the Seal of the first State of Texas. La Nell Aston of the General Land Office cheerfully handled my many requests for original grants and early maps from which to ascertain the meanderings of the early roads.

Anne Fox, Anthropologist at the Witte Memorial Museum, San Antonio, contributed valuable assistance and encouragement. It is she who has custody of the bones which I believe to be those of Colonel Menchaca. Former State Representative Jake Johnson spent several days)when he should have been campaigning) with me in the Losoya area seeking out the old river crossing, talking to local residents, and researching the files of El Carmen Church. In the later effort, the assistance of the pastor, the Reverend Charles Welter, C. M., and of the Reverend William Glynn, was a boon. For their permission, plus that of the Most Reverend Francis J. Furey, Archbishop of San Antonio, to conduct an archeological exploration of the site where remains of the Medina dead are supposed to have been buried, I am deeply grateful. The project awaits funding and the availability of qualified personnel to conduct the dig.

Francis N. Knight, District Soil Conservationist, Pleasanton, was most helpful in providing aerial photographs and soil maps of the area (and in interpreting them for me). Dr. George B. Jaggy, Jr., of Leming, who grew up within rifle shot of the battle site and who owns much land in the area, rendered invaluable assistance by loaning me his four-wheel drive pickup to prowl the blackjacks. Mr. Arthur Fassnidge, who went along to unlock the gates and to keep me from getting lost, made the venture doubly enjoyable. Dr. Jaggy's relative, Ms. Sadie Mae Bruce, who lives near the old Laredo Road, and Jerome Korus, across whose fields it ran, were not only great company but contributed much to locating where the old road once ran. Robert H. Thonhoff, history buff and teacher at Fashing, Texas, and an authority on the old fords and trails, did me the honor of brainstorming the Medina battle with his history class. Lobo Wolfe, professional dowser of La Puente, California, did his thing with aerial photographs of the area with startling, if inconclusive, results.

Of the Atascosans, perhaps Judge Joye H. Troell and his vivacious Ruth, made the greatest contribution to the completion of this book. Not only did Mrs. Schwarz and I park our motor home in their backyard in Pleasanton for days on end, but at every opportunity he joined me in field trips and in critical discussions of local history. He is the owner of several volumes of Bexar County Deed and Probate transcripts pertaining to Atascosa County before it was organized and copied seventy years ago, which he generously made available. Judge Troell also read the first draft of the manuscript and made many valuable suggestions.

Special acknowledgement must be made to Robert S. Weddle who made cogent and apt suggestions that were invaluable in shaping the quality and flavor of the book.

To all these my gratitude.

TED SCHWARZ

PART ONE

The Gutiérrez–Magee Expedition American Provoked Filibuster

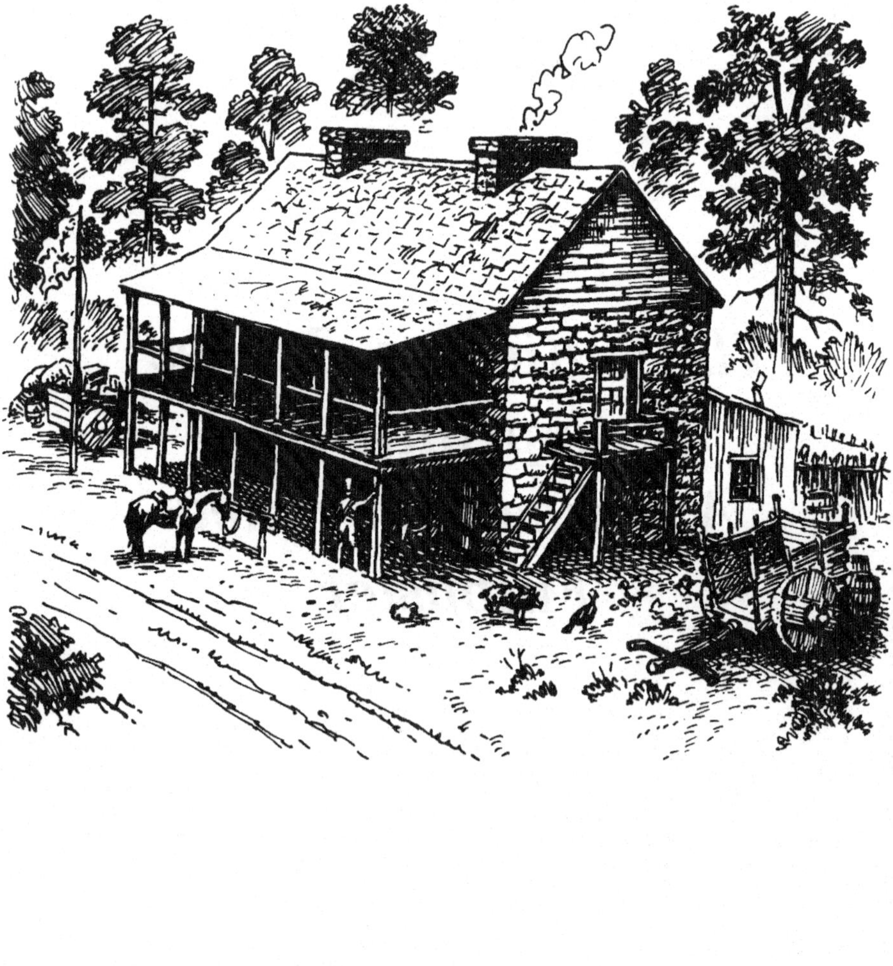

1 *The Prologue*

THE FEISTY LITTLE SPANISH CORPORAL DID not intend to be intimidated by the insolent deserter who now stood before him, nor did his face betray the forboding he felt. In the service of his king since he had been barely an adolescent, *Cabo* Ermenegildo Guillén had not gained his present responsible rank — and command of a detachment of men guarding the ford called *paso de las ormigas* — by being a quitter. Across the river this day in early June 1812, lay the Neutral Ground, and because somewhere in its semitropical fastness an invasion army was forming, he had been sent out from the Spanish outpost of Nacogdoches by Don Cristóbal Domínguez, the commandant, to guard the river crossing on the road that led from the Texas *pueblo* of Nacogdoches, to the town of Natchitoches, in Louisiana.

Until a few years before, all of Louisiana had owed allegiance to the Spanish king, and the Sabine had been an unimportant watercourse in the vastness of his realm. Then, due to the vagaries of European politics, Louisiana was suddenly American, and the *Rio de las Sabinas* was Spain's frontier, separated from the distrusted *norte americanos* by only a few leagues of Neutral Ground — a no man's land which had arbitrarily been agreed upon in 1806 by the Spanish commander, Simón Herrera, and the American general, James Wilkinson. Corporal Guillén remembered seeing then many mules, loaded with silver, they said, dispatched from San Fernando de Béxar by acting Governor Antonio Cordero, arriving in Nacogdoches and being sent on — to Wilkinson — he was told.

Ermenegildo did not understand these things. Nor did he understand the trouble they had had in Béxar earlier in the year — trouble that had spread to Nacogdoches, and led to the brief imprisonment there of Don Cristóbal and the other royalist officers. *La voz general,* rumor, brought word from Béxar soon thereafter that a highly respected old Indian fighter, Captain José Félix Menchaca, a native of that place, had somehow been involved in the business there and, to save his head, had fled south across the *Río Grande* to Revilla in the province of Nuevo Santander.

Official word then came from the governor to Domínguez, now again in command at Nacogdoches, that Captain Menchaca was guiding an insurgent leader named Gutiérrez de Lara across the wilds of Texas to the United States, and *Cabo* Guillén himself had been on several forays seeking to capture them, but without success. Now, according to the swaggering Mexican turncoat standing before him, Captain Menchaca was warning Guillén that he was returning with sufficient troops to force a passage of the river at the point the corporal's detachment was guarding. An old veteran of many campaigns for his king, Menchaca may have thought to spare the small Spanish outpost from his adventurous followers, or, if contemporary American accounts may be believed, there may have been an ulterior purpose of which Guillén seemed not to have been apprised. Since he was a *gachupín,* wearer of spurs, Ermenegildo Guillén's response was haughtily Spanish [*lo que es propio de un buen Español*]. He sent word ahead to Menchaca that none would pass that way unless they first dug out Guillén and all his men. He also sent a courier racing back to Domínguez with the threatening news, saying that if the captain attempted to cross the river, he was determined to make the greatest possible resistance, and, in case the enemy's forces were so superior that he could not resist them, he would withdraw while continuing the heaviest fire possible until he met up with reinforcements sent out from Nacogdoches.[1]

The veil of history then obscures the events that followed, to which we shall return shortly after examining the broader canvas on which Corporal Guillén's stand was but a cautious brush stroke in what would prove to be the first Anglo-American thrust by arms into the Spanish borderlands, a quest that once launched would not end until their manifest destiny had planted their flag on the shores of the Pacific.

In the bicentennial years, of 1976–1983, when our preoccupation was with Concord and Paul Revere, with Boston and John Adams, and with Philadelphia and the Declaration of Independence, we tended to forget that the American Revolution was not confined to the thirteen English colonies, as Herbert E. Bolton once pointed out, nor did it end in 1783, when Washington succeeded in freeing the eastern third of the United States from British rule. After having wrested Louisiana from Spain by the secret treaty of San Ildefonso, Napoleon sold the middle third of the Nation to Jefferson in 1803, but "all the rest of America from Cape Horn to Oregon was freed by revolution in the years between 1810 and 1826. . . . Hidalgo, Morelos, and Iturbide played the most conspicious parts in the movements which liberated from Spain all the country between Panamá on the south and Oregon on the north." Notwithstanding the misadventure in 1813, it would be Mexican patriots who soon separated the southwestern third of the United States from European domination.[2]

It should be remembered that from 1808 to 1815, Spain had been eclipsed by the gigantic policy of Napoleon. Although Spain still held possession of East Florida, and claimed West Florida and Texas, the United States likewise claimed the two latter provinces by virtue of the purchase of the Louisiana Territory. The entire southwestern United States was then an extension of the *provincias internas del norte* of New Spain, governed by bureaucrats headquartered hundreds of leagues in the interior. West Florida had declared its independence and was annexed by President Madison in October 1810. Napoleon's inability to support the Spanish cause beyond the Iberian peninsula left New Spain — and particularly Mexico — the seedbed of revolutionary conflict.

As a borderland whose early history was inextricably meshed into that of Mexico on the one hand and with that of Greater Louisiana on the other, Texas was inevitably involved in the revolutionary movements begun in Mexico. This was begun by the priest Miguél Hidalgo y Costilla when he summoned his first following of insurgents by ringing one of the bells of his parish church in the early hours of September 16, 1810.[3] In Washington City, New Orleans, and Natchitoches, President James Madison and Secretary of State James Monroe and their agents warmly welcomed and adroitly encouraged the spread of revolution in Spanish America. In the Neutral Ground which separated the English and Hispanic cultures, restless border men eagerly grasped the opportunity for adventure and profit in the guise of promoting the ambitions of their government.

This then was the explosive background for the not-so-clandestine efforts of both Napoleonic and American agents to give direction to the revolutionary struggle as it spread from central Mexico to the Louisiana border. It was the setting for the short-lived Casas uprising in San Fernando de Béxar, for the betrayal of the resolute Hidalgo at the Wells of Baján and his subsequent execution in Chihuahua, and for the Gutiérrez–Magee filibustering expedition from its organization in the Neutral Ground in the summer of 1812 to its crushing defeat by royalist forces in *el encinal de Medina* in August 1813.

Of the three men who captained that expedition — Gutiérrez de Lara, Magee, and Álvarez de Toledo, respectively Mexican, Bostonian, and Cuban — José Bernardo Gutiérrez de Lara dreamed the most improbable dream and trudged the longest road to bring almost to fruition the revolutionary doctrines he had embraced as a young man. A wealthy man in his mid-thirties, who for some unexplained reason followed the trade of blacksmith, Bernardo Gutiérrez owned two large estates, an important commercial house, and other properties in and near Revilla, one of the five Rio Grande *villas* of Nuevo Santander established in 1750 by José de Escandón. Renamed Guerrero, Revilla was inundated by the rising waters of the lake created by the completion of Falcon Dam in 1954. Gutiérrez is said to have had a cultivated mind, much sagacity and energy, and considerable refinement, attributes not usually expected of a *vecino* of a dusty frontier village. His older brother was a priest, and it is likely that among his family antecedents there may have been other clerics, thus accounting for the family's economic and cultural prominence.[4]

Bernardo's insurgency led him into the presence of the revolutionary Hidalgo and his chieftains, Ignacio Allende and Mariano Jiménez, both ex-officers of the king. After the defeat of Hidalgo's poorly disciplined and scantily equipped army in January 1811, by Major General Félix María Calleja, the insurgents had retreated to Zacatecas, where Hidalgo was stripped of command and Allende took over. Meanwhile, Jiménez pushed northward and, with help from the Gutiérrez de Lara brothers, achieved revolution in the provinces of Nuevo Santander, Coahuila, and Nuevo Leon. Allende then moved his forces up to Saltillo to join him. It was here that Bernardo Gutiérrez appeared before the military council, uninvited, in March 1811, and offered "my services, my hacienda, my life" to the faltering revolutionary cause. The council appointed him lieutenant colonel and ordered him to return to Nuevo Santander to recruit and organize troops. Before he left, however, word came from San Fernando de Béxar that the Casas government had been overturned and that revolutionary envoys en route to the United States were prisoners. Gutiérrez then offered to fulfill the envoys' commission, and the title of ambassador was conferred on him, also.[5]

Two months earlier, on January 22, 1811, a retired army captain, Juan Bautista de las Casas, with the aid of presidial troops, had engineered a *coup d'état* in San Fernando de Béxar. The governor, Manuel María de Salcedo, and the commander of auxiliary troops, Lieutenant Colonel Simón de Herrera, who was also the governor of Nuevo Leon, were imprisoned and sent in chains to Coahuila. Casas placed himself at the head of the government, proclaimed for Hidalgo, and notified Jiménez of his actions. Jiménez sent Casas his commission as governor of Texas, but Casas soon alienated many of his followers with a high-handed and disorderly administration. The opposition to him was deviously wielded into a counterrevolution some six weeks later by the Subdeacon Juan Manuel Sambrano, who restored the royalist regime. In the course of events, the two envoys from the Mexican revolutionists en route to the United States, and a large shipment of silver specie consigned to Casas, were captured by Sambrano. Casas was sent to Monclova, where he was tried for treason and executed. His head was returned in a box to Béxar where it was displayed on a pole in the middle of the *Plaza de las Armas*.[6]

Although Americans were beginning to refer to the capital of Spanish Texas as "San Antonio" by this time, the Spanish name of *Villa de San Fernando de Béxar,* or the shortened form "Béxar," will be used in this work. By 1810, the *Presidio de San Antonio de Béxar,* on present-day Military Plaza, had ceased to exist as a geographical entity, and the troops were then housed in the new *quartel* under construction in *La Villita* and in the compound of the secularized mission of *San Antonio de Valero,* referred to even then as the "Alamo barracks." Both were across the river from the city.[7]

With a party of about a dozen men, equipped at his own expense, and guided by Captain José Menchaca, Bernardo Gutiérrez de Lara's mission carried him across Texas and into the Bayou Pierre district beyond the Sabine. Governor Antonio Cordero of Coahuila had sent word to Governor Salcedo in Béxar that Gutiérrez and Menchaca were in Texas. Salcedo sent out patrolling parties, but it was not until the little band was beyond the Sabine that the royalists came up with them. Gutiérrez had found food and lodging for his party in the home of a Frenchman in Bayou Pierre, when Spanish troops, commanded by a Lieutenant Miguél of Nacogdoches, attacked them during the night of September 17. All but two members of the group escaped into the woods, but Gutiérrez lost his credentials and 300 *pesos.* James Gaines was to report later that Gutiérrez escaped with only his drawers and shirt. A deserter from the barracks in Béxar, also hiding in Bayou Pierre, fled to Natchitoches with the news that the Spanish soldiers were scouring the piney woods for Gutiérrez.[8] Rescued by a band of fifteen volunteers from Natchitoches, the fugitives were taken to that American outpost. There is little doubt but that the rescuers had been dispatched by Dr. John Sibley, United States Indian Agent at that place, who, along with Governor Claiborne of Louisiana, was keenly concerned that the revolution in the Spanish provinces assume a "proper direction." Sibley had been in the area since 1802, and he became an authority on Indians of the Red River region and Spanish Texas. From 1805 to 1814 he was Indian Agent for the Orleans Territory, and was successful in keeping the Indians as far as Matagorda Bay friendly to the United States, a fact that aroused Spanish authorities against him. He was an untiring letter writer, both to periodicals and to public officials, including the President.[9]

By mid-October Bernardo Gutiérrez and José Menchaca had parted, Captain Menchaca to return to Béxar to overturn the government of the Spaniards and, with the new government established, to send Gutiérrez new credentials, letters of credit, and funds for his mission. Although supported by several hundred American volunteers assembled in the Neutral Ground who were described as "the finest riflemen of our Country ... in high spirits flushed with the love of liberty & panting for glory," somehow Menchaca abandoned the expedition and joined the royalists. Whether it was Corporal Guillén's spunky opposition at *paso de las ormigas* that unnerved him or whether he was bribed (as Gaines wrote in 1835), we do not know. Gaines erroneously reported that when Captain Menchaca* returned to Béxar, he was executed by Governor Salcedo and his head was "exhibited publicly on the gate posts." [10] The embarrassed Americans backtracked to Natchitoches to await another day for their much visioned undertaking. Some months later, William Shaler wrote to James Monroe from Natchitoches that it was the general opinion in that place that the banditti gathered under the leadership of Menchaca would have succeeded in establishing a republic in Texas if they had not been deserted by Menchaca.[11]

Gutiérrez traveled eastward with an interpreter, a change of mounts for each, and a pack mule. He was entertained and encouraged along the way by important personages in Nashville and Knoxville. At Nashville, the interpreter, a boy, refused to accompany him any further than General Overton's place. The General, a scarred hero of the American Revolution, rode three leagues with Gutiérrez in order to put him on the right road. Gutiérrez reached Washington City on December 11.[12]

He was received "with the greatest cordiality" by Secretary of War Eustis and by John Graham, Chief Clerk of the State Department. Graham took Gutiérrez under his wing. Besides being an almost daily visitor at the State Department, Bernardo Gutiérrez had interviews with the British, Russian, and Danish ministers. He had several meetings with Secretary of State James Monroe. Back in 1805, while in Paris en route from Spain, Monroe had urged Jefferson to hasten diplomatic adjustment by seizing Spanish Texas. Now Monroe proposed to send an army to the Rio Grande to aid the revolutionists in the interior of Mexico, acting under the pretext of taking possession of Texas as a part of the Louisiana Purchase — an offer which Gutiérrez said he refused as being beyond his authority to negotiate. In a final conference on December 17, Monroe stated that in the event of war with Great Britain, the United States would immediately field an army of 50,000 men in New Spain, thus siding in the struggle for Mexican independence.

---

* Actually, when Captain José Félix Menchaca returned to Béxar, he was tried by a military council and was sent to Chihuahua, where he was placed under the protective custody of Don Nemesio Salcedo.

Since he was without credentials (those given him by Hidalgo had been lost at Bayou Pierre; meanwhile, Hidalgo himself had been captured and executed), Monroe advised Gutiérrez to return to Mexico and tell rebel leaders there of the favorable disposition of the United States. Before his departure, President James Madison received him with great courtesy in the "Palace of the President," which, with its many glass windows and crystal and gold lamps, made a proper impression on the rebel from the Rio Grande.[13]

While in Washington, Gutiérrez went sightseeing with José Álvarez de Toledo, who had also come to the young nation's capital to intrigue with Monroe, telling him of British designs to seize Cuba, Puerto Rico, and Santo Domingo. A Cuban and former Spanish naval officer, Toledo had represented Santo Domingo in the Spanish Cortés in 1810–1811. His denunciation of the regency caused him to flee to Philadelphia, where he arrived in September bearing a revolutionary commission from his fellow American delegates. A deepening friendship prompted Gutiérrez to join Toledo in Philadelphia, which city he reached on January 7, 1812. Detained from departing by bad weather and lack of ships, they spent the intervening weeks planning a revolution. They worked out an understanding that Toledo would remain near the United States government in the interest of Mexican independence, while Gutiérrez would initiate revolutionary activity along the northeastern frontier of New Spain.[14]

Gutiérrez departed from Philadelphia by boat on February 19, 1812. He reached New Orleans on March 23, and hurried to present himself to Governor Claiborne. In Claiborne's office he was introduced to Captain William Shaler, United States Special Agent, recently arrived from Cuba. Shaler had been a sea captain; then he held a consular post in Havana. Late in 1811 he was instructed to proceed to Mexico to obtain information concerning the revolution. Unable to enter the port of Veracruz, he left Havana for New Orleans, expecting to proceed to Natchitoches and enter Mexico by way of Texas.[15] Shaler appears to have had secret orders to cooperate with Gutiérrez, and, from the moment they met, Shaler took over Graham's task as Gutiérrez's mentor, even sharing his lodgings with the Mexican revolutionary envoy. Governor Claiborne called on Gutiérrez several times, entertained him, and together they walked about the city. Julia Kathryn Garrett probably best summed up the significance of this hospitality: "The Governor of Louisiana would not for days have taken walks with, or feted a stranger, unless he were of special significance." [16]

After a three-week journey by riverboats and on horseback, Shaler and Gutiérrez had finally arrived in Natchitoches on April 18. Gutiérrez had now reached his base of operations for the penetration and liberation of New Spain. Six months before, he had appeared there as a miserable fugitive. Now he returned, almost in state, accompanied by Shaler, an American of obvious distinction and importance. On May 7, he and Shaler were honored with a magnificent banquet at Fort Claiborne, the significance of which was not lost on the residents of Natchitoches, where intrigue permeated the very air.

Neither was the arrival of Gutiérrez and Shaler lost on the Spaniards. Several couriers were dispatched to Commandant Bernardo Montero at Nacogdoches from Spanish citizens who were then in Natchitoches. Among these was Peter Samuel Davenport, Spanish Indian Agent at Nacogdoches (and therefore, Dr. Sibley's opposite number), who was on his way to New Orleans to purchase supplies for the Texas Government. In Béxar several weeks later, Governor Salcedo was to endorse Davenport's letter, which Montero had sent on to him, to the Viceroy with the terse comment, "he knows more than what he expresses." [17] Davenport had come to Spanish Louisiana about 1790, and in 1798 he joined the firm that was to become the commercial House of Barr and Davenport in Nacogdoches. Although a Spanish subject and a civil servant who exercised considerable power, Davenport was about to cast his lot with the revolutionaries.[18]

With the war between United States and Great Britain looming ominously near, the frontier village of Natchitoches became the scene of international intrigue and conspiracy not unworthy of an European capital. Busily stirring this witches' cauldron was United States Special Agent William Shaler, ably assisted by United States Indian Agent Dr. John Sibley. In New Orleans, United States Territorial Governor William C. C. Claiborne conveniently looked the other way. At Fort Claiborne, a twenty-four-year-old West Pointer, Lieutenant Augustus William Magee, resigned his commission in the United States Army and began to organize the Republican Army of the North. Meanwhile, Samuel Davenport, merchant of Natchitoches and New Orleans who had been supplier of Spanish Texas for many years, began to assemble material for the filibusters. In the vortex of this seething activity, the Mexican revolutionary Bernardo Gutiérrez dutifully played his role of willing pawn of the American conspirators.

But for Bernardo the winds of fortune did not blow from just one quarter. In Philadelphia, he had been approached by French agents with ingratiating offers; during his stopover in New Orleans, Bonapartists again contacted him. On the Louisiana–Texas frontier he was approached by one Paillette, a former officer in the French Army and at that time, a local planter. Speaking for Napoleon's minister in the United States, Paillette offered to raise and equip four hundred men and to advance one hundred thousand dollars to purchase military stores. Other North Americans—whose identities Shaler chose not to reveal in his reports to James Monroe—promised Gutiérrez that in two months they would assemble five hundred men in the Neutral Ground equipped with two cannon and sufficient funds to march against Béxar.[19]

Then in mid-May Gutiérrez wrote Graham that word had come from the Rio Grande that all his properties had been confiscated, and that his family, his mother, and his brother were prisoners. The entire Gutiérrez de Lara family were ejected from their homes, despoiled of everything in sight, the immovable things seized; 4,200 *pesos* were taken from Bernardo's wife, his widowed mother suffered poverty and his clerical brother, Don José, fled to the mountains.[20] A lesser man might have succumbed to one of the flattering proposals, but Gutiérrez stuck with the advice of Shaler and kept him informed of the various propositions made to him. These propositions did not "comport with the policy or dignity of the United States" and required immediate attention, Shaler candidly informed his boss, Monroe. It would seem that William Shaler had now progressed from a passive observer of events in Mexico to an avid fomenter of rebellion, for he presented the American Secretary of State with a daring plan for moving United States troops across the Neutral Ground to the Spanish Sabine. He went even further and proposed the area about San Marcos, close to the center of Texas, as an ideal site for a United States reserve fort! He also reported that he had employed two deserters from the Spanish troops in Béxar as his couriers and that Dr. Sibley had provided them with rations, listing them on his accounts as Indians.[21]

Under the guidance of Shaler, Gutiérrez became the zealous propagandist. From Natchitoches he launched a campaign to show his countrymen the pathway to liberty. With the aid of one

José Francisco Banegas, deserter from the royal presidio at Nacogdoches, a heavy packet of subversive literature was distributed in that Spanish outpost. A Frenchman from Natchitoches, Bernardo Martín Despallier, became a valuable colleague because of his knowledge of Texas and a following of Texas friends. Despallier, who had held a military appointment in Louisiana under Governor Carondelet in 1794, had come from New Orleans to Nacogdoches in 1804, where he married María Cándida Grande. He moved his family to Villa Trinidad before its official founding in January 1806. Expelled from Spanish Texas for illegal trade with Natchitoches, he developed a deep hatred of Spanish officials. Despallier himself issued a twelve-point memo directed to the Creole inhabitants of the provinces of Mexico, explaining Gutiérrez's position.*[22] Copies of Toledo's booklet *el amigo de los hombres* found their way to Nacogdoches, and Indians along the Rio Grande were said to have been imbued with its theories. In Natchitoches, Shaler provided another one hundred dollars to equip couriers to carry more messages to Nacogdoches and to Nuevo Santander.[23]

Banegas, the Nacogdoches courier, was captured late in June, and a month later he was executed by Governor Salcedo in Béxar. For his part in capturing Banegas, Governor Salcedo promoted Corporal Ermenegildo Guillén to sergeant and gave him a medal.[24] Two emissaries, Juan Galván and Félix Arispe, both deserters from the Spanish forces, carried messages to the insurgent commander Ignacio López Rayón, who relayed them to Gutiérrez's brother, the priest Don José, in Revilla. From Béxar, Governor Salcedo wrote his uncle in Chihuahua, the Commandant-General Nemesio Salcedo y Salcedo, that the American Government had decided to win over the ruffians and revolutionists of Texas by propaganda. His troops, he knew, were better fitted to fight Indians than propaganda.

By June, Natchitoches was agog with speculative talk. The long-awaited and daily-expected declaration of war between the United States and Great Britian provided the major excitement. It would furnish the opportunity for the sons of liberty to march to Mexico's assistance and at the same time indulge their lusts for commerce and treasure. The United

---

* Uniquely, Despallier gave two of his sons in the war for freedom in Texas in 1835–1836. His oldest son, Blaz P. Despallier, fought in the Battle of Béxar, was wounded, and died of cholera a short time later. Another son, Charles Despallier, was one of the valiant thirty-two who went to the aid of the Alamo, fought, and died there.

States, they believed, would sanction their invasion of the Spanish provinces, if only to prevent a British invasion of Louisiana or to bring about a settlement of the Louisiana boundary problem. Rumors of expeditions planning to enter Texas provided provocative morsels of speculative talk. By day Sibley and Shaler took active part in the town talk and fed it with choice tidbits. By candlelight, they wrote lengthy reports to their respective superiors, the Secretaries of War and State.

They reported that hundreds of men were assembling near the Sabine. Some had passed through Natchitoches. The specter of the Aaron Burr conspiracy was raised again when it was rumored that General Adair, formerly a prominent figure in the Burr expedition, was to be commander-in-chief and that he had been in Rapides, from where he had contacted Gutiérrez. Sibley went so far as to inform the Secretary of War that "should such an enterprise be contrary to the views of the United States there is no force in this quarter to stop them, or should they want the military stores in Fort Claiborne they would probably take them." He intimated that the leaders hoped for the liberation of Texas, followed by United States annexation. Shaler wrote Monroe the same views. By the end of June, they were expressing anxiety concerning Gutiérrez. In spite of their efforts, they feared he would embrace one of the proposals made to him. Gutiérrez had told Shaler frankly that if American volunteers assembled on Spanish territory and offered to cooperate with him in the cause of independence, "all the world would regard him as a fool not to profit by the circumstances."[25]

By July, Shaler had cast his lot with an expedition. In a letter to Monroe, he expressed humiliation at having lost the confidence of Gutiérrez, but this seems only to have been a thin cover of his true role in the undertaking. Soon he was writing Monroe more details of the expedition, including the fact that several pieces of artillery from New Orleans had already rolled down the streets of Natchitoches en route to the Sabine. Nacogdoches would be taken within a month, he said, and success beyond the Sabine would be complete if the expedition were conducted with common prudence. He was assured, he wrote, that the expedition would make no movement until it was known that war existed between the United States and Great Britian.[26] That awaited news reached Natchitoches in late July. In the Neutral Ground an army of liberty was ready to move with the exciting news.

It would be nice to be able to credit José Bernardo Gutiérrez de Lara with the creation of this band of freedom fighters, this Republican Army of the North, poised on the Sabine awaiting only his signal to carry the sweet fruits of liberty to his Mexican brethren. But the facts belie that possibility. Other than playing the nebulous role of "Ambassador of Mexico, near the United States," and lending himself freely to the machinations of Shaler and Sibley, Gutiérrez had little to do with the formation of the force of revolutionaries. It was Augustus Magee, who, with consummate skill in a brief forty days, organized a heterogeneous group of brigands, adventurers, and gentlemen into an army. Shaler and Sibley, busy with their pens, prepared their Government for events to come, cautiously not mentioning names until the project was in action.

When names were finally out in the open, Shaler described Magee to Monroe as "a very tall, robust Bostonian, handsome of person and countenance, commanding in appearance, and withal prepossessing in manner," one of the best-informed officers of his age in the United States Army. Magee had stood third in his class at West Point and had been appointed a second lieutenant "artillerist" on January 14, 1809.[27] In the early part of the year he was busy clearing the Neutral Ground of bandits who had gathered in alarming numbers since the Casas revolution in Béxar had opened a lucrative trade between Texas and Natchitoches.

In December, the Indian Office ordered the Indian factor at Natchitoches, Thomas Linnard, because of the "considerable quantities of wool" brought there and "the scarcity of woolen goods [in the United States] to purchase 15,000 or 20,000 pounds . . ." Strictly forbidden to trade with Louisiana after it had been ceded to Napoleon in 1798, the *vecinos* of Texas had only the annual fairs at Saltillo and the markets at Monclova as outlets for their goods. The great distances involved, as well as the near desert areas to be traversed, left the citizens of Béxar, La Bahía, and Nacogdoches without a market for their wool or a source for manufactured and imported goods. Governor Salcedo, who had served as an administrator in Louisiana while his father was governor of that province and who had a genuine concern for the near poverty of his constituents, condoned — albeit unofficially — the continuation of the trading caravans between Béxar and Natchitoches.[28]

Magee's duty on the frontier, his contacts with the adventurers who frequented the borderlands, his dissatisfaction with the army, and his feeling of personal slight in having been passed over for promotion, all turned Magee to a brave new dream — that of becoming the North American liberator of New Spain! On the twenty-second of June he resigned his commission in the United States Army and began his career as a revolutionist.[29]

Behind the scenes, Samuel Davenport, with a corps of twenty men, undertook the job of Magee's quartermaster. Convinced that the outbreak of war between the United States and England would wrest Texas from Spanish dominion, he played for time while he surreptitiously assembled supplies for the Republican Army. Residents of Nacogdoches depended largely on Davenport for their necessities, and he used this leverage to convince them to receive the republicans when they would reach Nacogdoches. It was his wagons, arriving from New Orleans loaded with supplies, that would both support the invading army and sustain the residents of that Spanish outpost.

In mid-July Gutiérrez wrote to General James Wilkinson, commander of United States troops in the Territory, asking him to use his "influence and power" to obtain the glorious liberty of the Spanish provinces whose cause he knew the General favored. Wilkinson's interest in Texas had begun in 1789, when Philip Nolan first told him of the province. For his part in exposing the Aaron Burr conspiracy and in negotiating the Neutral Ground arrangement, Wilkinson is alleged to have received $120,000 in silver specie sent him by Governor Cordero on pack mules. Like Shaler and Sibley, Wilkinson used his pen to write the Secretary of War a lengthy plan for preventing Great Britian from gaining control of the Spanish provinces. Wilkinson also relieved the commanding officer at Fort Claiborne, sending in a Captain Wollestonecraft from Baton Rouge, who sat on his hands and did nothing to disband the army of men gathered in the Neutral Ground. Once Nacogdoches had been taken, Wilkinson ordered Wollestonecraft, with all the artillery and arms of the post, back to Baton Rouge. What schemes were being promoted under the guise of defense against the British! In Natchez, Nashville, Philadelphia, Baltimore, and Washington City, the press fanned public thinking into acceptance of this colossal conspiracy to violate the sovereignty of Spain.[30]

2 *Revolution Sweeps Texas*

ON AUGUST 7, A SMALL ADVANCE PARTY OF the Republican Army crossed into Spanish Texas at the pass where *Cabo* Guillén had stood off Captain Menchaca nine months earlier and headed west over the trail to Nacogdoches. The next day Colonel Magee led the balance of his force across the Sabine, and two days later José Bernardo Gutiérrez de Lara rode out of Natchitoches to join the army over which he was titular commander-in-chief. No sooner had the advance party entered Spanish territory than they were confronted by the curate Sambrano leading a trading caravan.

Awarded a lieutenant colonelcy for overturning the Casas government in Béxar the previous year, Sambrano had brought a pack train of sixty mules laden with wool and silver specie from Béxar, manned by a hundred mule drivers. Because of the large army of men gathering in the Neutral Ground, he had sent word to Natchitoches that his trading venture had the sanction of Governor Salcedo and requested assurance of a safe passage.

Only several months before, the United States had sent Lieutenant Augustus Magee into the Neutral Ground to protect this very trade, but Captain Wollestonecraft — no doubt

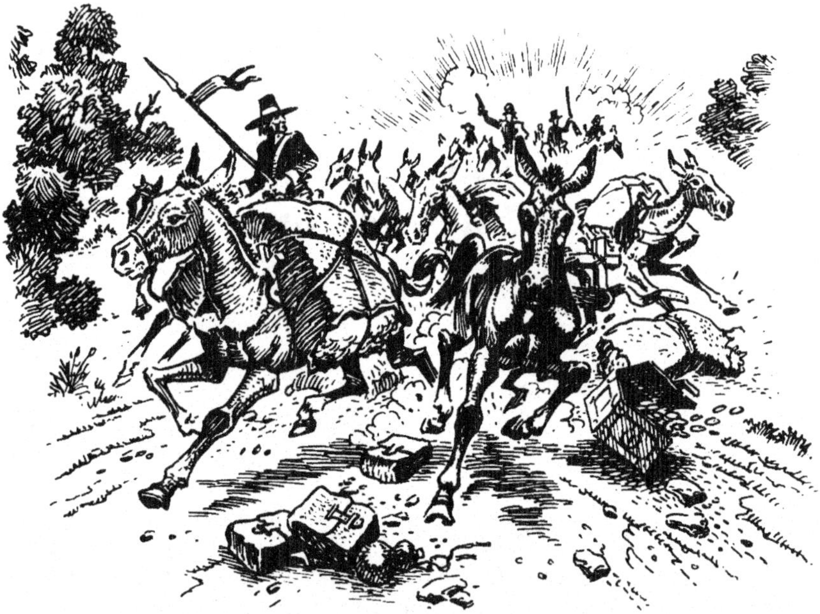

Revolution Sweeps Texas 19

acting on Wilkinson's orders — refused Sambrano the escort he requested. After waiting several weeks, Sambrano undertook the crossing in his own strength, guarded by some soldiers he had commandeered in Nacogdoches. Several of the Americans later suggested that Sambrano might have been leading a military force to head off Magee's army. James Gaines said he had rallied 300 militiamen; John Villars that he had "commanded the Royal Forces at Nacogdoches — about 300 or 400 men." Although his rank predated by some months that of Lieutenant Colonel Bernardo Montero, then commanding at Nacogdoches, and by his nature, Sambrano would have thrown his weight around, Montero was a professional soldier who would not have knuckled under to the Béxar subdeacon at such a dangerous moment. Also, contemporary manuscript sources reveal that the Nacogdoches garrison was then sadly undermanned, underequipped, lacking in horses, and totally incapable of mounting a guard of several hundred men. Therefore it must be assumed that, at this juncture, Sambrano's expedition was strictly a commercial one. Both Villars and Gaines wrote that he turned tail and fled when attacked by an advance party of only four or five men, underscoring the fact that he was not leading troops with the objective of halting the invaders.[1]

Juan Manuel Sambrano, who was about forty and a native of San Fernando de Béxar, was one of the truly colorful personages of the time. A subdeacon in the church, he spent his idle hours at gambling and in the *cantinas*. A *héroe*, with "his blond hair floating in the wind, his shirt open at the collar, his sleeves rolled up above the elbows, and a cavalry sword strapped to his waist," he arrogantly walked the streets of Béxar, engaging in frequent brawls — often over gambling debts. Commanded to leave the capital several times by the governor, he either ignored the order or managed to get himself forgiven. When things got too hot, he retired to his ranch, *La Laguna de las Animas*, where, according to the 1811 census, he had thirty-two servants and two slaves, immense herds of livestock and three registered carts. [He was at the ranch when summoned to lead the counter-revolt against the Casas government.] He wrote his name with an "S" but, beginning with his baptismal record, most historians have insisted on calling him "Zambrano" or, as the Americans called him, "Sam Brannon."[2]

Having learned of the imminent advance of the Americans, Bernardo Montero had stationed an ensign [*alférez*] and eighteen soldiers at Salitre Prairie, some twenty miles from Nacogdoches. They were attacked by a small advance party under Captain Samuel Kemper at daybreak on August 11, while at Mass. One Spanish soldier escaped and fled to Montero with the baleful news. A Virginian but a resident of West Florida since 1801, Kemper and his brothers Reuben and Nathan had been in frequent trouble with the Spanish authorities, leading an abortive rebellion in 1804.[3] John Villars said that the attack took place at Edmund Quirk's ranch on Ayish Bayou (now San Augustine) and that all those captured agreed to join the republican cause and were sworn in as soldiers by Antonio Flores. The new recruits were placed under Captain Despallier, and it was in this way that his company of republicans commenced.[4]

At Nacogdoches, Commandant Montero ordered the alarm sounded, but Gutiérrez's propaganda messages and Davenport's threats had prevailed and the citizens failed to respond. Montero then ordered the troops immediately to begin the march for Béxar. A short distance from town the militia and all but about ten soldiers deserted. The lieutenant colonels, Montero and Sambrano, and the ten fled westward.[5]

With the Spanish officials gone, the residents of Nacogdoches prepared to receive the advancing army. A delegation was sent to confer with Magee, and the next morning a procession of some 300 left the town to meet the army and escort the Americans into Nacogdoches. Archives and public property were placed in Magee's charge. Four hundred mules and horses, 80,000 pounds of fine wool, silver specie — much of it Sambrano's wealth — and public supplies and ammunition, swelled Davenport's quartermaster stores. Magee sent the mules and the wool to the United States with Reuben Ross, who bought clothing and stores with the proceeds.[6] The gateway to Spanish Texas had been breached. Nacogdoches, the Spanish bulwark against the threatening Americans, was now a stronghold of the filibusters.

A few soldiers missed the celebration in Nacogdoches. Bernardo Despallier and another captain, according to Villars, were sent in pursuit of Montero and Sambrano on their retreat toward Trinidad, pushing the Spaniards so hard that they left some of their provisions and lances behind. They arrived at the newly founded Spanish log village bastion a day behind the Spanish officers, and immediately entered the town and fraternized with the inhabitants.[7] As Despallier's company was made up of *Tejano* recruits, it is understandable that they could mingle freely with the Trinidad residents — Despallier himself having led a group of settlers there before the villa was officially established in January 1806. Montero and Sambrano, joined now by Captain Ysidro de la Garza and the Trinidad garrison, retreated to the Navasota River, where they awaited orders from the Governor. When word reached Nacogdoches of this development, a republican vanguard took possession of Trinidad with whirlwind speed. Only the Presidio La Bahía and Béxar remained as obstacles in the republican grand parade across Texas.

To make sure these bloodless victories might continue, the propaganda war was resumed. Gutiérrez issued three proclamations, dated "General Headquarters, Nacogdoches, September 1, 1812, of the Second Year of our Independence." He signed them "Colonel in the Armies of the Republic of Mexico, Deputy for her in the United States of America, and Commander-in-Chief of the Army of the North." One was addressed to the officers, soldiers, and inhabitants of Béxar, urging them to embrace the cause of independence, since an army of Americans, descendants of men who fought for independence of the United States, were marching to secure for them their liberty and protection of their rights. The second, addressed to his beloved and honorable compatriots in the Province of Texas, informed them that Gutiérrez had undergone great trials for their sake and had been received by the United States Government as well as by ministers of Europe and that great forces were coming by land and sea to liberate Mexicans. The third informed the people of Mexico that the Army of the North had come not to rob them but to unite with revolutionists in that country to establish economic and political liberty. The American volunteers were not overlooked. They too were given a propaganda dose, promising them the rights of honored citizens of the Mexican Republic, including, among other things, the right to tame and dispose of wild horses and mules found on the Texas prairies.[8]

Two couriers, Luís Grande, a revolutionist from Trinidad [and probably a relative of Despallier's wife], and Anselmo Bergara, a deserter from the veteran troops of Béxar, were sent to carry the messages to republican sympathizers in the latter city. Gutiérrez had previously sent out *Alférez* Miguél Menchaca, probably the nephew of Captain José Menchaca, and two soldiers with the incendiary documents, but they encountered Don Gabino Delgado, who had come from the capital and who told them the area all the way to the Guadalupe River was covered with spies. Delgado was correct. Grande and Bergara were intercepted on the road by four spies sent out by Salcedo who posed as deserters and who offered to guide the messengers into town. Instead, they betrayed the rebel couriers to the Governor, who had them shot.[9]

On September 13, the Army of the North — now numbering about 300 Americans and nearly 100 Mexicans and *Tejanos*, with three fieldpieces — departed Nacogdoches for Trinidad, where they planned to wait until cooler weather before advancing on Béxar. A rear guard, under Captain James Gaines, remained on the Sabine to sign up volunteers hurrying from the United States. Shaler wrote that the business of volunteering for New Spain had developed into "a perfect mania" during September. Deserters came from Béxar, reporting that consternation prevailed in the capital, that Governor Salcedo had withdrawn all outposts and concentrated his forces in Béxar. By October the liberty army numbered six hundred. Arms and equipage had been placed in the best of condition, and the army functioned with perfect military order. On October 12, an advance party was twelve miles beyond the Trinity.[10] Magee had done his job well!

Early in October Shaler wrote Monroe that he was so certain of being able to proceed to Mexico within the month that he would depart immediately if it were not for giving the appearance that he had some connection with the expedition.[11]

At this moment of high expectation, James Monroe, United States Secretary of State, dropped a bombshell into the proceedings. Actually, Monroe had made his move ten weeks earlier when he sent Doctor John Hamilton Robinson on a mission to Don Nemesio Salcedo y Salcedo, Commandant-General of the Interior Provinces, at Chihuahua. Robinson was to tell Don Nemesio that the President of the United States was concerned with recent activities of persons in the Neutral Ground who were disregarding the authority and endangering the welfare of both countries. He was to propose that the two countries establish commercial relations and settle their territorial boundary problems by amicable negotiations.

Dr. Robinson had been in Texas before, but as a political prisoner. In 1805–1806, he had explored the upper Rio Grande Valley with Zebulon Pike. Imprisoned by the Spanish authorities, the party was sent to Chihuahua, detained for a time by Don Nemesio, and then sent out of Spanish territory by way of Texas. It was Pike who had recommended Robinson to Monroe.[12] International observers placed different interpretations on Robinson's mission. A French agent opined that the "United States acted a double and deceptive part," sending Robinson to convince Spanish colonial authorities of the good faith of the United States toward Spain, while Shaler had been instructed to support the revolutionists. Republican victory or royalist victory, Monroe would be on the winning side.

Robinson appeared in the republican camp at Trinidad on the evening of October 15, displaying the United States flag on his baggage. Rumor and suspicion went through the camp. Magee, after calling a council of war, permitted him to proceed toward Béxar — after Robinson agreed to several conditions, among which was that he leave the flag and that he take a passport from the newly declared Texas Republic.[13] Robinson's journey was to have far-reaching effects on the causes and morale of both the Republican Army of the North and the Spanish population of Texas.

On the 18th, the Republican Army left Trinidad in high spirits. Gutiérrez reported they were united, well-armed, and "determined to besiege Inferno itself." They crossed the Brazos, and at the Colorado they learned that Salcedo planned an ambush for them on the Guadalupe. Magee decided to turn south to La Bahía, and they occupied that coastal presidio during the night of November 7. As they approached, the soldiers occupying the citadel surrendered, and the republicans found themselves in possession of a large square stone fort with two bastions on which they quickly mounted cannon. Because Salcedo had already withdrawn the presidial troops, the garrison consisted of militia only and was said by McLane to be about 200 men who surrendered on first summons and who, with an equal number of citizens, joined the Republican Army. Reports differ as to the number of cannon found at La Bahía. Yoakum wrote that they found in the fort some sixteen pieces of artillery of all calibers, some dating back to La Salle in 1685. McLane wrote that they found neither cannon nor a military chest [as Yoakum had reported], but did recover a good supply of small arms ammunition. They had spent several days setting their new stronghold in order before the governors Salcedo and Herrera captured their picket guard on the Béxar road and unexpectedly approached La Bahía. McLane wrote that the royalist force arrived about ten days after the Americans had taken possession of the fort. Davenport said it was six days; Yoakum three days. Such differences are typical of the reporting of the day and are cited to alert the reader to the hazards of giving credence to a single source. This is especially true of dates and, whenever possible, dates given in this work have been determined from manuscript sources. The Spaniards attacked but without success; their enemy remained holed up in the fortress. The royalist commanders decided to starve them out and began a four-month siege of the stronghold.

Fed by their own propaganda and by encouraging messages from Béxar, the Americans had fully expected that royalist troops would desert to the Army of the North when they arrived at La Bahía. When, instead, some of their own men went over to Salcedo, doubt and discouragement replaced the exhuberance they had felt in their earlier successes. Davenport placed the blame for their situation on Robinson's appearance in Béxar. Garrett wrote that republican confidence withered when the people of Béxar and royalist troops did not come out and welcome the Army of the North, as rumor declared they would. Instead, the royal authority before La Bahía, by its magnetism, drew some of the inhabitants of the town to join the royal army and attracted, as well, many of the soldiers from the revolutionary army who had deserted to them from the Spanish forces at Nacogdoches.[14]

Captain McFarland [whom Villars identified as a foreigner], leading a small party to the Nueces River, had captured a Mexican sergeant and twenty-five men, who, seeing the small force of Americans surrounded by Salcedo's troops, refused to join the Republican Army although "they expressed their wishes for the cause." Juan Galván, a deserter from Béxar who had carried messages to Revilla for Gutiérrez, had been made an officer and was placed in charge of the detachment guarding the *caballada*. Now Galván was bought up by Salcedo, and he went over to the enemy, taking with him 200 mules and horses. The resignation of a Captain Scott [after taking an *escopeta* shot through his coattail in one of the skirmishes], and the abandonment of the expedition about this time by the quartermaster, Davenport, further contributed to the general deterioration of morale. McLane wrote that Davenport had developed second thoughts about his possessions in Nacogdoches when his lieutenant, the officer of the horse guard who had sold the *caballada* to the enemy [probably Galván], sent word to Davenport that he intended to have the "skin of his belly for a drum-head." After promenading the square for two days with a gun under his arm, Davenport procured a horse and left in the night, making good his escape. Davenport's own account was that he was ordered to Natchitoches, and Magee wrote that Davenport "leaves me on particular business." [15]

Faced by an untenable situation, Magee is said to have called a military council which agreed unanimously to capitulate to the royalists. Salcedo and Herrera are said to have attended an interview with the American officers but no agreement was reached, and on November 23, hostilities were renewed. Warren D. C. Hall later categorically denied that Magee had agreed to surrender the fort, but Villars, McLane, Ross, and Davenport attested to such arrangements. The men rejected the terms, which essentially were the surrender of American arms, delivery to Salcedo of the Mexican and *Tejano* rebels, and the departure of the Americans with one gun per five [or ten] men to kill game on the return home. Gutiérrez may not have been consulted during the negotiations — McLane said he "kept close in his quarters, keeping his own council" — which may have later led to his charge that Magee had agreed to surrender him for 15,000 *pesos*.[16]

Discouragement lay hold of Magee and Gutiérrez. Both wrote gloomy letters to Natchitoches, the essence of which was that if the enemy continued to resist, the republicans would be forced to abandon La Bahía and fight their way to freedom. Gutiérrez urged Shaler to annex the land from the Sabine to La Bahía to the United States to prevent the Spaniards from putting the inhabitants to the sword for their acceptance of the revolution. Magee put it more bluntly, "We are differently received in this country to what we expected — indeed you have no conception of the treachery of these people." He also asked for annexation of Texas all the way to the Rio Grande. "My hopes of effecting a Revolution in this country with the means I now hold are entirely blasted," he said, "but still I am strong enough to open my road, whatever course I choose to go." [17]

Davenport arrived with their letters on December 19. His own report to Shaler on conditions at La Bahía reflected disappointment at the delay but not the discouragement shown by Magee and Gutiérrez. Perhaps at the safe distance, his outlook brightened. He said the army numbered six hundred dependable men in good spirits, with enough food to last four months

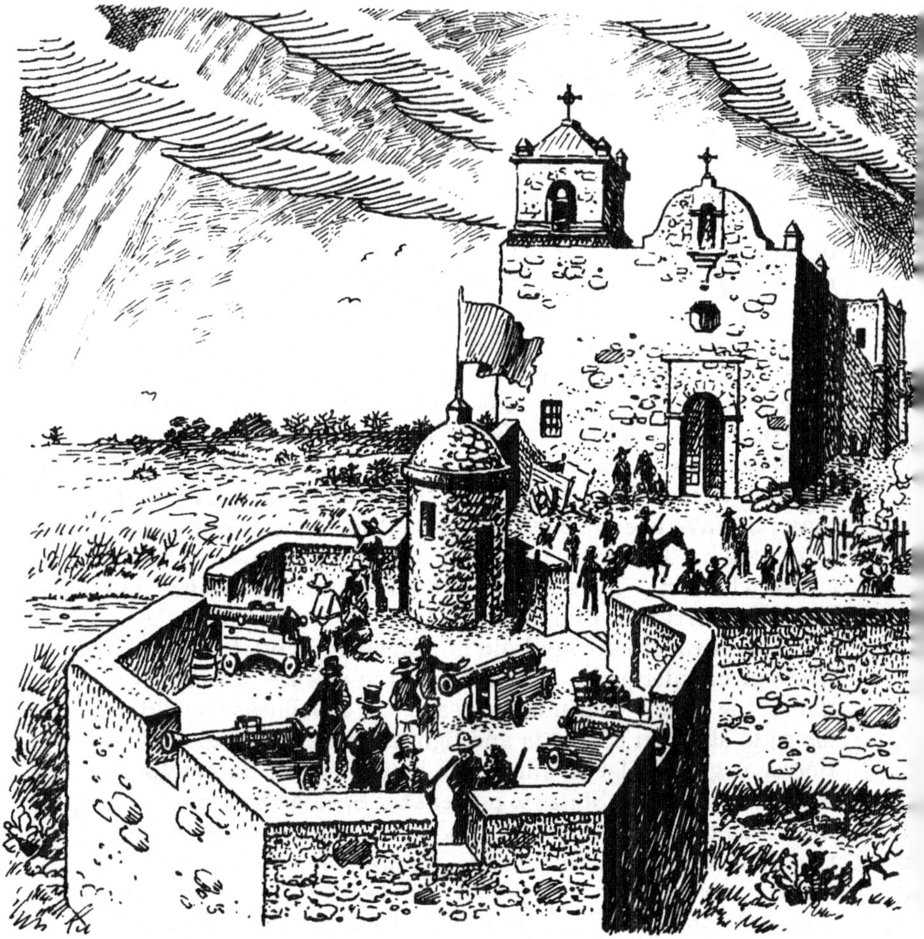

and plenty of ammunition. Gutiérrez had installed a forge and personally directed the men in repairing arms and equipage, leaving his anvil for his gun during the frequent skirmishes.[18]

The siege dragged out through December and January and into February. Many skirmishes occurred, in which the republicans were mostly victorious. Loyalist troops began to desert to the republicans in increasing numbers, so that toward the end it was the besiegers who weakened, their troops poorly clothed against the cold Texas winter, their powder chests empty, and their stores diminishing. A furious battle in early February 1813, resulted in yet another defeat for Salcedo and Herrera. On the 19th of February, the royalists evacuated camp before day and retreated toward Béxar, encumbered with wounded men and disgruntled troops, some of whom deserted on the way. The deserters were joined by inhabitants of Béxar, who, having learned of Salcedo's defeat and of his retreat, were on their way to join the republicans. Villars said that when Salcedo's troops took up the line of march for Béxar, they were followed by Menchaca and some Americans who cut off their baggage in the rear and brought it back to La Bahía. Included was wine, *mescal,* and other liquors "which afforded the garrison an opportunity of getting lordly drunk." Hall said it was a detachment of fifty men under a Captain Holmes who cut off the Spaniards' baggage, making no mention of the booze.[19]

In a dispatch to Colonel Rueben Ross, published in *The Boston Patriot,* Gutiérrez stated that on February 10, the army under his command, consisting of 500 troops and one piece of artillery — probably an understatement — defeated Salcedo's whole army in a general battle. Salcedo retreated from La Bahía at daybreak on the 11th, he wrote, and took the road to San Antonio. Actually, Salcedo's departure was a few days later, and Villars wrote that in the interim he evinced no further sign of fight, and that Menchaca, Delgado, and Sava harrassed his spies every night. On his return to Béxar, Governor Salcedo found that the inhabitants had been sorely tormented by frequent Indian attacks during his absence with the troops. Fifty-five persons had been killed and 5,000 sheep and 10,000 horses and mules stolen. There was a bitter rift among the people; some had already left Béxar to join the republicans when word came that they — 1,400 strong — were marching toward the capital. In the midst of these forebodings, Dr. Robinson appeared in Béxar on his return from Chihuahua. He found "everything in confusion, every person alarmed for the security of his person and property." When he left, Robinson was besieged by people wanting him to take their property with him to safety.[20]

Colonel Augustus Magee did not live to savor victory. Reuben Ross had brought word to Natchitoches on January 10 that he was wasting away with a fever that had plagued him since he left Trinidad. On February 8, he died, apparently of consumption. Gutiérrez was to say in 1815, that he took poison to avoid being shot for an attempt to sell him [Gutiérrez] to the royalists. James Gaines reported that some people believed that Magee had been given poison by some of the border ruffians — by whom Magee expected to be assassinated — in revenge for his actions in suppressing their activities in the Neutral Ground in the spring of 1812. McLane wrote that when Magee's body was taken for burial, "the enemy contributed their mite in honoring the dead, by discharging their cannon — rolling the balls around the graveyard." [21]

Victory at La Bahía spurred both Shaler and Gutiérrez to take up their pens. Shaler assured Monroe that the revolution would now succeed and its effect would be of great consequence in Mexico. Again, he was ready to leave immediately for the interior of Mexico; only fear of being regarded a partisan of the revolutionists prevented him!

Gutiérrez sent a messenger galloping after Ross, who was then gathering recruits and supplies in Natchitoches. Gutiérrez urged him to hurry — that the army was impatient to be on its way to Béxar. Ross returned on March 12, with twenty-five Americans under Captain James Gaines and a like number of Coushatta Indians under their half-breed chief, Charley Rollins. [Gaines had commanded rear guards on the Sabine and at Trinidad. A Virginian and a cousin of General Edmund P. Gaines, he had been sheriff of one of the eastern parishes of Louisiana, and was about thirty-seven at the time.] Captain John McFarland was sent to recruit among the Lipan and Tonkawa Indians, and the number he is reported to have brought in varies from less than fifty-five to as many as 300. Reinforced by some 170 or 180 Mexicans sent by José María Guadiana, the republican commandant at Nacogdoches, the Army began its march on the twenty-fifth.[22]

With Magee dead, command of the Americans now fell to Samuel Kemper, whom Gaines labeled a good officer and whom Shaler described to Monroe as a man of much courage and firmness, "an excellent executive officer, but of no education and of doubtful capacity for chief command." Lieutenant Colonel Reuben Ross seems to have been second in command while Gutiérrez, no longer overshadowed by the military faculty of Magee, undertook a more dominent role in leadership.

Before they marched, the Mexican prisoners and deserters at La Bahía were organized into three companies commanded by Miguél Menchaca, Antonio Delgado [who had deserted to the rebels during the siege], and Juan Sava. Captain McFarland and his scouts had captured a garrison of sixteen men commanded by an old Castillian officer at Refugio mission, and they, too, joined the republicans. The march was without cannon or baggage wagons, each man carrying everything on his back. McLane said that the livestock were very numerous and annoying, "tormenting the poor tired soldier during the night, and if they failed to get an ample supply of food, they would nibble and bite him on the march — many of the men not having a second shirt, were eaten raw on the backs and shoulders by these Mexican pests [probably donkeys and mules, and chickens]." The author suspects the beasts were hungry for the salt they found in the sweat of the marching men, a need which is supplied today by mineral blocks put out by cattlemen. There were about 270 American volunteers, 200 Mexicans and thirty Coushatta Indians, according to McLane. Ross wrote Shaler that there were about 600 effective men, a figure confirmed by Gutiérrez although he said their total strength was 900. Villars accounted for upward of one hundred Indians, including some "Bedi, Towakanays & Lepans, none of whom were any account except the Cochattes who fought bravely & suffered much." [23]

At about eleven o'clock on the morning of March 29, on the east side of Salado Creek about five leagues from Béxar, the republicans were marching on the lower or mission road, expecting to find food and take up quarters for the night at Espada mission, when their flankers discovered an enemy ambush on the upper road. The ambush proved to be the forces of Governors Salcedo and Herrera [McLane said "the entire male population of Texas"], consisting of some 1,200 men and six well-mounted brass cannon. The battle was bloody and brief, lasting no more than an hour, and resulting in the complete rout of the royalists and the capture of most of their arms and ammunition, the six cannon, and 1,500 head of horses and mules. Lieutenant Colonel Ross distinguished himself in this engagement by a swashbuckling sabre duel with a Colonel Montura. Miguel Menchaca received a very disagreeable but not dangerous wound, while Gutiérrez, after detailing some of his countrymen as his bodyguard, took a post in the rear. The victors spent the night at Espada mission, about eight miles down the river from Béxar, and the next day advanced five miles to the mission Concepción to take up quarters. Residents, militiamen, and presidial troops streamed out to join their ranks. The following day Kemper sent Captain Josiah Taylor to raid the royalists' horse herds, capturing all sixty guards and 300 horses and mules. Called the Battle of Salado in contemporary accounts, this battle on the twenty-ninth is generally known today as the battle of Rosillo — to distinguish it from another battle of Salado in 1842.[24]

On April 1, Kemper marched in battle formation to the gates of the city. As the rebels approached, Salcedo sent out three envoys carrying a flag of truce and a message addressed to "the Commanders of Troops in the mission Concepción." It proposed turning over the city on thirteen conditions — four of them "in the interest of humanity." He asked that the city not be looted, that the inhabitants not be deprived of their religion, arms, properties, or privileges, that no taxes be imposed, and that the sick be cared for. The remaining conditions asked that all troops with their cannon, ammunition, baggage, and provisions be allowed to withdraw to the interior, that those inhabitants who so desired also be allowed to leave, and that the Spanish officials not be mistreated. Crushed a second time by revolutionists, the king's men still had flair; and they had guts. Gutiérrez and Kemper accepted the four conditions in "the interest of humanity," but rejected the others and warned that their military titles must be used in future communications. A second proposal was also rejected, and Salcedo and Herrera surrendered unconditionally to avoid the city being besieged. Yoakum is responsible for the story that Governor Salcedo offered his sword to Captain Taylor, who referred him to Colonel Kemper. Kemper declined to receive Salcedo's sword, but referred him in turn to General Gutiérrez. This was too much! Salcedo stuck his sword into the ground in front of Gutiérrez and turned away.[25]

Manuel de Salcedo, Spanish Governor of Texas, and Simón de Herrera, Governor of Nuevo Leon and commander of auxiliary troops in Texas, along with twelve others, were made prisoners. Persons whom they had imprisoned, including seventeen Americans held in the Alamo, were released. The veteran

Revolution Sweeps Texas 31

troops, the militia, and the inhabitants of Béxar, along with the companies of the Alamo and of La Bahía, were incorporated into the invading forces and passed with their arms under the Green Flag of the First Texas Republic.[26] The flood of propaganda which Shaler and Gutiérrez had unleashed from Natchitoches and Nacogdoches, abetted by bigoted campaigns waged by American periodicals, had fanned a hatred and intolerance for the Spanish regime in Texas, which now rebounded. On the evening of April 3, Salcedo, Herrera, and twelve other prisoners were escorted out of Béxar under the guard of sixty mounted men. In command were Antonio Delgado, former corporal of the Béxar militia, and Pedro Prado and Francisco Ruíz of the Alamo Company. The Americans had permitted the release of the royalists because the ruling junta had assured them they were to be taken to Matagorda Bay, there to board a vessel and sail to safety in the United States. McLane said that Gutiérrez had proposed to the Americans that the prisoners had best be sent to La Bahía, where there were better security facilities, and the Americans, having no suspicions of his designs, readily consented to this arrangement.

The journey ended six miles from Béxar, near the recent battle site. The prisoners were dismounted, disrobed, and robbed of their valuables. Governor Salcedo's tongue was cut out. After being refused spiritual sacrament, they were beheaded with swords whetted on the soles of their executioners' boots. The bodies were left on the field unburied.[27]

American accounts of the execution vary with the teller. One frequent error that has been repeated into the twentieth century is that Manuel Antonio Cordero, longtime Governor of the Province of Coahuila, was among those butchered. One writer, Hunter, even embellished the fiction with a poignant story of how Cordero, "before his arms were pinioned about the tree" handed his watch and ring to one of his executioners and asked that they be forwarded to "wife, mother or relatives" in Mexico City. Cordero, in fact, served as Governor of Coahuila until 1817, having returned there in 1810 after five years in Texas. As for his wife, she was Gertrudis Pérez of Béxar, whom he had married in 1806. In 1804, her brother had bought the private residence on the west side of Military Plaza, once the *comandanciá*, and the probability of the Corderos having lived there affords legitimacy, in part, to its having served as home of the Spanish governors.

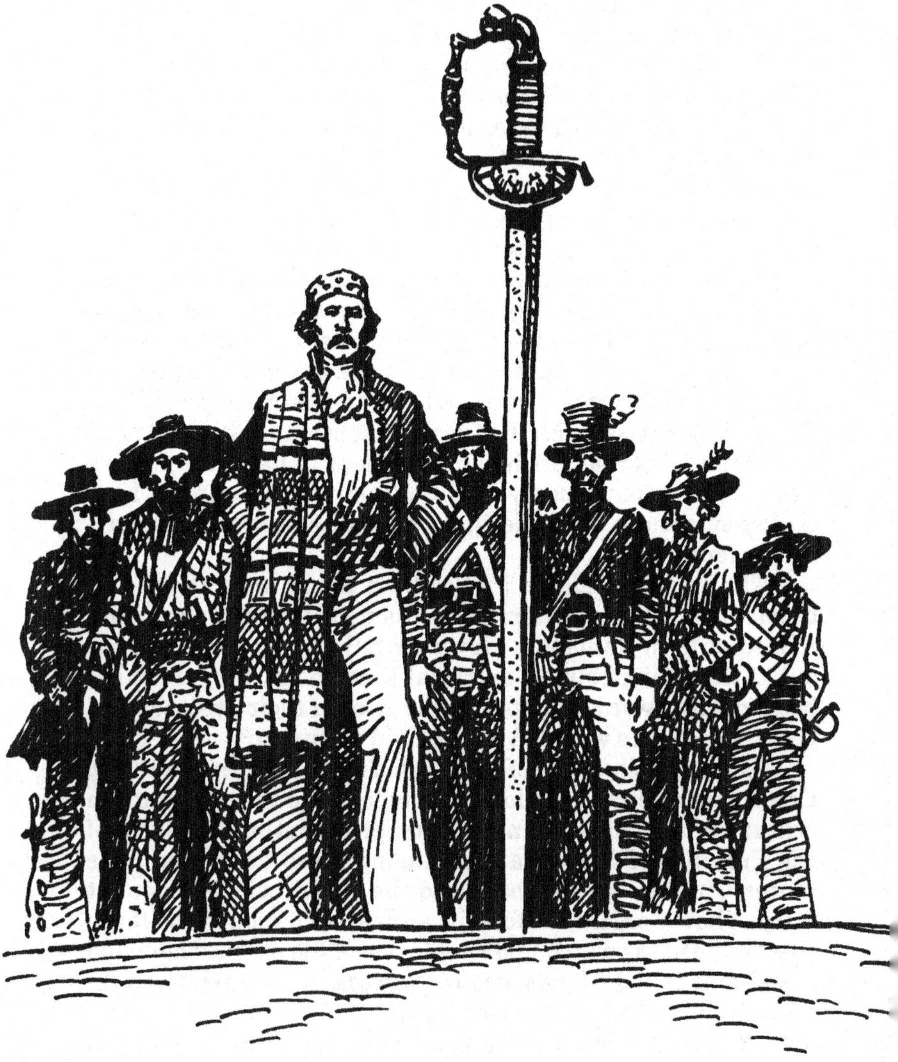

While we know the petulant character of Manuel de Salcedo only by what emerges from between the lines of his voluminous correspondence, we have a most favorable American appraisal by Zebulon Pike of Simón Herrera, former governor of Nuevo Leon who shared leadership with Salcedo. Salcedo, who seemed to have the interests of his provincial charge most sincerely at heart, had acquired experience in colonial administration when he served as his father's deputy in the governorship of Louisiana, where he also had married a New Orleans girl. But in Texas, in the shadow of his dominant uncle and immediate superior, Nemesio Salcedo y Salcedo, he became a bickering bureaucrat, pleading for help that his stern uncle did not see fit to provide and, when he felt the occasion warranted it, going over his uncle's head directly to the Viceroy.[28] According to Pike, Herrera, who stood almost six feet tall, with sparkling black eyes, dark complexion and dark hair, was "engaging in his conversation with his equals, polite and obliging to his inferiors; and in his actions one of the most gallant and accomplished of men." He had known President George Washington and held that hero in exalted veneration. When he entered into the agreement with General Wilkinson that established the Neutral Ground, he did it against the orders of his superiors and the advice of his officers — in the end, to receive the thanks of both the Viceroy and the Commandant-General for having disobeyed their orders! [29]

The following morning, when Delgado and his republican detachment returned to Béxar and informed Gutiérrez that the fourteen prisoners had been put to death, the native republicans applauded, but the Americans were horror stricken. They hurried to the site and interred the victims. Delgado was court-martialed but acquitted — he justified his action as retribution, claiming that Salcedo had taken the lives of his father and brother and had their heads dragged through the streets. The circumstances of this act are obscured. In a report which seems to have come from Kemper, *Niles Register* stated that the young Creole officer Delgado had witnessed many cruelties of Salcedo, and among them the beheading of his father, at which his mother was compelled to be present, and "by order of Salcedo the blood from the bleeding head of his father was sprinkled over his unfortunate mother." * James Gaines was

---

* José Antonio Navarro, an eighteen-year-old youth who lived in San Antonio during these turbulent years, denies this story. In his memoirs, Navarro

commissioned to justify the act to the American troops, and he later wrote a rambling rationalization for it, only partially factual. McLane said that on further investigation, the Americans found so many Mexicans justifying the act, they had no alternative but to submit. He attributed the fact that the Spanish officers had surrendered, rather than retreat from Béxar — as they had the time to do — to a lengthy conversation that Governor Salcedo had with Dr. Robinson regarding the treatment they might expect if defeated by the Americans. Robinson told them that if the Americans had entire control, they would have nothing to fear in such an event.[30]

The role of Bernardo Gutiérrez in the foul murders of the royalist officers is debatable. He avowed to the Americans that he knew nothing — that Delgado had acted on his own. Others implicated him indirectly. The effect on American morale was pronounced. The massacre, plus the turn of events in the next two- and one-half weeks, prompted Kemper, Gaines, Hall, and other competent officers to take furloughs and return to the United States.[31]

There the tragic blunder was lamented while the capture of the capital was applauded. Typical was a glowing account of the battle of Rosillo published in the Philadelphia *Democratic Press,* quoting a letter from Natchitoches dated May 8, which concluded,

> Now, my dear friend, could a veil be drawn over what is yet untold, I should feel happy; . . . I shudder at the horrid assassination; yet glory in the victory. This affair opens a door for Gen. Toledo who sends his respects to you from Nacogdochez; being on his way to join the army.

The letter's writer remains anonymous, but it bears the strong imprint of Shaler — particularly the reference to Toledo, of whom we shall yet hear much more. Six months before, Shaler had denied to Monroe that he had any connection with the letters that were appearing under Natchitoches dateline in the newspapers of the time. There can be little doubt, however, but that both Shaler and Sibley were managing the news from Texas, since articles appearing in *The National Intelligencer* and other eastern papers appear to have been copies of parts of their letters to their respective superiors.[32]

---

says instead, that Gutiérrez, like Pontius Pilate, ordered the killing, and Delgado's father died later on the Trinity River while attempting to escape Arredondo's wrath after the Battle of the Medina. Cf. José Antonio Navarro, "Apuntes Historicos Interesantes de San Antonio de Béxar," *San Antonio Ledger,* June 5, 1869.

PART TWO

The First Republic of Texas

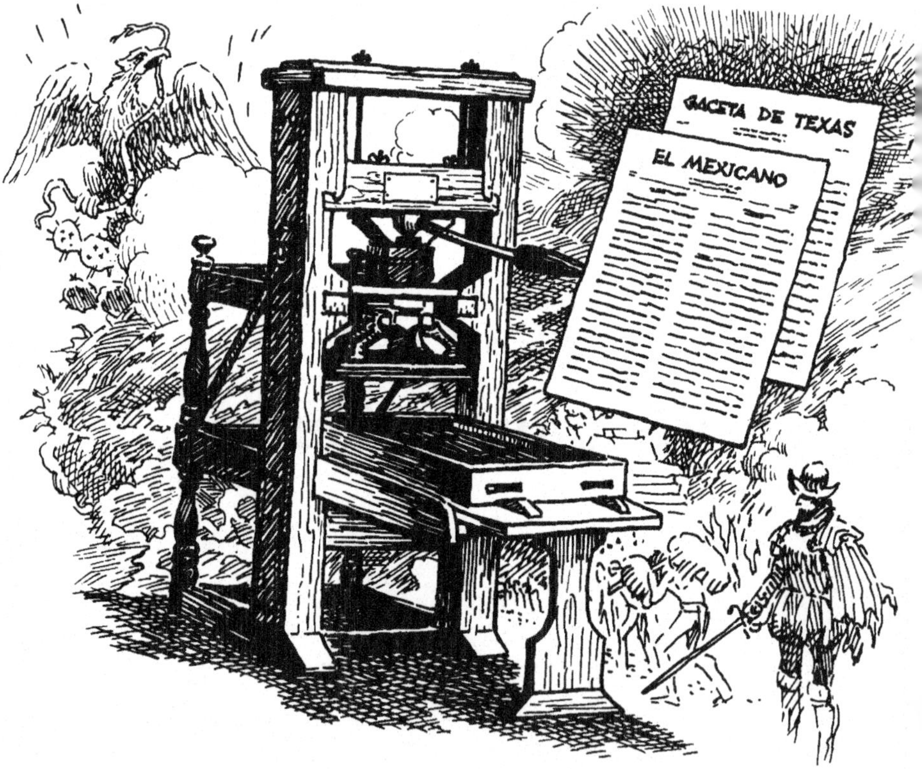
GACETA DE TEXAS
EL MEXICANO

3 Texas — An Independent State

THE MURDERS OF SALCEDO AND HERRERA removed all vestiges of Spanish power from the province of Texas, and the rebel government was unopposed from the Sabine to the *Río Grande del Norte*. In exalting letters, both Shaler and Sibley expressed their optimism to their superiors. Their joys were short-lived, however, as subsequent events unfolded.

In San Fernando de Béxar, a declaration of independence, "shaking off the yoke of European domination," was adopted on April 6, 1813 — the province assuming the name of the State of Texas for the first time. Authors of the declaration are unknown, but the phrasing clearly shows both Spanish and American influence. It cited the gamut of reasons that rendered the step necessary — a few of them somewhat specious, perhaps, but on the whole a noble statement. It reached a pinnacle of rhetoric with, "Man is formed in the image of his Creator: he sins who submits to slavery." It pointed to Spanish colonies of South America who had long since declared independence, and cited the United States's experience of thirty years as proof that "such a separation may be attended with national and individual prosperity." Samuel Kemper provided the editor of *Niles Register* with a copy of the declaration, which published a "hasty translation" of the principal parts in its July 17 issue.[1]

The declaration provided for the formation of a provisional government. Liberty ended there! Gutiérrez was empowered to name a president, a secretary, and five advisers to constitute a junta of seven, which would have full power to form a government and to write a constitution. Gutiérrez became president of the *Junta de Gobierno* which included among its *vocales* [board members] several Menchacas, two Arochas, and a Delgado, but not a single American. Samuel Kemper and the other Americans whose leadership had brought the filibusters to this point were excluded from the government-making process.[2]

The constitution Gutiérrez and his junta produced reflected their lack of training in statecraft. Reverting to type, the political system they imposed on the new Texas republic came out a rehash of the old royalist political regime. Gutiérrez was named governor of the State with the title of President-Protector, assisted by a twelve-man junta. Like the Spanish governor, the governor of the new republic remained the supreme authority; the Cabildo of San Fernando de Béxar was revived as the Supreme Governing Junta. Meeting one day each week, the Junta was a closed corporation that controlled public affairs, elected officials as well as the judiciary, and in all its acts was subject to the governor.[3]

The new nation had gained a government, but at a price which would yet destroy it. Disgusted with the gross murders of the Spanish officers, and grievously disappointed at having been excluded from the new government, Kemper, W. D. C. Hall, and several other American officers took furloughs on April 20, to return to Natchitoches. A great many of the seasoned volunteers also went home, only to be replaced by adventurous recruits who were streaming into Béxar. With the American leaders gone, discipline declined, while the army's strength shot up to over 1,500 men — almost entirely new recruits, former royalists soldiers, militiamen, and Indians. It became a disorderly multitude, rife with mutual distrust between Mexican and Anglo-American. McLane said the Americans spent their afternoons at fandangos, at which the ladies manifested more friendship for the Americans than for their countrymen, thus augmenting the growing hatred for the Americans. To avoid contact with them, some Mexicans left town in small parties, going into the interior, and there spreading the charge that it was the Americans who were responsible for the diabolical butchery of Salcedo and the Spanish officers, "which raised an universal storm of indignation against them throughout Mexico — causing men to vow before the alter [sic] to devote their time and means, and the women to sell their trinkets to raise men and money to exterminate these inhuman barbarians." He explains by footnote that the Americans, being ignorant of the Mexican character, yielded too readily to their counsel, thus subjecting themselves to the charge of complicity in their guilt. This turn of events "arrayed the whole country against the Americans, . . . The most ardent [Mexican] friends of the Republican cause became lukewarm, leaving the Americans to plan and fight their battles without their counsel or aid." [4]

Doctor Garrett summed up the situation thusly:

> Discord was everywhere in Béxar. The Republican Army, having much leisure, declined in discipline and spirit. Disorder was general and mutual distrust arose between Mexican and American troops. The arrival of multitudes of recruits added confusion . . . they were not grounded in the spirit of the early army of Magee and Gutiérrez.[5]

In the meantime, Lieutenant Colonel Reuben Ross succeeded Kemper as commander of the Americans.

Having put his house in order in Texas — or so he thought — Gutiérrez directed his efforts to liberating the neighboring provinces. Proclamations over his signature were sent to the several Rio Grande villas during April and May. They made known that the Texas Republic — with American help — was committed to the liberation of New Spain. Mexicans were urged to follow the example of Béxar by declaring independence and uniting with Texas in shaking off their yoke.

In April, while Gutiérrez busied himself setting his new Republican State in order, José Álvarez de Toledo appeared on the Louisiana–Texas frontier. What prompted him to abandon his role of behind the scenes co-worker in Philadelphia, is not entirely clear. For almost a year he had labored near the United States government, writing Gutiérrez at length, reproving, instructing, and cautioning him. A month before he left Philadelphia in December 1812, his dossier had been laid before Secretary of State Monroe, recommending Toledo as one in whom the "Government could place full confidence," whose knowledge of civil and military government would be an asset to Mexico. More important, the printer he had with him would be most useful in extending information and introducing civil government.

With an entourage of ten men and a printing press, Toledo appeared in Natchitoches early in April 1813. He carried a letter of introduction to Dr. John Hamilton Robinson, and, propitiously, Robinson returned on April 7, from his mission to Don Nemesio Salcedo in Chihuahua. To William Shaler, Toledo was presented as "General" Toledo, on his way to take command of the republican armies. Arrayed in resplendent gold braid, he cut a fine figure. Luis de Onís had described him as a person of "regular features, light colored, a very fine figure and very well proportioned," and both Shaler and Sibley took to him immediately.[6]

While he was in Natchitoches, Toledo, like Gutiérrez, was besieged with proposals. One was from General Adair's followers; another from Paillette, the French agent, who offered generous aid in exchange for free trade in Mexican ports. Also, like Gutiérrez, Toledo confided to Shaler all the proposals offered him. He was more interested in Dr. Robinson's report of conditions in Texas. Together they made extensive plans for the future, plans which Robinson was to present to Monroe on his return to Washington.

Toledo soon moved on to Nacogdoches, where he wrought order out of the turmoil which prevailed there. He established a public school, organized the militia, and equipped forty men for the army in Béxar. He won the confidence of the inhabitants, and they, in turn, elected him their representative in the new government at Béxar.

On May 7, Samuel Kemper and the other Americans on furlough reached Natchitoches. Their oral reports of the situation in Béxar, jolted Shaler from his complacent direction of affairs. Moreover, Gutiérrez's dispatches, brought by Kemper, which included a manuscript copy of the Constitution of the State of Texas, sent Shaler into a rage. That same day he fired off an angry report to Monroe, enclosing the Constitution which he called "an absurd revolutionary farce." With Bernardo Gutiérrez holding supreme power, he said, he now feared for the progress of the revolution. He put forth General Toledo as "a man of humility, with talents, and an enlightened mind," who should be given "the direction of affairs there."[7]

Dr. John Sibley was of the same opinion, telling the Secretary of War that he believed Toledo to be a man with talents, and that affairs in Texas would be set right when he took command.[8] Governor William Claiborne also registered sharp displeasure with developments in Texas. His chief complaint was Article One of the Texas Constitution, which declared that the State of Texas formed "a part of the Mexican Republic, to which it remains inviolably joined," thus removing categorically any American speculations as to whether Texas was included in the Louisiana Purchase or subject to annexation to the United States. Claiborne favored bold action. He wrote to General Flournoy, commanding troops in the Mississippi District, that since those in power in Texas,

> ...manifest no disposition to be dependent upon the American government or to grant any particular privileges to American people... [he desired it] to comport with the policy of the United States to occupy the country as far as the Rio Grande.[9]

Strong words from a Territorial Governor charged with responsibility for enforcing the Neutrality Act of 1794, and who two years before had ordered the arrest of "all persons engaged in — or against whom any well-grounded suspicion exists" of their engaging in a military expedition against the dominions of a foreign state "begun or set on foot within the Territory or Jurisdiction of the United States." [10] It had taken a hastily-drafted constitution, put together by a junta of frontier Mexicans and *Tejanos* — many of them illiterate or nearly so — to rip the masks of duplicity from Shaler, Sibley, and Claiborne, and to expose them as the eager imperialists they were.

That Shaler fully expected to play a pompous role in Texas is disclosed by a letter he wrote Doctor Robinson on May 7 — the same day he angrily sent Monroe a copy of the Constitution. He wrote, he said, because Robinson would understand the importance of a uniform and gold braid in New Spain. He explained that a sense of utility required him to request,

> ...a full dress uniform coat for a captain in the Navy [before he began his diplomatic career, Shaler had been a sea captain], a pair of gold epaulettes, a gold embroidered sword belt, a gold eagle and button, gold tassels for a hat and a few dozen Navy buttons for a waist coat.[11]

Shaler decided then to hightail it for Texas. Well attended by mounted men, he rode into Nacogdoches on May 20, 1813. He approved of what Toledo had accomplished there, sending Monroe a glowing account. But from San Fernando de Béxar,

Gutiérrez craftily thwarted Shaler's plans for Toledo. In an adroitly couched reply to Toledo's offer to join him in Béxar, Gutiérrez requested, instead, that he withdraw to Louisiana, explaining that he had been represented as a traitor to the Mexican independence. It seems that one Nathaniel Cogswell had written from Pittsburg in December, urging Gutiérrez not to permit Toledo to enter Texas; if he did so, he would "rue it in tears of blood," for Toledo was a traitor to Mexican independence — secretly in the pay of the Spanish minister in Washington — who plotted to end republicanism in Texas by seizing command. Cogswell had been a member of Toledo's entourage but, according to one of his aides, "had been discarded by the General and his party at Pittsburg on account of some dishonorable intrigues." [12] Be that as it may, Luis de Onís, minister in the United States from the Supreme Junta of Spain, wrote to Don Nemesio Salcedo, in August, that Toledo had made a proposal to him [Onís] before leaving Philadelphia, to betray the Republican Army. Before departing Nacogdoches, Shaler took sworn depositions from several members of Toledo's party. They declared Cogswell to have been a printer who was expelled from the group because of theft and falsehoods.[13]

Toledo returned to Natchitoches on May 29. Shaler followed on June 4 — but not until he had dispatched a blistering note to Gutiérrez, saying that his treatment of Toledo amazed him, that Gutiérrez was the "dupe of intrigues in which he would perish, and that all capable men would forsake him and his cause would fall." [14]

From Natchitoches, Shaler and Toledo mounted a vengeful campaign to remove Gutiérrez from command in Texas. At the same time Shaler undertook another vexing task, that of preventing French agents from taking over direction of the revolution. In this he had the dual duty of shielding Toledo from French emissaries, and of undoing the successes that French intrigues were having in Béxar. His reports to Monroe spell out some of the details.

Shaler told Monroe in June 1813, that Louis Massiot, whom Gutiérrez had installed as Secretary of State — he signed himself "The Sec. General of the Army" — was a French agent he had known in Havana. While Shaler was in Nacogdoches, a messenger from San Fernando de Béxar had met a courier from New Orleans and had delivered a packet of documents intended for Napoleon's agent, Monsieur Gerard. After he had turned over the packet, the messenger confessed his mission to Shaler. One wonders at the technique that Shaler may have used to obtain the confession.

On the Louisiana coast, six hundred Frenchmen from New Orleans and Barataria Island were ready to embark for Matagorda Bay — to aid Gutiérrez. Monsieur Gerard had already preceded them to arrange for the landing. [Texas was spared this invasion. The newspaper *El Mexicano* reported that Gerard was on a ship wrecked near Matagorda Bay; "Divine Providence" had saved Texas from the misery that nine vessels of banditti would inflict.] From Béxar, Reuben Ross reported that Gutiérrez, and Paillette — the French agent in Natchitoches — were arranging affairs through correspondence. Ross had been advised to eradicate this intrigue by wresting command from Gutiérrez, which course Shaler thought might be a good idea. Shaler wrote Monroe that he had taken every step in his power to save Texas, and "to sound and propagate alarm amongst the Americans" both in Natchitoches and in Béxar, and "I doubt not but the plan will be entirely disconcerted, and that the pretended Government of ignorance, imbecility, and fraud will be destroyed." [15]

Dr. John Robinson, too, warned the United States of the French menace. In his official report of his mission to Don Nemesio, he urged intervention in Texas and Mexico to frustrate French activities. He also reported that the French Consul in New Orleans had confirmed to him that Napoleon was prepared to lend liberal aid to the Texas revolutionists. [16]

It was to be Toledo's printing press and his aide-de-camp, Henry Adams Bullard, that were finally to be effective in cutting the ground from under Gutiérrez. In mid-June, Shaler wrote Secretary of State James Monroe that he and Toledo were about to publish a weekly political paper, *El Mexicano*, in English and Spanish, intended to contain an impartial account of the War of Independence. *El Mexicano* became a scathing defamation of Gutiérrez. Readers of the June 19 issue, which circulated on the streets of Béxar a few days after the Alazán fight, read that the "public voice" blamed the governor and protector of Texas for the most frightful calamities, errors, weaknesses, and monstrous crimes, "that we shudder at recording. We perhaps owe an apology to the public for introducing so insignificant and contemptible a character as José Bernardo Gutiérrez." [17]

Shaler realized that for the campaign to achieve its purpose, more than newspapers and broadsides would be needed.

He must have a campaign manager in Béxar. Shaler himself dared not go, so he sent Bullard, accompanied by one of General James Wilkinson's sons. He told Monroe that the participation of young Wilkinson was very indiscreet and in opposition to his [Shaler's] wishes.[18] One wonders whether Shaler was really successful in pulling the wool over Monroe's eyes or whether the future President was able to read between the lines — and that Shaler so intended.

4 *Spain Strikes Back*

IN ONE STROKE, AS IT HAPPENED, THE "weak monument of Texas independence" was to be brought down. Marching up from Mexico, the newly named Commandant-General of the Eastern Interior Provinces, Don Joaquín de Arredondo, was ordained to snatch Texas from republicanism — but not before his own forces also had made some arrogant, ill-timed moves, and intrigue, divided leadership, and personal jealousy had destroyed the military clout of the Republican Army.

Born in Barcelona, Spain, Arredondo was a career officer who had been instrumental in suppressing the Hidalgo and *Gachupín* revolts in the provinces of Nuevo Santander and Huaxteca, where he served as governor. Two years before, in March 1811, he had sailed from Veracruz with an expedition to crush revolution in Texas and to prevent Hidalgo and the Mexican revolutionary chieftains from escaping to the United States. Lack of maritime information concerning the Texas coast prompted him to disembark instead at Tampico, and to establish his headquarters at Aguayo, capital of Nuevo Santander. In 1812, he had left Aguayo to fight insurgents in the south — in the valley of Maíz, in San Luís Potosí. There news

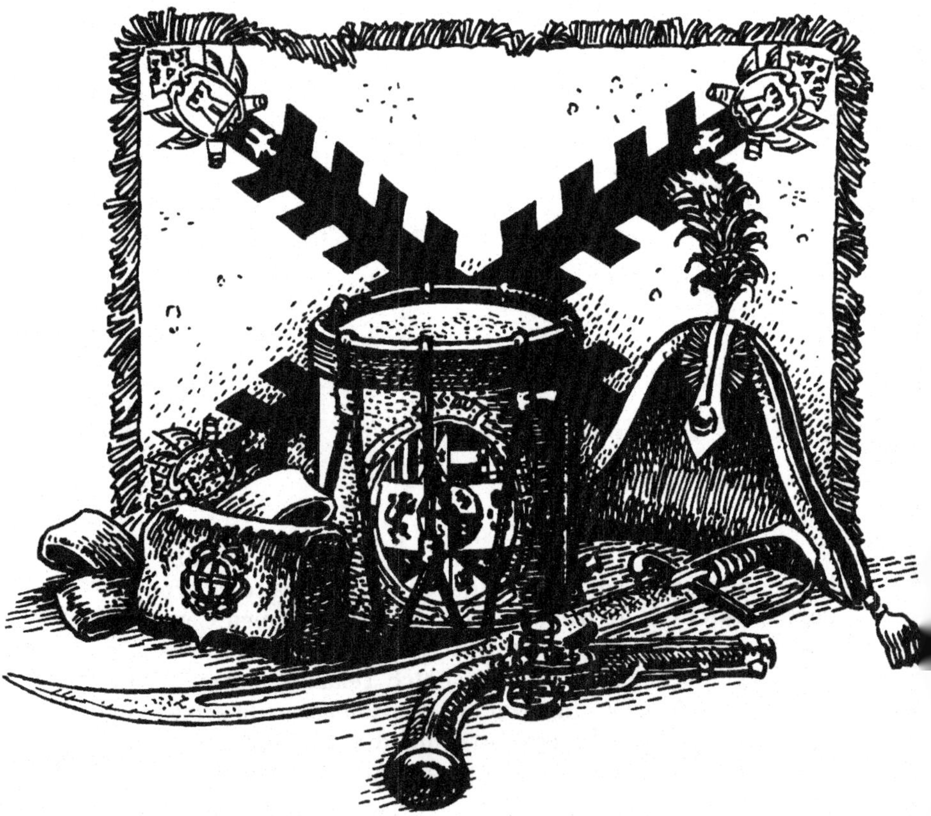

reached him of the deteriorating affairs in Texas. By mid-March 1813, Arredondo had decided that it was imperative to crush the revolution in Texas in order to uproot it in Mexico, and he wrote his superiors that he was marching to Texas. [It was about this time that Major General Félix María Calleja had been appointed Viceroy. It was Calleja who had chased Hidalgo's insurgent armies from Central Mexico. He had been Arredondo's superior, and he approved Arredondo's plan.]

On April 6, Arredondo left Aguayo. He was in Revilla on the seventh of May, and just missed seizing Gutiérrez's family, then on the road to join him in Béxar. On the way to Laredo — where he arrived early in June — he received word that Calleja had appointed him commandant-general of the four eastern interior provinces, if the death of Simón Herrera should be verified.[1]

The northern outlying [internal] provinces of Mexico had been separated from the viceroy's jurisdiction in 1776, and placed under a commandant-general responsible directly to the king. After various divisions and consolidations, Don Nemesio Salcedo y Salcedo was commandant-general for a number of years, headquartered in Chihuahua. In 1804, two separate jurisdictions were again ordered, but it was not until 1812, that Herrera was commissioned commandant-general of the eastern division. He was slain before actually taking office. Texas, Coahuila, and parts of Nuevo Leon and Nuevo Santander, made up the eastern division. During the last years of the Spanish regime, the Texas governors, in addition to being under the jurisdiction of the Commandant-General, were subject in fiscal matters to the *intendente* at San Luís Potosí, in judicial matters to the *audiencia* of Nuevo Galicia, and in ecclesiastical matters to the Bishop of Nuevo Leon.[2]

Also in the northern frontier at this time, at *Presidio del Río Grande*, was Lieutenant Colonel Ygnacio Elizondo. In March he had been gravely ill, and Dr. John Hamilton Robinson, on his return from Chihuahua, tarried a few days to administer medical aid. Elizondo's zeal had caused him once to join the ranks of the insurgents, but he became disenchanted when power and promotion were denied him. In 1811, at the Sanchez Navarro hacienda near Santa Rosa in Coahuila, he had been the jailer of the Governors Salcedo and Herrera — after they had been sent in chains from Texas during the Casas uprising. Salcedo then had reconverted the ambitious Elizondo to the royalist fold. Freed, both Salcedo and Herrera joined Elizondo in energetically reconquering Coahuila for Spain. At *acatita de Baján*, the renegade Elizondo he had seized the retreating insurgent chieftains Allende, Jiménez, and Hidalgo, and had sent them to their executions in Chihuahua — Hidalgo to become the immortal spirit symbolic of Mexican liberty. That ubiquitous soldier of fortune, known in Texas history as the Baron de Bastrop, was one of the spies who led the insurgents into Elizondo's trap.[3]

Elizondo had also served on the war council in Monclova which tried and convicted Captain Casas of high treason, had him shot, beheaded, and sent his head in a box to Béxar to be publicly displayed. "Unluckily, Casas, the man, did not become an heroic figure in the epic tales of Texas," wrote Dr. Julia Kathryn Garrett. "Unlike Hidalgo, the Texas insurgent has received only a few lines in historical annals. Some modern historians have even stated that Texas had no part in Mexico's struggle for independence."[4]

His health recovered, in April, Elizondo was assembling soldiers of Coahuila and fugitives from Béxar — the latter numbering some three hundred. About this time, he received an urgent entreaty from Gutiérrez, who, wishing to remove this obstacle to the advance of his forces beyond the Rio Grande, again invited Elizondo to join the republican cause. Elizondo held fast. In a rage, he replied that he would destroy Gutiérrez and his army by fire and blood, that he was determined "that in Hell shalt thou be put, thy body burnt and thy ashes scattered."[5] Poor Gutiérrez, how this curse floating up from the Rio Grande must have echoed later in his repudiation by Shaler from Natchitoches.

Toward the end of April, from Linares — while he was still marching northward — Arredondo ordered Elizondo into action again. He was to proceed to Texas, to camp on the Río Frío, to observe the enemy, to pursue them only if they fled with their cannon, but most emphatically he was not to engage them in battle, nor was he to enter Béxar. Before he left the Río Grande, however, Elizondo appeared to have had several meetings with Arredondo, in which they agreed on a plan to merge their troops for an all-out assault on Béxar. Elizondo was to await the arrival of Arredondo between the Frio and the Medina Rivers, and together they would destroy the rebels. Given to opportunity once again to play the hero role solo, Elizondo disobeyed on every count save one — he did not enter Béxar.

Taken in by reports brought to him by those who had fled

from the rebel capital, Elizondo hurried on to the León where he seized an outpost of nine men and forty horses on the morning of June 16. From them he learned that the rebels had a *caballada* of 300 horses at *el Puesto de Salado* guarded by seventeen renegade soldiers and six Americans. He captured them that night — killing three of the Americans — and, next morning, appeared on the Alazán where he claimed he seized fifty cattle and twenty-three hundred sheep and goats, plus three American spies. He wrote Arredondo that he had sent his pardon to all repenting insurgents in Béxar, that 300 soldiers and citizens had come out to join him, and that, but for the guards the rebels had, all the town would come out as the people were all disillusioned and recognized their error. What he did not tell his chief was that he had attached two of his own proposals to Arredondo's pardon. They were harsh: Within twenty-four hours, Béxar must surrender and twelve of the leading rebels [McLane said seventeen], including "the perfidious Gutiérrez," must be surrendered to him. He offered to pay the Americans 8000 *pesos* for Gutiérrez. Except for the twelve, all others were to be pardoned and the Americans would be permitted to return home.[6]

Needless to say, Arredondo was irate when word reached him in Laredo of Elizondo's disobedience of his orders. At three o'clock in the morning of June 21, he sped a courier to Elizondo with a message of rebuke for exposing the king's army and upsetting their planned strategy. Again, he reminded Elizondo of their plans and commanded him to await his arrival. But neither Arredondo nor Elizondo fully reckoned with the impetuosity and resourcefulness of the rebels who were once again to sweep all royalist troops from Texas soil.[7]

The republicans had not been unaware that there were great efforts being made in the interior to organize an army to invade and reclaim Texas. The native population was in frequent contact with friends and relatives on the Rio Grande, and Mexican scouts came in from time to time to report on conditions between San Fernando de Béxar, and the gateway villas of Laredo and San Juan Bautista — or *Presidio del Río Grande* — as the latter place was usually called. However, a fluke of circumstance had permitted Elizondo to slip through. It seems that John McFarland had been dispatched on the road to Laredo as a lookout. Hearing no news of an approaching army, for some reason he took off with his scouts down the

Nueces River, thus allowing Elizondo to reach the outskirts of Béxar undetected.[8]

With the reorganization of a civil government in San Fernando de Béxar, the Mexicans and *Tejanos* had assumed the police regulations of the city and countryside, while the Americans more or less abandoned themselves to a life of ease and dissipation. Sometime in the interval, Miguél Menchaca had organized and taken command of a force of three hundred mounted Mexicans and *Tejanos*. McLane said it was at the urging of the Americans that Menchaca, "an officer of some distinction," finally consented to organize and command such a force. Also, the Coushatta Indians, "finding no booty on the battlefield, and but little prospect of pay for their services," returned home a few weeks after their arrival in Béxar, much dissatisfied.[9]

So matters rocked along until June 14, when a rider entered the city announcing that a large army of royalists was approaching. This would have been Elizondo approaching on the Lower Presidio Road. Neither he nor the anonymous rider would have met with McFarland's spy party since they were on the Laredo Road — the rebels evidently expecting attack from that quarter. Panic followed. Gutiérrez wanted to retreat to the Trinity and from there offer Texas to the United States for protection. Soon word came that the report was unfounded — probably a dispatch from McFarland — whereupon confusion lapsed into indifference. On the eighteenth, Elizondo appeared near the Alazán Creek. He sent the three Americans he had captured at *el Puesto de Salado* into town with a long communication, which informed the inhabitants of Béxar, and the republicans therein, that their countrymen could not be relied on; that he had been one of the first to raise the standard of liberty and was betrayed and deserted by his pretended friends, and had been pardoned by the clemency of his king; that if the Americans would abandon the expedition and deliver to him certain of the rebels, he would guarantee them their pay according to their agreement with Gutiérrez, and they would be allowed to return home unmolested.

Disorder ensued. Ross advised retreat in the night; the men refused. He then proposed that they retire to the Alamo compound across the river and fortify it, but the men again refused to abandon the town. In the meantime, Ross had developed a liaison with a local girl whose father was one of Elizondo's soldiers, and she warned him that the native population had been won over. They planned — in conjunction with Elizondo's army — to fall on the Americans, and felt that Elizondo's promise to allow them to return home was only a part of the stratagem to trap them. She begged Ross to leave and save his life. Soon it was dark, and Ross rode off under pretext of placing the picket guard. Under cover of darkness and with a small escort, he abandoned his command.[10]

The Americans appointed a committee to ask Major Henry Perry,* to assume the command. Perry deferred until morning. During the night the men formed a square and took up their quarters around the cannon with their weapons at their sides. At dawn, Perry took command and ordered a general parade at eight. Not a Mexican showed up, which convinced the Americans that a plot was afoot to sell them out to Elizondo. Perry sent word to Menchaca that if he was not on parade at ten o'clock, with all his men, the Americans would proceed to hand over to Elizondo the prescribed rebels, Menchaca among them. When parade was called again, Manchaca's men were among the first on the ground, showing great eagerness to be led out against the enemy. The rest of the day was spent in making preparations, and all the men were ordered to report back to the plaza with their arms and to be ready to march at a moment's notice.

Sometime during the night — accounts vary as to the hour — the men were aroused and formed in marching order with their cannon drawn by hand in advance of their line. They proceeded in silence and arrived on a ridge in view of the enemy's quarters just as the daylight appeared. Elizondo had formed his encampment across a deep ravine near a pond of water. He had erected two log pens to the rear and mounted two cannon on the left to guard against attack around the head of the ravine. The royalists were at Mass — it being Sunday morning — when they were surprised by the discharge of the Americans' cannon. Elizondo immediately formed and posted his infantry in the ravine, with his cavalry placed behind his two cannon. William McLane described the battle that followed, thusly:

> ... The Americans advanced, playing their cannon on their cavalry and artillery — the infantry being protected by the ditches — dismounting one of their guns and driving their

---

* Major Perry was a near relative of Commodore Oliver H. Perry, who (two months later) defeated the British on Lake Erie, dispatching the memorable "We have met the enemy and they are ours."

cavalry [which McLane noted were few in number] back to a safer position. Elizondo sent a detachment to flank the Americans on their left where the Mexican infantry had formed, and Capt. Kennedy . . . was ordered from the centre to repel them. In the act of wheeling to the rear, your humble servant was shot in the back, the ball breaking a rib loose from the backbone, checking the force of the ball and turning it out through the side, which saved his bacon. . . . The Americans drove back the enemy's force on the left wing, and the whole line advanced leaving their cannon, and charging the ravine, driving the enemy out; and when the Americans advanced into the ditch their packmen and supernumerary force, being without arms except small swords, commenced pelting them with stones they had piled on the bank. The Americans mounted the bank and charged on the stone piles, driving the men back into their ranks, and attacking their whole line, which was defended with great skill and courage. The Americans pressing them at all points, they finally gave way, contesting every foot of ground until they arrived at their pens. Availing themselves of their protection, they made a last effort to repulse their foes. But the Americans, undaunted, charged the pens, shooting them down until they begged for quarter. The rest of their force, with Elizondo at their head, having abandoned the fight some time previously.[11]

McLane said the battle lasted about four hours and that the Americans lost five killed and had about twenty wounded. One of the wounded, Louis Massiot, died as the battle drew to a close. During the fight he had acted as aide to Colonel Henry Perry. He was shot through the body, and Villars, who was also wounded, said he died like a brave man.[12]

The battle of Alazán needs to be made the subject of an indepth study to sift fact from fiction, and to set straight confusing and conflicting data which have entered the history books. Prior to Dr. Garret's research, available contemporary sources — and the historians who drew from them — were in agreement that engagement took place on Alazan Creek about a half league northwest of Béxar, and that there was but one encounter between the republicans and the royalists. Doctor Garrett, however, advanced Sibley's version as he reported to the Secretary of War on July 10, 1813. Summarizing "many letters from different officers and persons connected with the Republican Army" which arrived from Béxar on June 30, and said that on June 18, upon receipt of Elizondo's demands, Major Perry and 1000 republican troops immediately marched out to attack. The royalists fled and were not pursued; the republicans returned to town. The next day, scouts discovered the royalists' camp, six miles from the city. On the morning of the 20th, Perry marched out again. "The Royalists discerned them in time to form on chosen ground a small distance in front of their Camp. The American Rifle Men began the Attack, the Royalists soon gave way & Retreated to their Camp which they Obstinately defended for about an hour; . . . when they all broke & ran in different directions." While we know that Sibley, with Shaler, was deliberately managing the news out of Texas, there still appears no point nor purpose in his having released a doctored-up version of the Alazán battle — one that differed so substantially from the facts reported by Villars, McKim, McLane, and Elizondo, all participants. Fernando Veramendi's appraisal of the articles confiscated from the enemy, dated seven days after the battle, placed it at *Paraje del Arroyo del Charco Alazán*. In his proclamation of July 4, 1813, Gutiérrez spoke of the "banks of *El Charco del Alazañ*" and the "plains of *Charco del Alazañ*, where the heroes of La Bahía and Salado so nobly distinguished themselves." Thus, the preponderance of evidence is that there was only one confrontation, on the morning of June 20, and that it took place on Alazán Creek.[13]

As was usually the case, the several chroniclers of the battle of Alazán gave varying accounts of the casualties. Probably the most reliable figures are those reported by William Shaler to James Monroe: "American volunteers killed and since died of wounds, nine; Mexicans twenty. Volunteers wounded, seventeen; Mexicans, none." One Indian was reported to have been wounded. The enemy's loss was estimated to have been 350 killed, with about 130 prisoners taken, of whom 52 were wounded.

Blundering Elizondo fled to *Presidio del Río Grande*. His foray from there to Béxar and back to the Rio Grande must have set some sort of a speed record. He had left the Río Grande on June 12. On the 17th, on the León, he had reorganized his division, forming the cavalry into three squadrons of 150 men each, and the infantry into four battalions of 150 men each — for a total of 1050 men. On the eighteenth — six days after he had left *La Peña* — he wrote Arredondo while awaiting a reply to the communication he had sent into Béxar. On the morning of the 20th, the battle of Alazán was fought. On the 23rd, from the Subaltern Quarters at *Presidio del Rió Grande*, he reported his defeat to Arredondo. It would not be unreasonable to presume that Elizondo outdistanced his battered troops and camp followers on the flight from the Alazán. In fact, he reported to Arredondo that it would be three days before all his dispersed people would be reunited.[14]

The victors returned to Béxar with their booty. According to lists sent to Shaler and Sibley, the quartermaster collected into his stores 5000 pounds of gunpowder, 350 stands of arms, and 4000 pounds of biscuits, forty pecks of flour, 1000 mules and horses with saddles and bridles, $28,000 worth of goods and clothing, $7,000 in specie and twenty-five packs of salt, besides Elizondo's two cannon [considered worthless], baggage, tents, liquor, cigars, coffee, beans, and sugar. The Republican Army was reequipped and refinanced by this windfall. Perhaps this explains McLane's comment that the republicans were not disposed to pursue so brave and magnanimous a foe, although they could have cut up the whole Royalist Army had they chosen to do so.[15]

When Félix Maria Calleja, the new viceroy, learned of Elizondo's blunder, he was uneasy. He insisted that Arredondo be cautious, to retreat before risking a defeat, because another such disaster would augment the evils of the moment to a point difficult to face. He notified Arredondo also, that he was sending a regiment of 1200 infantry recently arrived from Spain, that they had sailed from Veracruz and would disembark at Tampico and come overland to join him. Arredondo's rebuke to Elizondo was sharp, and sufficient to humble him for the remainder of his career. Again — for the third time — Elizondo was ordered to wait for the coming of Arredondo.[16]

In Béxar the republicans took new courage. From Natchitoches, the dispatches of Sibley and Shaler revealed the new spirit, Sibley writing the Secretary of War that Elizondo's invasion was, no doubt, the last effort to prevent the Republican Army from crossing the Rio Grande, that Toledo was on his way from Nacogdoches to Béxar with between 400 and 500 men, and that the Americans in Béxar were manufacturing swords and guns with great success and had mounted sixteen cannon. He added that the Government of Coahuila awaited the arrival of General Toledo "to make Some Amicable Arrangements with him & that their Example will be followed by Several Other Provinces." [17]

But it was for Bernardo Gutiérrez that victory at the Alazán presaged the greatest significance. Although he had remained well in the rear, well guarded, he counted on the victory to restore him to the confidence of the citizenry of Béxar and the Mexican troops, as well as to quiet his enemies among the Americans. True to form, he issued another proclamation inviting American colonists to settle in Texas, since the liberties of the Republic were "now perfectly secure." He chose the thirty-seventh anniversary of the American Declaration of Independence, July 4, 1813, as the date for his appeal, and in reporting the battle of Alazán, he stretched the fabric of fact somewhat. He credited Elizondo with 16,000 troops, while "my little band of renovated heroes . . . offered him battle with only 750 strong." [18]

When he was not busy with his pen, Gutiérrez enjoyed the companionship of his family. He had sent for them in April after independence was proclaimed, and his wife and two small sons arrived from Revilla, just as he was departing for the Alazán fight. It is said that Gutiérrez did not tarry to greet them, saying, "Forward! My country before my family." He took delight in their presence, however, and felt that fortune had indeed made amends for his long months of failure and frustration. Surely his mentor in Natchitoches, would now regret his harsh condemnation of a few weeks prior and the affectionate relationship they had enjoyed would be restored. He seemed unaware of the powerful ploy that Shaler was mounting in Natchitoches to unseat him! [19]

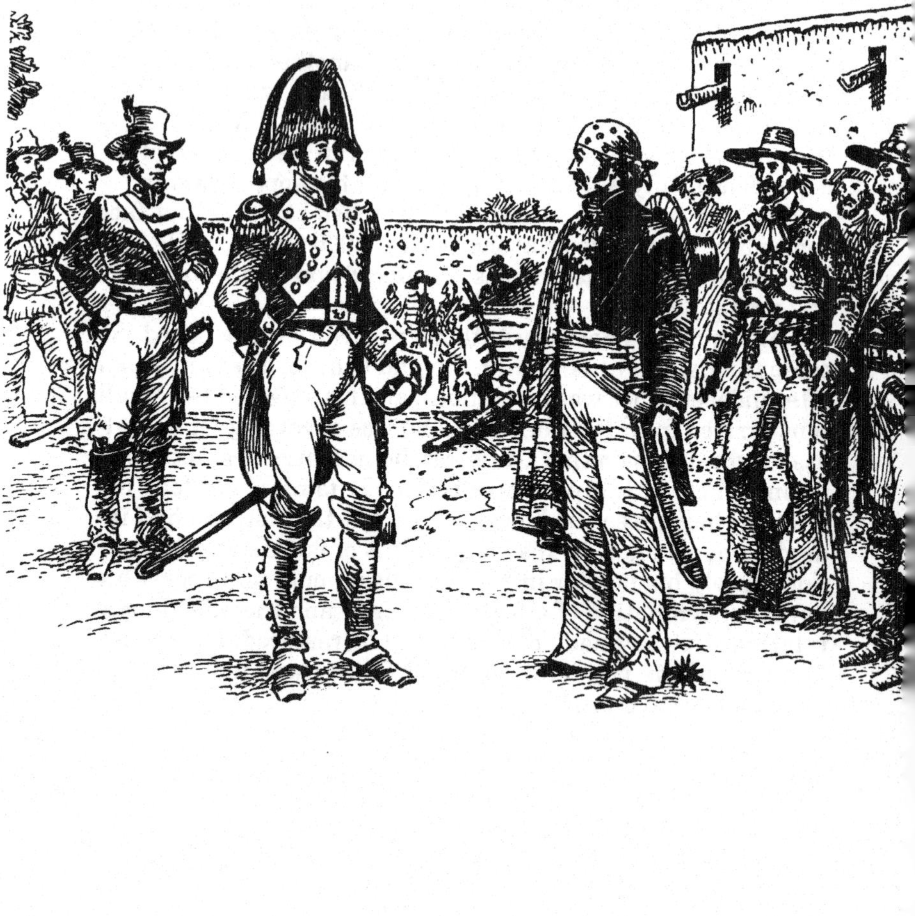

5 Shaler Switches Commanders

WHEN JOSÉ ÁLVAREZ DE TOLEDO departed Philadelphia to join his colleague in Texas, he carried with him a commission, signed by all but two of the delegates from the American provinces to the Spanish Cortés, granting him broad powers to take command of any forces which he might find in arms to sustain the independence of Spain's possessions, and to establish a government in the *Provincias Internas*. He was authorized at the same time to draw on Cádiz and Cuba for such sums as he might require.[1] In his entourage were Henry Adams Bullard, a fledgling lawyer; Juan Picornel, an old man and longtime South American revolutionary; a quartet of printers, Samuel Alden, Nathaniel Cogswell, Godwin B. Cotton, and Aaron Mower; one Colonie, a Frenchman from Marseilles, who served as *chef de cuisine*; and one La Tour, a New Orleanian who had changed his name from Calinette. Cogswell, as we have seen, was left in Pittsburg.

It was not until March 1813, that Toledo's little party finally reached Natchez, having suffered much from the cold and hardships endured on the Ohio River. From Natchitoches, as we have already seen, he and Shaler proceeded to Nacogdoches, after having sent Picornel on to Gutiérrez to tender the cooperation of Toledo and his group. Gutiérrez's imperious order for him to quit the State, incited by Cogswell's letter, caused both Toledo and Shaler to retire again to Natchitoches.

While in Natchitoches, and also in Nacogdoches, Toledo was joined almost daily by the arrival of fresh volunteers, whom he proceeded to organize into a well-disciplined force. Before Shaler left Nacogdoches early in June, he dispatched Bullard toward Béxar with about forty of these men, well-armed and in uniform. Of the original party, Juan Picornel and Samuel Alden accompanied the group. James Biddle Wilkinson, son of the General, was second in command of the party. They had traveled as far as La Bahía, where Gutiérrez learned of their presence and sent Bullard an order to remain there to guard the presidio. Bullard disregarded the order, and the party set out for Béxar. On the road he received another message from Gutiérrez offering him the post of Secretary of the Supreme Governing Junta of the Republican State of Texas, the office held by Louis Massiot, before Massiot was killed in the Alazán fight. The setup was perfect. Not only had Massiot been a thorn in the side of Shaler, who was fearful of his French intrigues, but from this high position Bullard could now proclaim to the citizens of Texas the evils of their new regime, and he could persuade both the Mexicans and the American volunteers in Béxar of Toledo's unique abilities to save the situation.

Once in Béxar, Bullard ruthlessly exploited his new office to mount a campaign to unseat Gutiérrez. Gutiérrez removed him from office, but he and his cohorts still had power. Their first objective was to win the American volunteers to their cause. Propaganda barrages from Natchitoches had prepared the ground; Bullard's speeches and promises now reaped a harvest. Among the promises, both Mexicans and Americans were told that with Toledo in command they would all receive their past and future salaries. Gutiérrez later charged that the people were told that the Congress of the United States had sent Toledo two million dollars for this purpose.[2] Another commitment to win over the native population was that Texas would remain free and be placed at the disposition of the hoped for Mexican republic. When a letter arrived from Shaler explaining that Toledo's leadership would solve all of their problems, the Americans signed a petition inviting him to Béxar.

Next, the Junta had to be won over. Bullard requested a meeting, which quickly resolved into a shouting match between Gutiérrez and Bullard. Gutiérrez accused Toledo of planning to deliver Texas to the Spaniards. He said that when Elizondo had appeared before Béxar, he asked whether Toledo had come, saying that if he were present, the business at hand would soon be settled. To discredit him further, Gutiérrez claimed that Toledo intended to introduce freedom of conscience and freemasonry into Texas — both heinous offenses to the Catholic members of the Junta. If Toledo came, Gutiérrez warned, blood would be shed. Bullard proceeded from argument to threats, vowing that unless Toledo were sent, all American volunteers would leave, taking with them all equipment. Henry Perry, speaking as commander of the volunteers, backed up Bullard in this threat.[3]

Without the American volunteers, the Mexicans and *Tejanos* knew well what the unbridled vengeance of Arredondo would be. By accepting the American presence in San Fernando de Béxar and by participating in the rebel government, they had painted themselves into a corner. The Junta gave its oral consent on June 27, and without waiting for the invitation to be put into writing, Captain William Slocum — one of the earlier filibusters — raced for Natchitoches with a letter from Bullard to Shaler. Bullard wrote that independence depended upon Toledo's presence in Béxar; the time had come for ruin or success. The Americans wanted Shaler to come, too, Bullard said, and, quite immodestly, he took credit for having saved "the independence of a nation" — aided by Shaler's letters. In the eyes of twenty-four-year-old Henry Adams Bullard, king-making was probably seen as a heady business! During the American Revolution his cousin, John Adams, had maneuvered the appointment of George Washington as Commander-in-Chief of the Continental Army. It is possible Bullard now saw himself playing a similar role in Spanish Texas.

Captain Slocum also carried letters from General Wilkinson to General Toledo and to William Shaler. In his letter to Shaler, Wilkinson revealed that his role in the conversion of the Junta was not entirely a supporting one. For the purpose of forestalling any intrigue, Wilkinson had sent Bullard and Colonel Henry Perry to make a deal with Miguél Menchaca. For American support of Menchaca, he and Francisco Ruíz were to put aside their previous fear of an open expression of their opinions and "that they will speak out boldly . . . for they carry with them the voice of the people and the army." Considering Menchaca's intransigence later, Wilkinson had probably oversold himself on Menchaca's enthusiasm for Toledo.[4]

Next day, the Junta drew up a formal invitation to Toledo in which it set forth six conditions under which he might come to Béxar. Although they had been intimidated and bewildered by Bullard's propaganda, their stipulations reflect that the Junta members were Mexican patriots first, their thoughts still with their people. Toledo was to be second in command to Gutiérrez; he must not introduce freedom of conscience, sectarian schools, nor Freemasonry; the army he brought must not exceed a thousand men, and when independence was achieved, they were to return to the United States unless each swore allegiance to Mexican soil. Considering the pressures that had been brought on the Junta members, their capitulation was hardly a *carte blanche,* but for Bullard it was enough — for the moment.

A fast courier brought the formal invitation to Toledo, who was again in Nacogdoches. On July third, he departed for Béxar, but with only one hundred volunteers instead of "between 4 & 500" reinforcements, as Sibley had predicted to General Armstrong, the Secretary of War. McLane noted that one of the first acts of Bernardo Gutiérrez, after the battle of Rosillo, was to,

> ... send a private express on the road to Nacogdoches, notifying all persons advancing to join the Americans — that if they proceeded they must serve without pay or emolument — that their services were not required. This order, from such authority, turned back all those on the road, promulgating this infernal edict throughout the country on their return.

Such an order may have accounted for Toledo's inability to raise a larger force at that late date, although, considering the heavy influx of recruits earlier, it did not seem to have deterred many already on their way.[5]

On July 10, in a letter to Monroe, William Shaler confirmed just how extensive his activities in Texas had been. He admitted that he had presented Toledo to the Americans, pledging his word for Toledo's honor and integrity, and that the Americans had responded with a declaration that they would receive Toledo or any person he recommended. They had asked Shaler to come to Béxar also. Shaler was elated. He would go to Texas as soon as Toledo had nullified Gutiérrez's "absurd government." Four days later he wrote Monroe that he was leaving at once for Texas, to support Toledo "to the extent of my power — consistent with my situation." On July 20, he again headed for Nacogdoches, only to be overtaken there by an earlier dispatch from Monroe ordering him back to Louisiana.[6]

Shaler was properly humble. He regretted having taken "a step not approved by the President," but explained to Monroe that he had tried to adhere strictly to the "spirit of his instructions." He reassured Monroe that events would still happen as planned, that Toledo would arrive in Béxar about August 1, where he would be hailed as their savior. Dr. Samuel Forsythe had written from Béxar that Toledo would be vested with all the powers Gutiérrez held, and then the Republican Army would march for the Rio Grande.[7]

Toledo did arrive on August 1, and the Junta immediately assembled to install him in office. Two days of bitter quarreling ensued. Gutiérrez's followers opposed his surrendering all his authority. Gutiérrez pleaded to be allowed to remain in command until after the impending battle with the approaching royalists. It appears the republicans knew then that Arredondo was on the march toward Béxar, after which he would turn over the command to Toledo. On the third day, the army forced a decision: Gutiérrez was to be removed from command and exiled to the United States. The next day, August 4, Gutiérrez resigned, and Toledo was named Commander-in-Chief [but not Governor] by the Junta in sort of a default commission signed by interim President Tomás de Arocha, and Mariano Rodríguez, *Secretario*.[8]

On the night of August 6, his long odyssey at an end, José Bernardo Gutiérrez de Lara moved slowly out of San Fernando de Béxar. His family, Dr. Forsythe, and a small band accompanied him toward Natchitoches. The tenuous cord of Mexican liberty, that had stretched from Father Hidalgo's *grito* on the church steps in Dolores, to the plazas of San Fernando de Béxar, had finally been severed.

In his victory Shaler was also defeated. He had failed to reckon with the *Tejano* character. Discord ran deep in the plazas and through the adobes and *jacales* of the century-old capital of Spanish Texas. The *vecinos* of Béxar, and the *Tejano* troops were steadfast in allegiance to their countryman, the deposed Gutiérrez. To them Toledo was a foreigner and a traitor, a *gachupín* who deserved no obedience — a native sensibility that soon would run to emasculate all of Shaler's planning and effort.

Leader of this disaffection was Colonel Miguél Menchaca, a nephew of the José Félix Menchaca who had guided Gutiérrez to the Neutral Ground in 1811. Miguél Menchaca had been one of the three commanders of Mexican companies at La Bahía where his loyalty never faltered, and he was characterized as a brave and gallant officer. His conduct in the Alazán fight had cast him in the role of a hero — albeit a disenchanted hero — who mirrored the discontent of the native population with the foreign leader who had been forced on them by Shaler's scheming and Bullard's brutal tactics. General Toledo sensed this discontent, and in a letter to Shaler, said he would purge the government and army of all of Gutiérrez's adherents if a royalist army were not approaching, but time only permitted him to prepare to meet Arredondo.

The time was all too brief. To restore confidence, Toledo proposed a reorganization of the Junta and issued proclamations envisioning future happiness. He renamed the army the Republican Army of North Mexico, and proceeded to reorganize it, thereby making a fatal mistake. In the battles of Rosillo and Alazán, American volunteers, Mexican troops, and Indian allies had fought as a unit, and standing together, they had won overwhelming victories. Toledo divided the troops along ethnic lines, the Mexican forces and the Indians forming one division under Menchaca, and the American volunteers under Perry forming another. Beyond that, Toledo's talents, which Shaler and Sibley had touted so highly, seemed to have failed him. He was simply unable to cope with the obstacles and opposition he encountered from the Mexicans and *Tejanos*, who refused to compromise or come to terms until the enemy was approaching the outlying ranches. Even Colonel Perry, commander of the American division, became irked with Toledo and declined to move when Toledo ordered the army to advance because so many of his men were "sick." Whether prompted by distrust, jealousy, or simply greed, the intransigence of the Junta and the army was Toledo's undoing, and on the tenth day after he had grasped the fallen scepter, rebel scouts brought word that a large Spanish army was advancing on Béxar.[9]

Commanders of troops in battle are prone to understate the numbers of their own forces and to blow up the strength of the enemy. For the winner such deceit enhances the glory of victory; for the loser (perhaps) it salves the wounds of defeat. The battle fought in *el encinal de Medina* was no exception. Versions of the sizes of the opposing armies ranged from the plausible to the ridiculous, with second- and third-hand reporters advancing the more improbable figures.

Historian Harry McCorry Henderson summed up the situation in Béxar.

> The determination of the strength of the Republican Army at this time is a problem. It is probable that the commander of the Republican Army did not know the strength himself.[10]

Henderson agrees with John Henry Brown that there were 300 Americans in Perry's command, a band of Coushatta Indians of undetermined strength, and about 600 Mexicans under Toledo and Menchaca.[11] Yoakum wrote that Toledo's force "consisted of 850 Americans, under Perry and Taylor, and about twice that number of Mexicans, commanded by Menchaca," making a total of around 2500.[12] Bancroft, who compiled his history from both American and Mexican sources, wrote that when Toledo "marched out with all his forces" to meet Arredondo, his army numbered "over 3000 men, and was composed of 850 Americans, about 1700 Mexicans and 600 Indian allies." [13]

Arredondo had reported from the battlefield that,

> ... the rabble ... had the boldness to come out to the field to fight me, in number about 3000, among these 600 Indians of different nations, all well armed ...

Later, to Viceroy Calleja, he said he had the satisfaction of engaging 3200 of the enemy.[14]

Bullard, Toledo's secretary and aide-de-camp, said in 1836, that Toledo's force amounted to about 1500, "of which about four hundred were American volunteers." [15] Young James Wilkinson, who wrote the first account of the battle, ended his report with, "We *know* that the strength of our own army did not at fondest including Indians much exceed twelve hundred men."[16] Dr. Sibley upped the number to 1400, the Americans consisting of between three and four hundred, when he wrote to the Secretary of War.[17]

The *Niles Register* in reporting the battle said, "It is probable 300 Americans were lost..." Adding three hundred to the ninety-odd who escaped across the Sabine, plus those taken as prisoners to Monterrey, brings the total to around 400, Bullard's count of the American volunteers. McLane gave the most conservative estimates: less than 300 Americans, 400 Mexican foot soldiers and about 200 mounted Mexicans under Menchaca. He made no mention of Indians. The Coushattas went home after the battle of Rosillo and there is no documentary indication that they rejoined the Republican Army. Arredondo failed to mention them in his reports. McLane did write that some one hundred "Sonkawanas" [Tonkawas] joined the Americans on the morning of the Medina battle.[18]

As can be seen, there is nothing definitive on which to gauge the strength of the Republican Army when it stirred itself to meet the approaching royalist force. On August 5, Toledo had ordered the American volunteers to organize into two battalions of 504 men each, not including the artillery company, plus a general staff of eight — a most optimistic table of organization which, no doubt, had at least twice as many vacancies as staffed billets when the army finally marched.[19] James Biddle Wilkinson's account was the first to reach the outside world. Both he and Bullard had been on Toledo's staff; therefore, it can be assumed that their figures are closest to what Toledo's own appraisal might have been. The author is inclined to accept 300 or 400 American volunteers and 800 to 900 Mexicans and *Tejanos* as plausible, with perhaps a hundred Indians, mostly Lipan Apaches, with a scattered representation of several other bands, for a total strength of between 1200 and 1400 men when the army marched out of San Antonio.

As for the royalist forces, most modern historians have been satisfied to accept Arredondo's own report of marching on Béxar with 1830 men, consisting of 635 infantry and 1195 cavalry. Bancroft listed 1930 men [as the result of a typesetter's error in *Gaceta del Gobierno de Mexico,* as can be verified by consulting the bound volume in the Bancroft Library, which has marginal notations by Bancroft's researcher], and in a footnote added eighty artillerymen. Foote set the figure at 2000, and Brown doubled that to 4000. Villars agreed with Brown [who may have taken his figures from Villars], and James Gaines reached the ridiculous with 10,000, of whom he sent 5000 out with Elizondo's reconnaissance party! Neither Bullard nor Wilkinson ventured an estimate of Arredondo's troops, but Wilkinson reported that the Mexicans had stated it at 3000 — a figure which must have included the packmen, mule drivers, and camp followers.[20]

The royalists arrived with a train of eleven cannon, of which two were dismounted and two were captured by the rebels in the pursuit of Elizondo before the battle. Toledo advanced with seven pieces of artillery, which Arredondo later reported were all three-pounders.

Thus, the opposing forces in the Medina battle were not too unevenly matched. Arredondo may have had the edge in manpower but not in logistics. His army had just marched more than sixty leagues through barren country, while the Republican Army was no more than a day's hard march from its base, giving it the choice of several advantageous positions. Had the rebels remained holed up in the city, made a defensive stand behind the Medina River, or even stood firm in the place Toledo had chosen for their ambush of the royalists, the history of the American Southwest might have been vastly different.

PART THREE

Defeat in El Encinal de Medina

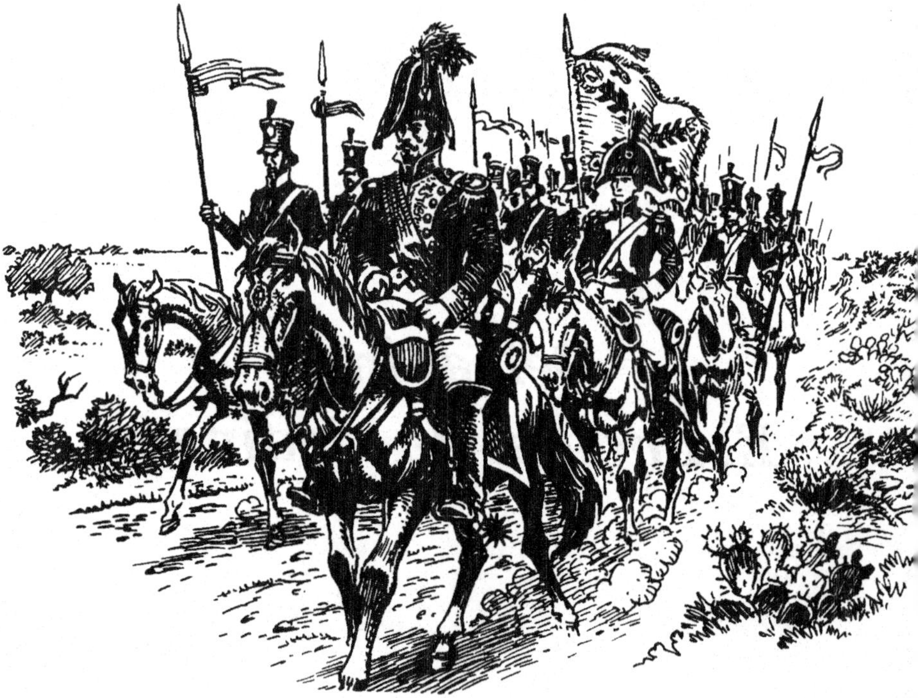

6 *Arredondo Probes for Advantage*

HAVING FOLLOWED THE VICISSITUDES OF the American-sponsored Gutiérrez-Magee filibustering thrust into the Spanish borderland, and having witnessed the formation of the first Republic of Texas — followed by the ruthless deposing of its Mexican president-protector by United States agents Shaler and Bullard, and having seen the ineffectual efforts of the *gachupín* usurper Álvarez de Toledo to grasp the helm and right the strife-torn ship of state, we now must attend that bloodbath in *el encinal de Medina,* which so decisively brought the entire effort to utter ruin.

It had been four months since Joaquín de Arredondo marched from his capital at Aguayo, Nuevo Santander, leaving Lieutenant Colonel Don Juan Fermín de Juanicotena as provisional governor of that province. Before he arrived at Laredo in June, he had received word from the Viceroy of his *ad interim* appointment as commandant-general of the *Provincias Internas Orientes,* a position of such broad civil and military powers that he was responsible, in most matters, only to the viceroy. Félix María Calleja del Rey, the newly appointed viceroy, who had decisively defeated the insurgent army of Father Hidalgo at *el Puente de Calderón* in January 1811, had great confidence in Arredondo's military and administrative abilities. Since the exchange of communications between the northern frontier and Mexico City required many weeks, Arredondo found himself, by default, possessor of almost autocratic powers over the king's subjects within his four provinces.

As previously stated, Arredondo had planned military strategy with Elizondo during several meetings at Linares and along the Río Grande. Also, Elizondo, captor of Hidalgo at *acatita de Baján,* had sought to gain further glory [and promotion] by leading a lightning-like strike to the outskirts of Béxar, only to be disastrously routed by the republicans commanded by Perry, Menchaca, and Bernardo Gutiérrez.

Now, Elizondo's bungling delayed the joint expedition against the rebels perhaps a month. After dressing down Elizondo, Arredondo sent him ammunition and 8000 *pesos* from the royal treasury to reequip his division. Then, about the first of August, Arredondo moved his troops up from Laredo to a place called *Cañada de Caballos,* where he expected to meet Elizondo. Four days later Elizondo showed up, and Arredondo merged the two divisions into an army of 1835 men, roughly two-thirds of which were cavalry. They rested a few days while he taught the men the "most necessary and indispensible formations and maneuvers in an action or battle," a discipline in which Elizondo's troops seemed to be lacking. He then took up the march toward Béxar, moving north on the Laredo road. He observed that from Laredo the country had been an immense desert, in a wretched state of nakedness — as was the case with the troops, most of whom were bare of foot and leg, many covered only with loincloths. Nevertheless, if we may believe Arredondo, they were most eager to engage the "wicked rabble" as soon as possible.

On the Seventeenth of August, Arredondo later wrote, he arrived with his army and made an overnight camp a league and a half "toward this direction [that is, toward Béxar] from a place called *Rancherías."* From *Campo del Atascoso,* he sent out a corporal and four soldiers to reconnoiter the country and to note the enemy's movements, with orders to proceed as far as Béxar if they found no rumor of the rebels. At that time, he claimed, he had absolutely no information of their location — a circumstance which would profoundly affect events on the morrow. The spy party noticed a great many signs of people on foot and on horseback, so they returned to camp.[1]

Neither *Cañada de Caballos* nor *Rancherías* has come

down to us as an identifiable place name on modern maps. *Cañada de los Caballos* was mentioned by Fray Solís some forty-five years earlier, while he was en route from *rancho del Atascoso* to Laredo, and, assuming it to be the same place, the rendezvous site of Arredondo and Elizondo was some fourteen miles southwest of present-day Tilden in McMullen County. Bullard wrote that the meeting place was a three or four day march from Béxar. There was also a newspaper account some months later which claimed that Toledo had received word as early as August 4, by way of La Bahía, of Arredondo's presence at *Cañada de Caballos*. However, McLane wrote that the royalist army was encountered while they were on the march on the Laredo road — some fifty miles from San Antonio — by Captain McFarland's spy company.[2]

More obscure perhaps, but documented throughout Spanish colonial times, was the great San José mission ranch *El Atascoso*, with its droves of mares, yokes of oxen for plowing, and hundreds of cattle and thousands of sheep and goats, all tended by the mission Indians without supervision from outsiders. *Rancherías* was probably its headquarters, located somewhere in the vicinity of present-day Poteet, near the *camino real* crossing of the Atascosa River. Throughout the colonial period, Spanish writers referred to Indian settlements as *rancherías*. *Atascoso* was mentioned as early as 1736, as being some thirty-five miles from the San Antonio [Alamo] mission on the way to the Rio Grande, that is, on the *camino real*. Fray Solís had been on his way to Laredo from Béxar when he stopped at the ranch, and he subsequently crossed the La Parita and San Miguel Creeks and the Frio River,[3] but his route does not necessarily locate *Rancherías* on the Laredo road. *El Atascoso* ranch had been in existence for some years before the *Villa de Laredo* was founded in 1755, and Solís's itinerary merely confirms that by 1768 there was an established trail or trails permitting travelers to switch from the old *camino real* to the newer road, or vice versa. For some miles below the Atascosa, the roads ran roughly parallel and only a few miles apart.

It must have been such a bypass or connecting trail that Arredondo chose for his army to follow on August 17, as they made their way to a campsite some four miles past *Rancherías*. A careful reading of his report establishes that he probably had this in mind when he crossed the Medina in order to outflank the rebels, all of whom he expected would come out to meet him on the Laredo road. He wrote that in view of the information that his scouts had brought him,

> ...before starting on my march [on the eighteenth] — which I directed toward the river Medina, proposing to change my course [*extraviar camino*] in order to cross it by a different pass from the direct one ... I sent forward Lieutenant Colonel Don Ygnacio Elizondo ... I informed him of the route by which it had been arranged to cross the river Medina, and the road, which was a short cut, [*camino que cortaba*] for him to follow in his retreat until he joined me.[4]

Arredondo had not been in the *encinal* before and would not have known the roads, but one of his aides, Don José María Cespedes, was from the presidial company of La Bahía and must have known the area well, as did Elizondo, Captain Ygnacio Pérez of the Béxar militia, and many others of his entourage.

Now, if Arredondo's army had still been on the Laredo road when he sent out Elizondo, and if it intended to continue up that road, there would have been absolutely no reason for Elizondo to be told of a shortcut to Arredondo's intended position later in the day. As there is no documentary basis whatever for assuming that Elizondo did *not* use the shortcut for his retreat after flushing the rebels, one must conclude that daybreak on the eighteenth found Arredondo in camp somewhere to the west of the Laredo road, and on a course which would take him to some point on the Medina River other than the Laredo road crossing.

The American chroniclers also have pinpointed Arredondo in areas that must have been westward of the Laredo road. In his *Memoirs,* Antonio Menchaca said that the American spies had watched Arredondo's movements,

> ... until he got this side of the Atascosa ... that Arredondo stopped at the water holes called *Charcos de las Gallinas* on the hill this side of the Atascosa Creek and about five miles from the Medina River.

Menchaca, who was only thirteen at the time, would have gotten his facts from others, and it is not improbable that — writing many years later — he got his place names confused and that his *Charcos de las Gallinas* referred, not to Arredondo's campsite, but to Toledo's at *Laguna de la Espada.* His reference to "*the hill ... about five miles from the Medina River,*" fits the contemporary description of the site chosen by Toledo for his ambush of the royalists.[5]

John Villars, who was captured and taken to Monterrey by Arredondo, wrote that Arredondo fixed his camp some ten miles west of the Medina. "*West*" meaning on the right bank and not necessarily in a westerly direction. The Medina flows west to east in this area.[6]

James Gaines, who was not present when the battle was fought, but who nine years later helped Mexican Governor Trespalacios bury the bones of the fallen, reported that Arredondo "now advanced to a small lake where he fortified distant about 6 miles from the Medina." In reporting his trip with Trespalacios to San Antonio in 1822, he again placed the battle site, "*at the lake 6 miles from the Medina where the Patriots were defeated in 1813.*" Later he was to remark that while they buried the bones at the site, "*the skulls were taken on 6 miles further to Medina where at the foot of a pecan tree [we] buried them in the honors of war.*" There is no rationalization for Gaines's repeated reference to "6 miles" — the campsite and the battleground could not possibly have been equidistant from the river.[7] He was not always accurate in some of his reporting. Perhaps the passage of time had confused his recall.

McLane stated in his narrative that, after the Republican Army had made camp for the night, "The spies came in after dark and reported that they had kept the enemy in view, until they encamped for the night, *about six miles from the Americans.*" As a point of reference, McLane at the time had the Americans, "*4 or 5 miles South West of the Medina river* [crossing], *at a small stream of water,*" a location that is confirmed by other contemporary accounts.[8][Italics added in this and preceding paragraphs.]

Mirabeau B. Lamar obtained information from James Gaines in 1835; and from John Villars in about 1847. Menchaca wrote his *Memoirs* late in life — all after passage of sufficient time to allow for some distortion of memory. McLane's narrative was not published until 1860–1861; however, he must be accorded credibility if but for two reasons: One, his purpose in writing was to correct Yoakum's "multitude of misrepresentations and erroneous assertions," and, two, he had lived in San Antonio since 1854. McLane was a wealthy, retired businessman, and had had ample opportunity and means to have revisited the battle sites to refresh his memories of the terrain — and it can be assumed that he did so. Although McLane wrote almost forty years after the events of the summer of 1813, his narrative cannot be discounted because of possible confused recall of terrain features — as could have happened to anyone who only saw the area once, and then in the heat and confusion of battle.

Without digressing further into corroborating detail or speculation, the preponderance of the available evidence seems to establish that Arredondo, in approaching his hour of triumph over the republican rebels, moved his army thusly:

After leaving Turkey Creek, where he may have camped at the waterhole marking a burned out, forgotten Spanish outpost that since the 1920s has gained fleeting notoriety as "Dead Man's Tank," he crossed La Parita Creek by the Laredo ford. Then, somewhere within the next several miles — probably in the vicinity of Parita Hill — he struck out in a northwesterly direction, following an established trail, possibly even the one Fray Solís had traveled. He went over high ground which marked the divide between the watersheds of present-day Bonita and Goose Creeks, across the site where Jourdanton was to be laid out a century later, arriving at the Lower Rio Grande Road [the *camino real*] before it crossed Salt Branch, probably a bit north of where the Camino Real historic marker is now placed on State Highway 173. The distance between the two roads by this route would be approximately three leagues, or eight miles, of fairly level ground with no ravines or creeks to cross — an easy shortcut and one which would offer good visibility and virtually no cover to conceal an enemy ambush. He then moved his army and train on the Lower Rio Grande Road, crossed the Atascosa at the old *camino real* ford about one mile southwest of present-day Poteet, and continued on past *Rancherías* to his campsite, which he called *Campo del Atascoso*.[9]

The campsite might have been anywhere in what is today called Rutledge Hollow, but most probably it was in a shallow draw three-quarters of a mile to the east, where even today there are several shallow ponds alongside the faint ruts of the ancient road. Wherever Arredondo chose to stop for the night, there had to have been a waterhole of sufficient capacity to supply the needs of some 2000 or more hot and thirsty humans and perhaps twice as many animals. This may have been a natural pond, or it might well have been a stock tank or reservoir built by the mission Indians in the heyday of *El Atascoso* ranch. Solís noted that *El Atascoso* had "some watering places of good and permanent water with fish *robalo, vagre*, eels, etc." [10]

Having reached his campsite, Arredondo would have been about twelve miles south of the Perez crossing of the Medina River, between thirteen and fourteen miles southwest of the Laredo Road crossing, and about the same distance from the intermediate ford at the Garza ranch. He anticipated that the enemy would come out to meet him on the Laredo road, but, unlike his adversary, when Arredondo lay down in his tent that night, he did not know his enemy's whereabouts; nor did he know that Toledo had spotted his camp and was preparing to ambush him just six miles ahead.

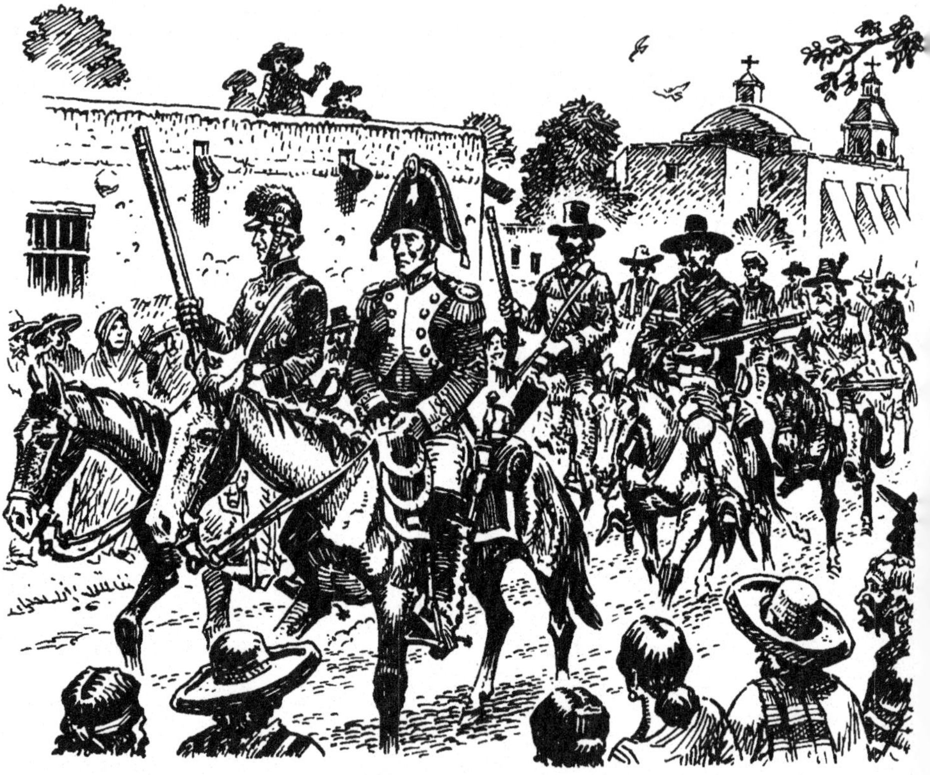

7   Toledo Moves to Set a Trap

WITH TRANSPARENTLY CLEAR AND SIMPLE hindsight, students of history have speculated as to why General Toledo abandoned a defensible position in San Fernando de Béxar, to march out and challenge Arredondo's army in the sandy wilderness below Gallinas Creek. McLane offered an explanation — of sorts. He wrote that the Spaniards had been discovered by Captain McFarland's reconnaissance party on the Laredo road about fifty miles from Béxar, and, having received this intelligence, Toledo proposed to march out and meet them. The American volunteers preferred to await their arrival near the town, but went along with Toledo's plan because it was favored by the *Tejanos*. They, no doubt, preferred that any fighting take place elsewhere than around their homes and families.[1]

On August 13, Lieutenant Colonel José María Guadiana, acting adjutant, had issued an order of march. The Washington Regiment of American Volunteers was to march at the head of the column, followed by the Mexican infantrymen. McLane said these numbered about 400, mostly prisoners and deserters from the enemy's ranks, including the captives taken in the Alazán fight. The Madison regiment and two pieces of artillery would bring up the rear. An advance guard of twenty Mexicans and Americans, under two officers, were to reconnoiter 200 paces ahead of the column. The munitions train, escorted by a section of artillery, was to fall behind the Madison rear guard, followed by the mounted civilians — numbering between 200 and 300, under Colonel Menchaca — with the Indian allies bringing up the rear. It is not known whether this order of march was observed when they finally moved out two days later, but McLane said the exodus was "cheered with the sound of martial music and smiles and salutations of the ladies." [2]

Some months after the Medina battle, the *Lexington Reporter* printed a lengthy letter from an anonymous person who claimed to have been "an eyewitness of the operations since the arrival of General Toledo in San Antonio." The letter went into considerable detail concerning Toledo's problems not only with Colonel Menchaca, but with the President of the Junta, and the Americans, which thwarted the General's efforts to move the army out of Béxar. It was undoubtedly written by someone close to Toledo, perhaps Bullard, since his name is conspicious by its absence in the account, and observations of the writer closely follow those made by Bullard in the *North American Review* in 1836.[3]

The letter [which probably gained a strong pro-Toledo bias in its translation into Spanish, and suffers further by retranslation back into English] stated, in essence, that Toledo gave orders for the army to march as early as August 5, with the objective of attacking Arredondo before Elizondo joined him. Somehow, it was mid-afternoon on the eighth when Toledo moved out with the Mexican troops and camped outside San Antonio at a place called *la Garita*. Perry failed to follow with the two American regiments, although Captain Josiah Taylor's company and another company did show up at eight that night. Toledo sent Captain James Biddle Wilkinson back to find out what was keeping the rest of the army from moving out. Wilkinson was back at nine to tell the general that Perry was sick.[4]

Several days of political maneuvering and countermaneuvering followed — including Toledo inviting his archenemy Menchaca to supper in his tent and arranging a dance at his encampment for the citizenry. In the end, a heavy rain forced the general "to abandon the only plan which would have been able to save the State of Texas and they returned to San Anto-

Toledo Moves to Set a Trap

nio and each one returned to the old idleness and inaction in which they had been since they occupied the capital." [5]

According to this account, the Republican Army finally moved out on the fifteenth, arriving the next day at the *Rodeo de la Espada*. After a detailed reconnaissance of the terrain and the road "by which the enemy must direct its march," Toledo selected "an extremely advantageous" place some distance forward where he planned to ambush and attack the enemy on its march — to which place he advanced the army, arriving between eight and nine o'clock on the morning of the eighteenth.[6]

Except for the anonymous letter in the *Reporter*, of the several contemporary American accounts, it is McLane's narrative that gives the most distances and directions, and also identifies several terrain features. In summary, McLane said that after two days of preparation, the Republican Army marched out of town "on the morning of the eighteenth [fifteenth] and encamped two nights later 4 or 5 miles South West of the Medina river, at a small stream of water ..." [7] This would have been Gallinas Creek. Bullard, in his essay, described the Medina that summer as,

... rather a deep ravine than a river [which] at that season is almost dry; but its banks are so steep, and the passes so narrow, as to impede the crossing of artillery. The republican army crossed this stream, and occupied such a position as to watch the only two fords, by which San Antonio could be approached from that quarter.[8]

In 1813, in this sector, there were three fords over the Medina River which served the roads to the south: the one at the Garza ranch below the confluence of Leon Creek [erroneously marked in 1918 as the Camino Real crossing]; the *camino real* crossing at the Pérez ranch several miles above; and the Laredo Road crossing below. Bullard's reference was to the two upper fords at the Pérez and Garza ranches, for the Republican Army was encamped on the Laredo road, thus denying that crossing to Arredondo. Bullard's use of "from that quarter" confirms that Arredondo was not then on the Laredo road but poised to approach the Medina at one of the two upper fords.[9]

Antonio Menchaca, in his *Memoirs*, wrote that the American spies were incessantly on the lookout, watching Arredondo's movements, and when Toledo was told that the royalists were across the Atascosa and advancing,

... Toledo prepared to meet them starting from here [Béxar] in the direction in which Arredondo was coming, slept at *Laguna de la Espada* the first [night], on the second [day] he crossed the Medina River and on a hill, a short distance the other side, he thought a convenient place to take the enemy at a disadvantage.[10]

As previously mentioned, Menchaca wrote his memoirs late in life, and he quite obviously garbled the sequence of events somewhat. The anonymous letter writer had the army camp on *Arroyo de la Piedra* the first night, making a permanent camp at *Rodeo de la Espada* the next day [the sixteenth], which was, no doubt, the same place as Menchaca's *Laguna de la Espada*. Such a cattle roundup station, with both corrals and ample water, would have provided an ideal bivouac area. It was located either between the Medina River and Gallinas Creek — an unlikely spot due to the nature of the terrain — or on Gallinas Creek itself. Fray Agustín Morfi recorded in 1778, that the mission Espada pasturelands then extended for more than two leagues beyond the Medina River.[11]

Bullard also observed that Arredondo was approaching on "the great road." The sandy trail that led through the *encinal* would hardly qualify as a great road, even though it was then a branch of the Laredo road. His reference would have been to Arredondo's approach earlier on *el camino real*, which for a century and a quarter had served as the main thoroughfare from the south.[12]

Wilkinson's report telescoped the march from the permanent campsite into a few terse lines:

> Learning that Arredondo was near at hand, we marched on the 18th Augst to the ground pitched upon by Genl Toledo as the position, where we would await the enemy and give battle. We arrived there early in the morning, formed our line of battle and had reason to believe, we should see him [the enemy] in an hour or two.[13]

Neither James Gaines nor John Villars, both usually voluble reporters, gave more than a few random words to Toledo's advance from Béxar. We know James Gaines was not present that day, and Villars's very brief report strongly suggests that he was not a participant in the Medina battle. He had been severely wounded in the Alazán fight and probably was still on the sick list when the army moved out of Béxar.

H. H. Bancroft, who drew his material from Mexican as well as American and Texian sources, had this to say of Toledo's movement of his troops:

Toledo Moves to Set a Trap

... Moving along the road to Laredo, on the 18th of August, he came upon the advance troops of the Spanish army shortly after crossing the river Medina, and the engagement began ... It had been his [Toledo's] wish to wait for the enemy on the left bank of the Medina, the advantage of which position was obvious; but he had been outruled by both the Mexican and American officers, who flushed with their victories, were eager for the fray.[14]

Then, citing the evident want of harmony and confidence between the general and the native portion of his army, Bancroft copied almost verbatim from Yoakum:

... and perhaps this was the cause of [Toledo] making the grievous mistake in forming his line of battle. Placing the Mexicans in the centre, he divided the Americans, and posted them on his right and left wings...[15]

Both historians probably were thrown off here by Guadiana's order of march which had the Mexican infantry between the two American regiments, as it was the consensus of accounts left by the American participants in the Medina fight, that Toledo's battle line on the morning of the eighteenth was formed with a company of Americans and one of Mexicans, alternately in line, in single file. This is, perhaps, an instance of Bancroft taking his cue too literally from Yoakum, whose reporting of the Gutiérrez–Magee expedition was bitterly assailed by both William McLane and Warren D. C. Hall.[16]

In summary, General Toledo was beset with the most vexatious problems in getting the Republican Army to march out of Béxar. Not only did Colonel Menchaca, the charismatic leader of the mounted *Tejanos*, oppose him [he even convened a court-martial of his officers and proposed to imprison Toledo on the pretext that he planned to deliver the republican army to the royalists], but the president of the junta, Don Tomás de Arocha, and the *alcalde* (mayor) of the city, countermanded Toledo's orders, once withdrawing 200 men from Toledo's command. The American Volunteers, under Colonel Henry Perry, seemed equally reluctant to cooperate and, except for two companies, failed to move out on August 8, when Toledo marched the army out to *la Garita*.

When they finally did march a week later, some unanimity seems to have been restored — perhaps because of word received the day before that Arredondo and Elizondo had joined forces and were marching on Béxar. Cheered on its way by martial music and the good wishes of the women, the Republican Army camped the first night on the *Arroyo de la Piedra,* a creek no longer on the maps but which probably was between Espada mission and the Medina River. The next day the Medina was crossed, and that night camp was made either on the Gallinas Creek or near it, at a place called *Rodeo de la Espada,* where the Espada mission ranch had once maintained watering holes and corrals to work its livestock. By 1813, the San Antonio missions had been secularized, and the ranch improvements had been abandoned.

While the army bivouacked for two nights at *Rodeo de la Espada,* Toledo personally made a thorough reconnaissance of the terrain before him, and of the road through it, by which the enemy was expected to direct its march. He chose "an advantageous position on the Laredo road," several miles forward from the main camp, where he proposed to surprise and attack the enemy from an ambush. Two parties of spies were kept busy reporting to Toledo on the enemy's movements, and, at nightfall of the seventeenth, he got the intelligence that the royalists had made camp that afternoon, nine miles from the republican camp.

At four the next morning, the eighteenth of August, the army was roused, and with the general at the head of the column, it marched to the place selected for the ambuscade, arriving between eight and nine in the morning. Contemporary reports indicate that officers and men all were well-satisfied with the position Toledo had chosen for their stand.

8   *Discovery, Pursuit, Mutiny*

MORE OFTEN THAN WE REALIZE, IT IS NOT the herculean efforts of the chief protagonists that decide the outcome of a battle, or change the course of history. Sometimes it is the impact of an unknown contender, who, in one brief moment onstage, may alter the histories of nations — only to fade again into obscurity like a meteor that has burned itself out in one brief flash against the eternal sky.

Such a force was *Alférez* Don Francisco López, who became separated from a reconnaissance party Arredondo had sent out and, riding casually across the open prairie in front of Toledo's ambuscade, was fired on by the trigger-happy Americans. He escaped, but Toledo's expertly-set trap for the advancing Spaniards was irreparably exposed. What followed was bitter tragedy for the insurgents and only a providential victory for the Commandant-General. Save for the mention of his name in Arredondo's report to the Viceroy, *Alférez* López appeared no more in the annals of the Southwest.[1]

When General Toledo arrived at the site he had selected for his ambush of Arredondo, he immediately formed the troops in battle line. According to McLane, Toledo placed a

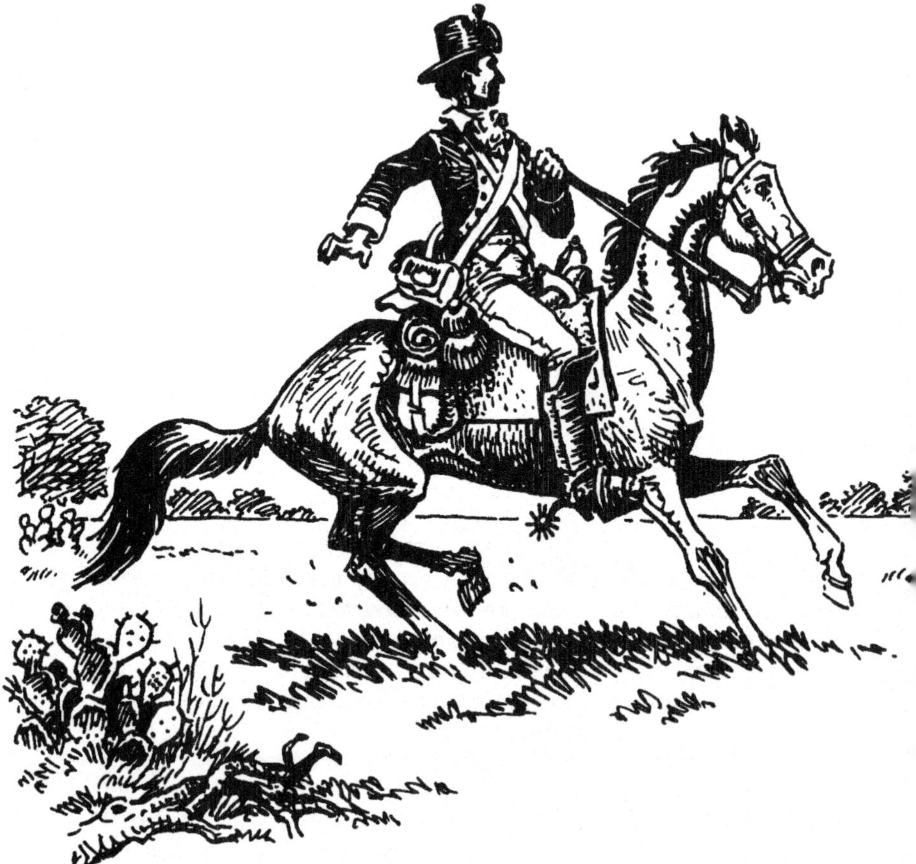

company of Americans and one of Mexicans, alternately in the line, in single file, leaving at their backs a thin stand of post oaks, and anchoring both his right and left flanks on hills which had impassable woods beyond them. McLane's version is corroborated by the *Lexington Reporter* account:

> ... To the front we had a plain one mile in extent beyond which continued a dense oak forest [*un encinal espeso*] on an extremely sandy terrain [*terreno sumante arenoso*], through the middle of which ran the Laredo road [a most admirable position, in McLane's words].
> ... We set our advance guard in this *encinal* with orders not to attack and to retire when the enemy approached without being seen by them since, as has been said, the General's idea was to surprise them on their march on their exit from the *encinal* ... Then we waited for the enemy which, although very superior to us, could not take advantage of all his forces since the terrain would not permit him to form his battle line except under our fire.
> The General-in-Chief gave the order that immediately when the enemy started to form its battle line, Captain Taylor [in command of a company of marksmen in ambush] was to flank him on the left, the Cavalry [formed in two divisions] was to encircle [the enemy] through the cover on both flanks and charge his rearguard, while the infantry made a bayonet attack on his front. Most unfortunately, none of these plans succeeded.[2]

At ten-thirty, the vanguard was attacked by the enemy and encircled. Toledo ordered the Army to leave its position and go to the aid of the advance guard. After his troops succeeded in this maneuver, he gave the order that they return to their first position.[3] McLane's account bears out the story to this point, stating that when the advance guard was attacked, "instead of falling back, the whole line was ordered forward to their support. When they arrived at the advance post, they repulsed the enemy, it being a small party of Cavalry."[4]

Neither the anonymous letter writer nor McLane mentioned the lone rider, but his untoward intrusion on Toledo's planned ambush is well-documented. Captain Wilkinson reported that is was not long after they had formed their line that the advance guard sent back word that the enemy was not far off, and

> ... thinking it probable he might not know of our being there our guards were called, so that his first information might be the sight of our line. Soon after this was done a stranger, who

appeared from his dress an officer, rode within 60 or 70 yards of our line apparently without seeing them — when he reigned in his horse, wheeled and went off at full speed, six or eight shots were fired at him, and probably he was struck, as his body was afterwards said to have been seen lying dead —[5]

Twenty-three years later, Bullard, then a member of the Louisiana Supreme Court, wrote that when Toledo had drawn up his line, his troops faced a small prairie, and such was their position that the enemy might approach within rifle shot without suspecting their presence. It was Toledo's intention to take Arredondo by surprise on his march, while encumbered with a train, which always accompanied a Spanish army. The republicans knew that the royalists had taken up their line of march when they heard the enemy's drum at daybreak, and,

... confident expectations were entertained that the plan would succeed. It was defeated by an untoward incident. While waiting anxiously for the approach of the royalists, a single horseman, well mounted, rode slowly through the centre of the prairie, and approached within a short distance of the republican lines, apparently without suspicion of finding an enemy there. As soon as he perceived his situation, he turned suddenly and disappeared, notwithstanding many rifles were discharged at him. It was then concluded, that, as the position of the republican army was discovered and would immediately be reported, it would lead to no result if they continued in the same position, as the enemy would certainly have time to form in battle.[6]

The decision was made, according to Bullard, to attack the Spaniards before they could make any new disposition of their forces. The whole republican line advanced "at the same moment," and soon the right wing engaged the enemy. It proved to be an advance party and was soon dispersed.

There is yet another view of this interesting vignette of history — the enemy's. This makes it one of the few incidents of the entire day that was specifically documented by both sides. Arredondo, in his report to the viceroy, stated matter-of-factly,

At a short distance from the above mentioned Medina River, Alférez Don Francisco López was separated from the main party. He was seen by the enemy, and they instantly fired a volley at him; but by a miracle, no damage was done him.

In view of this occurrence, Elizondo instantly ... commanded that the line be extended and that answer be made with a rapid and well-directed fire. The enemy charged bravely and with their whole force so that a circle was almost formed about him.[7]

One needs speculate at the circumstances which prompted young Ensign López to wander away from his party and at what his musings might have been as he cantered nonchalantly across an open prairie, well in advance of his companions, and in territory where he might expect to flush the enemy at any moment. Whatever they were, history merely confirms that the incident happened.

What the republicans thought to be the Spanish advance guard, was a detachment of 180 cavalrymen under Lieutenant Colonel Ygnacio Elizondo, which Arredondo had sent forward about three hours earlier. Arredondo had directed Elizondo to proceed with the greatest caution and vigilance until he saw the enemy, then to make a careful observation of their number, but not to engage them in battle unless he thought himself strong enough to inflict an exemplary punishment on them; otherwise, he was to keep up a slow fire while retreating. It was then that Arredondo had informed Elizondo of the shortcut he was to follow in his retreat. Arredondo had expected to be ambushed, but he thought the trap would be set where the *camino real* crossed the Medina; therefore, he had proposed to change his plans and move the army over the Garza ranch ford.

Now, finding himself almost encircled by a large force and remembering his orders, Elizondo turned his troops around and began his retreat, keeping up a sustained fire. As fast as he gave ground, the republicans advanced. Arredondo reported that after a short space of firing on both sides and various discharges of cannon by the rebels, the firing stopped. He said that the reason was that Elizondo's men had reached open country and needed to assess the movements of the enemy, as well as take a breather. [A more likely explanation is that the Spaniards on horseback simply outdistanced the republicans, many of them on foot and, in addition, dragging along seven fieldpieces.]

Arredondo wrote: "The rabble soon began to direct their fire with more vigor and force, advancing strongly. They were calmly answered by our troops who were forced to begin a new retreat in the same manner as in the first encounter." He said that this second skirmish soon ended, the republicans having suffered some losses. Two royalist soldiers were wounded, one gravely, and some horses were injured. Wilkinson reported that four royalists were killed but that the rest escaped.[8]

Arredondo told the Viceroy that during the latter action Elizondo had sent him an update of what was happening, and he [Arredondo] immediately responded by extending his line and deploying the main army in battle array. He also sent forward the subdeacon Lieutenant Colonel Juan Manuel Sambrano — the same Sambrano of the Casas uprising and, of the time the republicans had crossed into spanish Texas — with 150 cavalrymen and two small cannon [*cañoncitos del calibre de libra y media*] to reinforce Elizondo. Immediately following the last action, Arredondo's aide-de-camp, Lieutenant Cespedes, returned to give him private information of what had taken place. En route, he met with Sambrano on his way to reinforce Elizondo. This meeting was on the *camino que cortaba,* the shortcut that ran from *El Atascoso* Ranch on *el camino real* to Espada Mission by way of the Laredo Road crossing of the Medina. Sambrano had been given the same instructions as Elizondo — to continue luring the enemy toward the main force. Arredondo continued,

> I followed after him [Sambrano], but abandoning my first plan, and ordering the army to form a column, I resolved to attack the rabble.[9]

If Arredondo meant that he was abandoning his plan to place his army between the rebels and the city, by sneaking across the Garza Ranch crossing, than it was indeed a major change in tactics. He could now divest himself of a cumbersome train — which may have numbered as many as 600 or 700 mules and a hundred oxen, an equal number of carts, plus numerous children, women [camp followers and wives], *curanderos* [herb healers], and even speculating merchants who preyed on the soldiers and their limited supplies. Now, having reduced his command to less than 1300 men — by sending 330 out with Elizondo and Sambrano and detailing the rest in the rear to guard the ammunition and train — Arredondo was in a much better position to maneuver his forces than he had been earlier when he made the decision to cross the Medina River by a ford other than the Laredo crossing.

The three American chroniclers who left us with detailed accounts of the chase of Elizondo were substantially in agreement that there was no further contact with the fleeing royalists for quite some time after the earlier skirmishes. McLane observed that the march began about midmorning, "as hot as it ever gets," and that it extended for about four miles through heavy post oak sand, without water, the troops drawing their cannon, their teams having been turned out on the previous night. The four mile distance, of course, refers to the entire pursuit. The observation concerning the mules is significant: releasing them at *Rodeo de la Espada* was in keeping with Toledo's plan to wait in ambush below the Gallinas; also, it would save the animals from slaughter during the fighting.

Wilkinson's account introduced several incidents not found elsewhere. For one, he asserts that immediately after the lone rider incident, Colonel Henry Perry, believing that the whole Spanish army was near at hand, suggested that the republicans might obtain an easy victory if they advanced quickly to take advantage of any confusion that might have been created by the driving in of their advance guard. Toledo gave the order to march, and the rebels moved forward in battle order. The day was extremely hot, the men were thirsty, and those who had pulled the cannon through deep sand were dead-tired. After proceeding about two miles without again seeing the enemy [this would be after the second skirmish with Elizondo] the General gave the order that they return to their first position. For some reason — Wilkinson said it was because it had been ascertained that there was water just ahead — they continued after the retreating Spaniards. Toledo was determined to bring the enemy to action that morning, Wilkinson said, and after a brief rest at the waterhole, the advance continued, flanked by the Mexican cavalry and the Indians.[10] Wilkinson is guilty here of sugarcoating the facts — perhaps because he was reluctant to expose the Menchaca-Kemper mutiny, which will be examined later in this chapter.

When they got near the enemy — this time Elizondo was reinforced by Sambrano — the *Tejano* cavalry and the Indians were again sent forward to commence the action. They repulsed the royalists' rear guard [which Wilkinson called "the advance posts," believing that they had now reached Arredondo's main army]. Two pieces of artillery [the *cañoncitos*] were taken. As the Spaniards retreated, the republicans continued to advance in battle order through a thick scrubby oak growth. The sand was very deep and heavy, with the cannon sometimes sinking half-wheel deep. At times a piece of artillery would be forty to sixty yards behind the line, with a company marking time while waiting for it. Of the seven cannon taken out, several had to be left stuck in the sand, "not being able to get them up, and I believe but two were used with any effect [in the battle]." At other times, sighting from right to left, one wing would be considerably in advance of the other. "Our men undisciplined and unacquainted with military maneuvres," Wilkinson wrote, "got in a state of confusion. In this manner we approached the enemy — in this manner we went into action."[11]

Bullard wrote that when the republicans again encountered the Spaniards, this time reinforced by Sambrano, they confidently believed they faced the main body of Arredondo's army. The question immediately comes to mind: How could the republican command possibly have mistaken 330 cavalrymen for the entire Spanish army? The only plausible answer is suggested by both McLane's and Wilkinson's references to thick chaparral and thickets, which would have screened the royalists enough to prevent an accurate estimate of their numbers. After a smart skirmish ensued, during which a few prisoners were taken, together with "2 or 3 pieces of artillery," Bullard introduced a most significant factor not recorded by any other American combatant:

> ... It was now discovered that Arredondo had amused the republicans by sending forward these two parties with a view to check their advance, while he prepared for their reception in a position more favorable to his views. His [Arredondo's] true position was then ascertained at a distance of two or three miles, and that the intervening space was so sandy as to render it almost impossible to drag along the cannon, and there was no water to be had.[12]

McLane's narrative seems to have suffered an omission or an abridgement when it was first published in the San Antonio *Tri-Weekly Alamo Express*. The February 20, 1861, installment takes up near the end of the republican pursuit of the royalist cavalry detachment:

> On approaching a thick chapparal, skirting the next stream of water, they were fired on from the thicket by two pieces of cannon. They returned the fire from their artillery, but finding the enemy protected by the timber, they charged, leaving their cannon, which had broken down one-third of the Americans dragging it through the thicket, which prevented any correct estimate of their numbers.[13]

Although a bit garbled at this point, McLane's narrative sheds light on several phases of the pursuit. For one, it tells us where it led — to "the next stream of water," which had to be Galvan Creek. He confirms Wilkinson's comments about leaving several cannon stuck in the sand. He makes the remarkable assertion that one-third of the Americans had been broken down dragging the cannon through the sand [not the thicket as was printed]. He speaks of being fired on from the thicket by two cannon, cannon which would have been in Arredondo's line. And he concluded the sentence with a rationalization for the rebels having been taken by surprise when they burst unexpectedly on Arredondo's army. He said the thicket had prevented any correct estimate of their numbers. Examination of microfilm of the *Tri-Weekly Alamo Express* confirms that an omission just prior to the word "thicket" occurred in the original printing. The *Express* was a strong Union paper which suspended publication on May 3, 1861, without having printed corrections of "several mistakes of the printer" mentioned in the March 13 issue.[14]

Perhaps because the action had deteriorated from brilliant tactics to stupid chase, the *Lexington Reporter's* eyewitness devoted less than four lines to the pursuit. "The Royalist army retreated," he said, "and ours was in their pursuit until we arrived at an *arroyo* where the regiment of Vera Cruz had taken cover in such manner that neither our Cavalry nor the Infantry could attack them." He further explained that their artillery had remained in the rear because of the bad road and "the fatigue which we all had."[15]

Now let us see how all this furor and disorder appeared to the Spaniards. Arredondo, in his report to the Viceroy, wrote that Sambrano joined Elizondo and that his arrival was noted by the enemy, as follows:

> They thought it was the entire strength of the army for they believed it to be my troops. They, therefore, resolved to pursue Elizondo even more hotly.[16]

Here Arredondo was reporting after-the-fact intelligence, probably obtained from the prisoners after he arrived in Béxar.

He said the republicans charged again, showing even greater bravery, and keeping up a slow fire, which was returned by the Spanish cavalrymen who accompanied their fire "with a cannonade which was kept up until the enemy's force could not advance from fear of the damage they might suffer from our balls." Here Arredondo probably exaggerated. None of the American combatants mentioned a royalist cannonade. With only the two *cañoncitos*? He contradicts himself immediately. Elizondo, he wrote, was absolutely unable to resist so strong a force and beat a hasty retreat, being forced to abandon the two small cannon.[17]

While this was going on, Arredondo continued his march with his army drawn up in column. When he saw the haste with which Elizondo was retreating to join him, Arredondo formed his remaining troops in line for battle. The republicans, thinking they were already victors,

> ... advanced intrepidly but with excessive blindness [until] they found at their front the main body of our army in position for attack, with the artillery placed on the flanks of the infantry. This surprised the rabble, and they stopped for the purpose of restoring order. They did this, being aided by the great number of oaks [*encinos*] with which the country was covered.
> Placed in total order — this being observed by the company of guerrillas, ... which I had assigned to reconnoiter them — they advanced upon my army with great courage until they were within pistol shot.[18]

Thus the two armies, the republicans and the royalists, found themselves eyeball-to-eyeball in an open area [McLane called it "an open post oak flat"] just across Galvan Creek. But before we can examine and evaluate the grim battle that followed, the grave charge of mutiny that was brought against Colonel Menchaca, and possibly Colonel Samuel Kemper, needs to be studied and fitted into proper perspective.

After his splendidly staged ambush of the Spaniards was nullified by the lone rider incident, Toledo's control of the situation progressively fell apart as the day wore on. Regarded as a Spaniard, a *gachupín,* Toledo was looked upon with disfavor by the native-born *Tejanos*. Almost from the moment he arrived in Béxar, his nemesis had been the leader of the mounted provincials, Colonel Miguél Menchaca. Menchaca, whose influence with the Mexicans was unbounded, was characterized as a man having great vigor and charisma. In the few months that the republicans had controlled Béxar, and especially since the Alazán victory, young Menchaca had achieved the stature of a true leader who could appeal to his countrymen and receive a desired response. With the ambush at the Gallinas rendered ineffective, Menchaca challenged the General for leadership and, in a sense, he won.

The first confrontation occurred immediately after a smart skirmish when Sambrano reinforced Elizondo and two *cañoncitos* were captured along with a few prisoners. McLane said that Toledo ordered the troops to return and resume their former positions and await the approach of the enemy. Menchaca told Toledo that his men were not in the habit of retreating, and if they were not led on to meet the enemy, they would abandon the lines and return home. Getting no support from his assembled officers, Toledo finally ordered the line to march forward.[19]

Variations on this theme were reported in all the American accounts, except those of Villars and Wilkinson. Villars, it appears, was not there to report it, and Wilkinson, being a West Pointer, the son of a general, and aide to Toledo, must have found the mass insubordination repugnant, and he chose to gloss over the perfidy of his fellows.

Bullard's account affords a plausible summary of the sequence of events that day. He wrote that after the second skirmish with the retreating Spaniards, Arredondo's true position was ascertained, probably from interrogation of the prisoners, at a distance of two or three miles, and the intervening terrain was so sandy that it was almost impossible to drag along the cannon. Additionally, there was no water to be had. Bullard continued:

> Under these circumstances a council was called on the field, and it was determined that the army should retire to the position first occupied in the morning [that is, below Gallinas Creek, where the ambush had been set and from where both upper crossings of the Medina could be watched], and await the movements of the enemy, and at all events attack them if they should attempt to cross the Medina.
>
> This plan, the only one which could have saved the army, was thwarted by the obstinacy of Colonel Menchaca, . . . He positively refused to obey the order; and such was the danger to be apprehended from his defection, that Toledo yielded to the wishes of a majority of the officers, and the impetuosity of his troops, and gave orders to advance upon the enemy at all hazards.[20]

The anonymous letter writer to the *Lexington Reporter,* who may have been Bullard, said that when Toledo gave the order that the army return to its first position, "Menchaca disobeyed, continuing to advance against the enemy." The letter writer also reported the following extraordinary account, which is not found elsewhere, of Menchaca's defiance of Toledo that had occurred the previous night:

At nightfall of the 17th, the General received the news that the enemy had encamped that afternoon in a position nine miles from ours. [Toledo] immediately ordered Colonel Menchaca with 50 horsemen of his command and the mounted Indians to go out to attack and disperse the enemy's horseherd, an easy undertaking as it was not expected by the Loyalists. The General's object was to keep the enemy on its arms all night while we relaxed tranquilly and in good state so that the next day we should meet them fatigued by the bad night and by the march over an extremely sandy terrain. Adding to this was the much greater advantage to us of leaving the enemy on foot while at the same time all the train and equipment was on the ground.[21]

Menchaca, far from obeying the order, formed a junta of his officers, presented them with the confidential order he had just received from the general, and convinced them at the same time that if they went now and dispersed the enemy horse herd, they would not benefit from the horses and mules. The officers agreed with the colonel, and Menchaca went back and informed Toledo that he and the officers of his command had determined not to attack the *caballada,* planning instead to obtain the animals after the battle. Toledo countered that the objective which had conducted the army to this place was to destroy the enemy and not to go on a horse hunt, "but this reflection and various others were useless and the General remained disobeyed and filled with desperation." [22]

James Gaines, not always a reliable reporter since he repeated hearsay, squarely implicated Colonel Samuel Kemper as a co-mutineer with Menchaca. Kemper, on furlough since April, had rejoined the Republican Army the night before while it was in camp at *Rodeo de la Espada.* Toledo had conferred upon him, in *absentia,* command of the Madison battalion in an order dated August 5. Gaines said that after running battle that lasted for some time, the enemy retreated in such haste as to lose their artillery. Toledo, conceiving that the men were getting too far from water, called a halt and ordered a retreat back to the river.[23] Gaines wrote the following account in 1835:

This order caused great contention and confusion among the officers. Kemper had returned and taken command of the American forces, and Monchack [Menchaca] the principal Colonel commanding the Mexicans. The two colonels were opposed to Toledo personally, so that when he gave the order to retreat to the river, Kemper and Menchaca galloped violently up and down the lines countermanding the order and swearing that there should be no retreat. Toledo was ... already unpopular in the army, and the consequence was that Kemper & Menchaca charged vigorously on the enemy, who still kept retreating but still fighting.[24]

Antonio Menchaca, kinsman of the mutinous Colonel, goes into considerable detail concerning his insubordination. Again, it should be remembered that young Menchaca would have gotten his information from others, and the Colonel, being a folk hero and having died a soldier's death, would be remembered kindly, of course, and his exploits recounted in a favorable light. Nonetheless, Menchaca's *Memoirs* places the stigma of mutiny squarely on Miguél Menchaca's head.

> They [Elizondo's detachment] came up to the American troops and trying to engage them, upon seeing which Miguel Menchaca ... came up to Toledo and asked him what his intentions were. Toledo remarked ... that [the] manouvering was only intended as a decoy ... to ascertain the strength of his troops, that he [Menchaca] might take some of his men and engage with them but under no consideration to follow them far if they retreated; that Arredondo merely wished to get him out of his position in order to take him at a disadvantage.
>
> Menchaca went to attack them and did not return. He followed the detachment of Mexicans [Spaniards], killing all he could until he got up to the Main Body. [This probably referred to Sambrano's reinforcements.] He took two guns from the cavalry, but was attacked by the artillery [obviously before the Colonel was successful in capturing the two guns, the *cañoncitas*] and he retreated for about 1/2 miles from where he sent word to Toledo to Advance with his troops, for he [Menchaca] would not turn back. Toledo then sent word to him that it would be worse than Madness for him to attempt to move forward and leave his position, for he would be sure to be defeated if he did.
>
> Upon receiving this word, Menchaca, infuriated, himself came over to where Toledo with the balance of the force was and told the troops that the fight had commenced; that under no consideration would he, having already commenced the fight, quit until he and the men under him had either died or conquered; that if they [the troops with Toledo] were men, to act as men and follow him, whereupon all the forces became encouraged and moved in a body to follow Menchaca. Toledo, though unwillingly, followed.[25]

By the time he got around to writing his memoirs, Antonio

Menchaca, an honored veteran of the second Texian war of independence, was an old man, and his memory may have played him false on details. But his account sheds a cold, clear light on the men who made command decisions on that hot August day. Granted that it may have been a bit biased in Colonel Menchaca's favor, it certainly was not a whitewash, and it still revealed the pathetic picture of the distrusted *gachupín* general, who trailed unwillingly behind his troops while they followed a charismatic pied piper to their doom.

9 Disaster in the Encinal

ONE OF THE POPULAR STORIES CONCERNING the battle fought in *el encinal de Medina* is that of a carefully planned ambuscade which Commandant-General Arredondo is said to have set for the Republican Army and into which the rebels, like lemmings, rushed impetuously to their distruction. While the melodramatic story was reported widely in American periodicals of the time and later was taken up by Texas historians, it is significant that Arredondo, vainglorious as he might have been, did not take credit for such a stratagem. Perhaps, having failed in their own efforts to set a trap, the American combatants were preoccupied with the ambush idea and found it a convenient alibi. Yoakum gave the story historical credence in 1855 in his *History of Texas:*

> On the south of the Medina, he threw up a breastwork: it was in the form of the letter V [lying in its side], with the apex in the road, and open end in the direction of San Antonio . . . The breastwork itself was concealed by an artificial chapparal, formed of bushes set up in front of it, and giving the appearance of a natural growth.

Thrall repeated the story almost verbatim twenty years later, except that he referred to the breastwork as "fortifica-

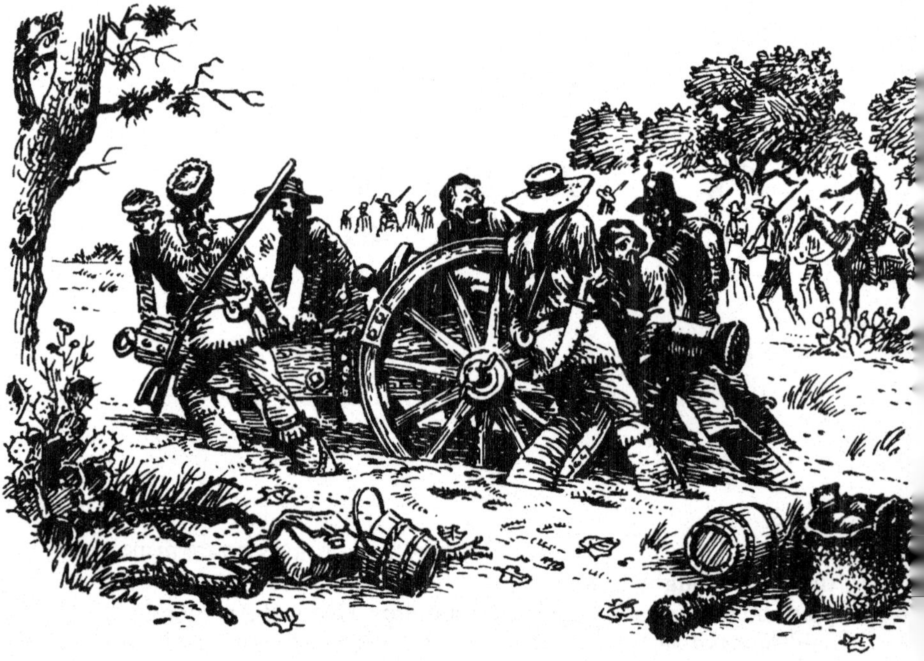

tions." A decade later Bancroft cited Yoakum in a footnote, but went on to say that no allusion to such an ambush was found in any Spanish document that he had examined.[1]

Oddly enough, Wilkinson's report, which was the first to reach the outside world, — made no mention of an ambush. It simply stated: "We found the enemy well posted and they received us warmly."[2] But six weeks later, the *Niles Weekly Register*, quoting a letter from a "gentleman of the first respectability, dated Natchitoches, Sept. 4," printed the news of the defeat of Toledo's forces which "with indescribable enthusiasm and impetuosity . . . rushed into the ambuscade where many pieces of the cannon of the enemy were opened on them by which they were mostly destroyed." The account states that it was Wilkinson, "who was in the battle acting as aid to General Tolledo," [sic] who had brought the news.[3]

By the strangest coincidence, on the same day, September 4, and from the same place (Natchitoches), Dr. John Sibley wrote his superior, the Secretary of War, the same news — in almost the same words! He credited "several persons of undoubted Veracity" who reported that the Americans "with the fury of Mad-men rushed on, running over their officers, & filed into an Ambuscade & were most of them destroyed."[4]

None of the American combatants mentioned an ambush, but most of them remarked on their coming unexpectedly on Arredondo's main army. Even Gaines, with his penchant for embroidering the hearsay he reported, stated only that Elizondo's retreat was a strategem "not discovered until they were in 40 yds. of the breast works." McLane gave the most graphic account of the meeting, writing that, "on approaching an open post oak flat, they perceived, to their surprise, a line of temporary breastworks, and the phantom they had been pursuing clambering over it, and the next moment they were saluted by the enemy's whole line of artillery, tearing off the brush and limbs over their heads, scattering the fragments into their eyes and faces."[5]

By this time, Bullard — and therefore Toledo — knew of Arredondo's whereabouts soon after the skirmish with Elizondo and Sambrano — no doubt from prisoners taken. Bullard was fluent in Spanish and must have taken part in the interrogation. We also have followed Arredondo's progress through the *encinal* and know that he would have had no more than an hour, at the most, to form his line when he saw the haste with which Elizondo was retreating. Arredondo's army was then marching in column on a narrow road through an oak woods, and it must have taken him every available minute to move his foot soldiers up to the line, to haul his seven cannon through the sand and place them on the flanks of the infantry, and to position his remaining 865 cavalrymen.

The contemporary documention, therefore, confirms that there had been no royalist ambush. That fiction was passed on to the waiting world by Sibley, who, with Shaler and others, had gambled heavily on the success of the expedition and, when it failed, needed to temper the truth in breaking the tragic news to his countrymen. He leaked the story of the ambush to media of the time, and thus a bit of historical myth was contrived.

The temporary breastwork over which the fleeing royalists were clambering would have been a line of hastily piled up camp gear. Santa Anna himself used such a defense at San Jacinto, which can be seen in the foreground of Henry McArdle's painting of that engagement.[6] McLane's comment that Arredondo's artillery salute tore off the brush and limbs over their heads is also in character. Spanish armies were historically notorious for overshooting their enemies with both artillery and hand-held weapons, the latter usually because of recoil and lack of proper sights. At La Bahía, McLane said the enemy made quite a display discharging their "scopets" (*escopetas*), poised on the left arm at an elevation of forty-five degrees. As late as the Mexican War, Mexican infantrymen fired from their hips to avoid the bruising recoil of their weapons.[7]

McLane reported the surprise attack as follows:

This sudden and unexpected attack by the enemy they supposed they were driving before them so alarmed the Mexican Infantry that they had fled and hid in the chapparal, leaving the Americans in scattered detached parties.[8]

The fact that the line ceased to be continuous when the Mexicans fled confirms the premise that Toledo had formed his line of alternate Mexican and American companies, rather than the Mexicans in the center with Americans on their flanks — as historians Yoakum and Bancroft wrote, and which the latter even termed a "grievous mistake", implying that it cost Toledo the day.[9] The timidity of the Mexican foot soldiers, most of whom had been presidial troops, prisoners, or men who had defected from Colonel Herrera's auxiliary forces, was described by Wilkinson, who said they hung back "most shamefully, creeping up like men rather prepossessed with fear than like soldiers resolved on victory."[10] Gaines wrote that they fled at the first fire, leaving the Americans in a state of disorganization and confusion; also, that having deserted early, they lost but few men in the slaughter that followed the fight.[11]

Such cowardly conduct did not characterize the mounted *Tejanos* under Colonel Menchaca's command, many of whom would have been propertied citizens of Béxar, each with a vital stake in the outcome of this fight. They rode into battle with audacious gallantry, and it was not until Colonel Menchaca was struck down by grapeshot in the neck and fell, that they became discouraged, frightened, and disordered.[12] Even then, they were twice rallied, and the second time they made a furious charge on Arredondo's rear to cut off the ammunition wagons, only to be repulsed with considerable loss.[13]

Although the battle in the *encinal* lasted nearly four hours, there is a dearth of knowledge of how the fighting actually took place. Arredondo devoted a scant two dozen lines to the first three- and one-half hours. Wilkinson and McLane each gave about the same amount of general information from the American vantage points — not enough to plot the ebb and flow of the fight as it raged between Galvan Creek and the ridge to the southwest. Bullard supplied two enlightening incidents, and bits and pieces reported by the noncombatant reporters make up the sum of our knowledge.

Arredondo wrote that when the rebels had restored order and had advanced to within pistol shot,

> ... my brave and daring soldiers, ... began to return a lively, sustained, and well-directed fire which was returned in like manner. So there was a most hard fought battle, reaching the extreme of having their artillery placed within forty paces of ours. We kept up this most harsh struggle for more than two hours, and still no decisive result was recognized by either side.
>
> The enemy, seeing such strong and tenacious resistance, and in consequence of the excessive damage which our fire did their troops, ... Toledo tried to surprise us on the right and the left flanks and in the rear. But he was not so quick in his movements as I was in commanding an advance guard sent out on both flanks and a considerable picket force detailed as a rear guard, ... We gained much advantage by this prompt arrangement, because the accursed plans and the fire of the enemy were met on all four sides.

After three and a half hours of this determined and hard fought battle, it was seen that victory was on our side; for the most tenacious Anglo-Americans had been completely routed. Seeing this, I ordered the music to start up and my drummer to beat a reveille. This caused such an effect on my troops and reanimated them so much that it seemed as if they were going to advance.

Confusion now seized upon the enemy; and they began to abandon their artillery. I, therefore, ordered a picket to advance on the right to seize it. The commander of the infantry, Don Antonio Elosua, advanced on the left with another detachment for the same purpose.

At the same time, I ordered the cavalry to set out to overtake those who already fled. They did this with intrepidity and resolution, making an end of as many scoundrels as they found on the way, continuing [*llegando*] as far as the Medina River.[14]

"Consequently," Arredondo concluded, "after four hours of this bloody battle we were the masters of the enemy's ground." In a letter from the battlefield to Juanicotena, Arredondo said he was writing at four in the afternoon, indicating that the fighting had ended an hour or so earlier. He was able to give Juanicotena a body count of 600 enemy dead, plus 100 prisoners "who are now being executed." Later, in reporting to Viceroy Calleja, he upped the number of dead to a thousand, "*más que menos, la mayor parte anglo americanos,*" saying the field was covered with cadavers, among these the son of General Wilkinson, Colonel Menchaca, and various other officers.[15]

Apparently Arredondo was preoccupied with Wilkinson. More than three years later, when transmitting a copy of his 1813 report to Apodaca, the new viceroy, he still contended that the rebels were commanded by Toledo and "a son of General Wilkinson." Neither Wilkinson's nor Menchaca's body was among the battlefield trophies. Antonio Menchaca wrote that "Menchaca was struck by a ball on the neck . . . was brought with them, died on the way and was buried on the Seguin road at the place called . . . *Cañada de Menchaca.*" [16]

From the American viewpoint, Wilkinson observed that the action was commenced by the Mexican cavalry under Menchaca and the Indians, but it was not severe until the main body came up, after which it continued for more than an hour. He said the enemy used their artillery well and poured a heavy fire with their small arms, the brunt of which was directed against the American lines. While the Mexican infantry hung back most shamefully, the Mexican cavalry and Indians were smartly engaged on the left, and a few Americans "took better care of their persons than to annoy the enemy." At last the Mexican cavalry broke and retreated. They met General Toledo, who rallied them for a short time. Then the American infantry began to drop off. About this time, Captain Taylor was shot and had to leave the line, which had a discouraging effect on his company.[17]

By then, the republicans had gained on the enemy. They had taken one or two pieces more of their artillery and were fighting the royalists on the ground they had first occupied. "Fifteen minutes more," Wilkinson wrote (and he underlined the word "fifteen"), "would have given victory entirely in our hands, — but our men were hot — thirsty — and exceedingly fatigued — in some companies they had suffered severely — they got discouraged and not long after broke." [18]

Wilkinson said the rout soon became general. The right wing was entirely broken, and the royalists on that side were moving toward the ammunition wagons. A few men were still engaged on the extreme left, but a party of the enemy came around and took them in the rear. Arredondo said that these pincer movements were effected to seize the republicans' artillery.

Colonels Kemper and Perry, in the meantime, "finding that the day was indienably [sic] lost, that nothing could save it, that the men had all either retreated or were moving off — that the enemy were approaching them — turned their horses heads and left the field of battle." Toledo had been in another part of the field when a soldier, "seeing the enemy advance, took hold of his bridle reins, turned his horse and told him to save himself by flight or he would be taken directly, which he did." Wilkinson may have been that soldier; at any rate, he accompanied Toledo in his flight.[19]

Bullard wrote only a few lines about the battle itself, but he related a most extraordinary development. Being already exhausted with heat and want of water and obliged to leave several pieces of artillery behind on account of the sandy ground, the republicans had fought under great disadvantage; "yet the battery of the enemy was twice silenced by the American rifles, and *the singular spectacle presented itself of two armies flying from each other, each thinking itself defeated.*" [Italics supplied.] [20]

McLane's narrative supports Bullard's account and adds

some details. All the Americans that were able, he said, advanced up to the enemy's breastworks and picked off their men at the guns, until they had silenced their whole line of artillery. He continued:

> ... They [the royalists] had kept up such an incessant fire that the elements around them were a dense mass of smoke ... When their cannon were silenced, their whole line gave way, and Arredondo having taken position on commanding ground in the rear, perceiving his cannon silenced, his cavalry gone, and infantry retreating, ordered his aid to draw the men off and prepare for a retreat.[21]

From this point, McLane and Bullard diverged in their reporting of the battle. McLane wrote:

> ... When the aid advanced to their lines, the smoke having blown off, he discovered that there were but a handful of Americans opposing them, and he rallied their men and returned to their works and resumed the fire of their cannon. The Americans having discovered their own hopeless condition, retired from their position, leaving the enemy a clear field ...[22]

Bullard, however, introduced the story of the defection of "one Musquis" with a squadron of provincial horsemen, late in the afternoon, which, he said, changed the fate of the day. Bullard reported:

> Turning the left of the enemy's line, he advanced to the rear, and surrendered to Arredondo, whom he found mounted on a fresh horse, having already given orders to retreat. The information conveyed by Musquis induced him to return to the charge; the whole line advanced with little further opposition, and no quarter was given on the field.[23]

Among the contemporary reporters, only James Gaines supported the Músquiz defection version, and he may have gotten the story from Bullard. Embellishing it somewhat, he wrote that the Spanish cavalry fled,

> ... and Arredondo commenced packing up his mules for a retreat; at this crisis, a traitor in the patriot ranks, Col. Musquis father of Ramon Musquis [later Mexican governor of Coahuila and Texas], galloped over to the enemy's ranks and informed the genl. that the Americans were whipped; that they were feinting [sic] from the want of water. On hearing this Arredondo rallied his disconcerted cavalry & other companies, and coming again to the fight with renewed vigor soon compelled the Americans to give back. Their defeat was

now certain — a dreadful slaughter ensued — they broke but more then one half who had not fallen in the Battle fell in the retreat.[24]

This turncoat may have been Miguél Músquiz, who had been commandant at Nacogdoches in 1801, and who had succeeded in killing Philip Nolan, an earlier American interloper alleged to have been in the pay of General Wilkinson. He may also have been the Miguél Eca y Músquiz, who was a member of Sambrano's junta following the overthrow of the Casas government in the spring of 1811. Such strong royalist antecedents would explain his proclivity to switch sides again when he saw the rebel cause faltering.[25]

The self-effacing Bullard, who never once mentioned his own name in his report, may have been an eyewitness to Colonel Músquiz's going over to the enemy. And if he was, then Bullard had pinpointed a most important element in the defeat of the Republican Army in the *encinal*. Arredondo, it will be recalled, wrote that Toledo had tried to surprise the royalists on both flanks and in the rear. Bullard reported that Músquiz had turned the left of the enemy's line and advanced to the rear, where he surrendered. Another source, albeit suspect at to its validity, stated that Toledo's aide-de-camp, "Captain Bullard, succeeded in rallying a force of Menchaca's men, a sufficient number to make a charge on the Royalist rear with a view of cutting off his ammunition wagons, but this charge was repulsed with considerable loss." [26] If this account may bear belief, was it Bullard then who drove around Arredondo's right flank in a charge to the rear, while Músquiz turned the line on the left? Somebody led these flanking movements, and, if the commanders were Bullard and Músquiz, then the Músquiz defection becomes a most critical factor in the rout of the rebels. It may even be conjectured that Músquiz might have been captured, instead of surrendering, and, to save his life, told all to the Commandant-General.

Whatever the precise particulars of this incident might have been, those facts we have, point to the strong probability that it was not brilliant generalship on the part of Arredondo that turned the tide of battle in favor of the king's soldiers (as he would have the viceroy believe); rather, it was but an aborted maneuver that luckily saved the day for him as he sat upon a fresh horse ready to lead what was left of his army in a hasty retreat toward the Rio Grande.

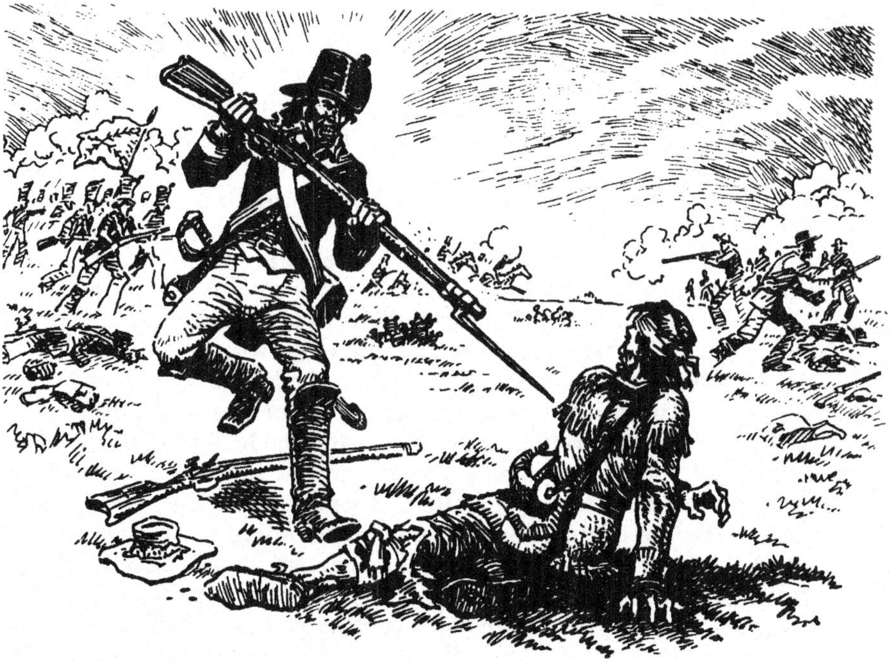

10 *Swift Vengeance*

HOWEVER PROVIDENTIAL HIS VICTORY MAY have been, Arredondo's vengeance was swift and cruel.

From the battlefield, he wrote Juanicotena that a hundred prisoners were then being shot — adding to the more than 600 bodies already on the ground. He directed the battle areas to be searched and all booty seized. "This rabble lost their seven Cannon, Wagons of muskets and carbine Ammunition, much Plain shot, grape and Lead, many fire Arms, Banners, War Chests and Medicine Box," he told Juanicotena. Later he gave the viceroy a detailed accounting of the booty he had seized on the site and in the city, ranging from twenty-two cannon of different sizes, to three iron buckets. The loot included 1085 firearms and 396 bayonets, sabers and lances, as well as 286 cannonballs, 217 shells, 108 sacks of shot, and 7260 carbine and rifle balls. As the fighting abated, Arredondo ordered Elizondo, with 200 cavalrymen, toward San Fernando de Béxar, to apprehend those who fled early in the action and to take possession of the town.[1]

Royalist reprisal begat eager retribution at the hands of the Mexican turncoats who had fled the battle early and now sought to make points with the conqueror. McLane described the general slaughter of the retreating Americans thusly:

> They butchered most of those who had broken down, cut them in quarters, and suspended them on poles and limbs of trees like beef or pork for the packer; and when the enemy advanced, they displayed them as trophies of their loyalty.[2]

Villars said that the Americans were slaughtered in great numbers — all who were taken prisoners, the wounded and all were "shot and hung up by the heels on trees. The slaughter continued to Béxar; no quarters were given to any overtaken of the Americans." Gaines confirmed that "more than one-half who had not fallen in the Battle fell in the retreat." Villars reported that some forty-five or fifty Americans managed to reach Béxar, but the citizens took them prisoners and delivered them to Elizondo. Among the "miserable recreants and traitors was a brother-in-law of Bernardo, ... but this did not save him; he was shot with the prisoners."[3]

En route to Béxar, Elizondo picked up several more prisoners. He reached the panic-stricken town shortly after a frantic group of some 300 rebel families had fled toward Louisiana. Among them were the Delgados, Arochas, and Leals — scions of the *familias pobladores* that had figured prominently in the affairs of the Villa of San Fernando since the 1730s, as well as in independence movements of the current decade. Toledo, Kemper, Perry, Bullard, Wilkinson, Taylor, and other surviving American officers were already in full flight toward Nacogdoches. Arredondo later claimed that those who fled the city had carried away "the best of everything, as they had arranged to do in case they lost the battle." This, too, was probably an exaggeration to impress the viceroy, for it is known that the Delgado–Leal family and some of their Arocha in-laws took only a sack of dried corn, plucked from their own fields.[4]

Meanwhile, Arredondo moved his army and military train up to the Laredo Road crossing of the Medina, where he treated his wounded, had his soldiers' clothing washed, and shot a few more prisoners. His camp probably was made on the tongue of land at the confluence of Losoya Creek with the Medina — a location pointed out today by longtime residents of the area as the battle site.[5] Then, his wagons loaded with wounded and dying, he proceeded in triumph into Béxar, where he arrived on the morning of the twentieth.[6]

Menchaca said that the parish church in San Antonio was

filled with men praying that their lives should be spared. According to him, "All were taken out, some placed in the old Spanish Guard house, and others crowded into the house of Francisco Arocha." Of the latter, eight suffocated during the night. Menchaca also said,

> On the following day, they were all taken out in a line to ascertain which of them deserved to be put to death, and which to be put to hard labor ... Arredondo selected forty which should be put to death, and the balance, 160 were handcuffed in pairs and sent to work upon the streets. Of the forty who were selected to die, every third day they would shoot three, opposite the Plaza House, until the entire number were disposed of.[7]

Yoakum's version, was that some 300 were imprisoned during the night in one house, and that eighteen died of suffocation. Hunter wrote even a more lurid account. The story may well be apocryphal.

John Villars, who was one of the prisoners, reported that in Béxar, Arredondo had about three hundred male prisoners, whom he put in irons;

> ... and daily executed some of them, then dragging them round the public square, and then cutting off their arms and heads and placing them in public places — These scenes continued until he dis[posed] of most of the unfortunate fellows. — The few who were not executed were liberated on the birthday of Ferdinand.[8]

Arredondo said that 112 prisoners taken during the battle were shot "on this and the following day." On the way to Béxar and in Béxar, 215 more were captured, of whom those deserving death were shot, and "the less culpable were sent to prison." His prisoner count, therefore, is somewhat more modest than those claimed by American writers, which aggregate five hundred or more.[9]

It should be understood here that these prisoners were mainly the *Tejano* inhabitants of Béxar and former royalists soldiers who had been unable to flee before the arrival of Elizondo. Both Villars and McLane mentioned American prisoners being held in Béxar: McLane, "eight or ten ... who were saved by the intercession of Elizondo;" and Villars, who said thirteen or fifteen were taken to Monterrey the following April and set free, Villars among them.[10]

Arredondo caused the wives and female relatives of men

suspected of cooperating with the revolutionists to be arrested and held in a building known as the *Quinta,* where they were made to grind corn and make *tortillas* for Arredondo's soldiers. Villars wrote that, "they were treated with great brutality, whipped, ravished and maltreated in every possible form; and they constituted the best portion of the population." Their overseer, a sergeant named Acosta, was a "black ferocious villian who violated some of the prisoners daily and whipped others for their resistance." They endured this harrowing experience for fifty-four days and, when released, went into the streets destitute, their homes and possessions having been confiscated.[11]

To impress proper respect for the king's officials, Arredondo had the bodies of Governors Salcedo and Herrera exhumed and, with great solemnity, given fitting burial in the parish church, now San Fernando Cathedral. The officiant was Reverend Don José Dario Sambrano, curate of Béxar and brother of the Subdeacon Lieutenant Colonel Juan Manuel Sambrano.[12]

Shortly after his arrival in the prostrate city, Arredondo ordered Elizondo with 500 mounted men to pursue fugitives fleeing toward Nacogdoches, with orders to put to death every man he caught. McLane reported that Elizondo refused the commission unless Arredondo would temper the order to allow the Americans to proceed home, the *Tejano* citizens to be pardoned, but all those who had been in the king's service executed. Another detachment of eighty men was sent to restore the royal authority in La Bahía, where eleven republicans had been seized and put to death by the inhabitants.[13]

Although plagued by fatigue, and with exhausted and broken horses, Elizondo arrived at the Trinity on the twenty-eighth — ten days after the Medina battle — and established a base of operations two leagues west of the stream. He had been forced to leave eighty horses and half his men at the Colorado, to follow *poco a poco.* The same day he had come upon a fresh track. Taking forty men, he raced ahead of his party. At eight the next morning he overtook seven Americans and a Spaniard on the *Arroyo de Nuncio,* where he apprehended three, the rest escaping into the thick woods. Two hours later he was on the Brazos, where he noted a "small crowd of rebels" on the far bank. Shouting across the river, he diverted the fugitives by offering them a pardon while a picket of his troops doffed their clothes, crossed the stream bareback, and captured sixteen men, women and children. Two managed to escape. Four of the men were executed. Leaving a corporal and seven soldiers with thirty-seven worn out horses to wait for the troops he had left on the Colorado, Elizondo rejoined the main body of his men.

Two days later, he again encountered a fresh track. He followed it all day without overtaking his prey, so he sent ahead a party of forty-five men under the *Alférezes* Fernando Rodríguez and Tomás Saucedo in pursuit of the rebels, instructing them also to spy on the village of Trinidad. The next morning, the advance party sent word that they could not reach Trinidad because the river was in freshet; however, on their return, two leagues from the river, they succeeded in seizing the Delgado family, killing Antonio Delgado. Villars said that Antonio Delgado was about to resist, but surrendered upon being assured his life would be spared. Another source says, "They instantly killed Antonio Delgado with a ball, and when he fell before his mother they began to stab him with their lances . . . ordering that he be stripped and left as food for the wild beasts, which was done." Infuriated by the supplications of Antonio's mother, *Alférez* Rodríguez upended his lance and beat her until he separated her from her dead son. The mother was none other than Angela Arocha, who had been previously forced by Governor Salcedo to witness the beheading of her husband as noted in chapter two; she also lost two other sons and several nephews at the Trinity.[14]

Elizondo established a base of operations on the edge of a plain, about two leagues west of the Trinity, where the road from La Bahía joined the *camino real* and where travelers on either road could not escape his ambush. He sent Rodríguez and Saucedo out again with two rawhide boats and forty men to cut off the escape of Toledo from Trinidad, but they were prevented from crossing the river by an Indian of the Jaraname tribe who fired on them. The same night he sent *Alférez* Manuel Chapa with twenty men to *paso del Salto,* where he had heard the Arocha family had assembled. The next day Elizondo himself led a party of fifty men, all that could be mounted on his weary horses, to take Trinidad, only to find that the rebels had fled to Nacogdoches in the night. Elizondo now had spread himself so thin that the best he could do was to send three inhabitants of Trinidad on to Nacogdoches "to see their kinsmen" and to form a counterrevolution — promising the town a general pardon and immediate assistance.[15]

He left thirty-five men in Trinidad and returned to his

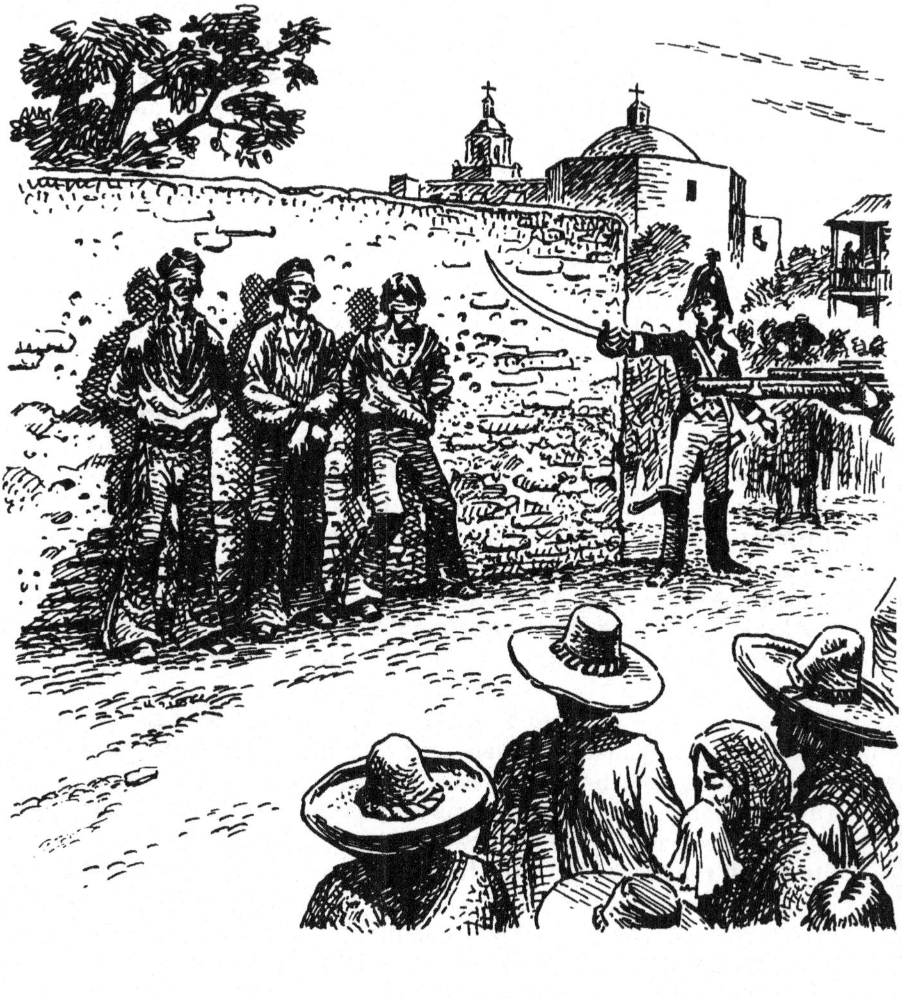

Swift Vengeance 113

camp, which he called *Campomento Español en el Puesto de Trinidad*. There Chapa sent him word that he had seized the family of Francisco Arocha. Although wounded, Arocha escaped across the river along with a number of rebels, Chapa did seize nine men and much booty, including twenty-odd horses and saddles. On his return to camp, Chapa, with the aid of twenty men sent him by Elizondo, captured twenty more men, fourteen women and seventeen children at *Rancho de Bemen*. Although his troops were mostly without mounts by this time, Elizondo boasted to Arredondo that he had captured rebels every day since reaching the Trinity. To date, he had executed twenty-seven soldiers and thirty-one *paisanos*, while pardoning seventeen soldiers and nineteen civilians, pending Arredondo's judgement. Among the executed were several who had participated in the butchering of the Spanish officers in April. He had also seized nine Americans, and these he naively dispatched to Nacogdoches to capture Toledo for him.[16]

According to information Mirabeau B. Lamar received from a Mr. Navarro [most likely José Antonio Navarro] years later, the men condemned to execution were confessed by a Padre Camacho, chaplain of Elizondo's detachment. He had received a wound in the thigh at the battle of Medina, and, as each made his confession and asked for absolution, the padre would dismiss him by saying, "It is possible that you may have been the one who shot me, and if so, may the Lord have mercy on you." Arredondo failed to list a Camacho among the Medina chaplains — although he named seven — so the story loses some of its veracity. Also, it is unlikely that he would have sent a wounded priest as chaplain on Elizondo's mounted pursuit halfway across Texas. Padre Camacho may have been the priest who was wounded in the Alazán attack, whose name is not documented, except by Hunter as "Padre Senobio." Villars mentioned the priest Camacho who was stabbed by Elizondo's assassin and who was also named as having confessed the Delgado and Leal men before their execution by Elizondo. Although Arredondo did commend a Chaplain Don Manuel Camacho in his report to the viceroy, he did not identify him as one of the wounded.[17]

Yoakum and other historians are responsible for the story that a long trench was dug and those to be executed by Elizondo were placed on a log laid across the trench, tied together ten at a time, and shot, their bodies falling into the trench.

While the story smacks of practicality, it fails to find confirmation in any other authority.

Although Elizondo acknowledged capturing only nine Americans, Shaler wrote Monroe, "upwards of fifty were taken prisoner." He treated them well, provided them with pack trains for provisions, a rifle for every fifth man, and passports to return home. Shaler talked with several of the men on their arrival at Natchitoches, and they all agreed that Elizondo had treated them in the most affable and friendly manner, that he told them he had no complaints against the Americans, that they were at liberty to stay in the country should they wish, and that he was in favor of establishing relations between the two countries.[18] In August 1819, the *National Intelligencer* published a very lengthy essay "On the Texas Expedition," by one William Darby, which lauded Elizondo in the most glowing terms for his kindness to the American prisoners. "Such an exhibition of talents, bravery, greatness of mind, and generosity of sentiment, if made upon a theatre more within the view of mankind would secure to Illesondo the meed of an immortal name," wrote Darby.[19]

On September 5, Elizondo started to Nacogdoches, but fell the victim of a ruse when he believed a message brought to him that the town was deserted except for several loyalist families. Actually, Toledo was already there rallying fugitives with about a dozen officers and some fifty men. Shaler informed Monroe that Toledo was unable to muster enough men to make a stand at Nacogdoches, and retreated to Natchitoches on September 7. Elizondo dispatched a general pardon to the hundreds of fugitives scattered throughout the wilderness of the Louisiana–Texas frontier, and then he returned to the Trinity.[20]

Having executed a total of seventy-one insurgents, Elizondo began his return march to Béxar on the seventh. With him were one hundred men and as many women captives, numerous children, and all the plunder his troops had gathered in their sweep across Texas, plus the provisions taken from the fleeing inhabitants. Four days later a camp was made at the Brazos to rest men and horses. There, one of his officers, Lieutenant Miguél Serrano, crazed by days of brutal tension, attacked Ygnacio Elizondo while he rested in his tent at daybreak on the twelfth. Serrano succeeded in killing Elizondo's cousin, Captain Ysidro de la Garza, and in wounding the Chaplain Camacho. Elizondo received a saber wound in the hand and a thrust of "notable consideration" in the right side. He wrote Arredondo informing him of his misfortune and asked that a physician be sent to him.[21] Elizondo ordered the march resumed, directing affairs from a stretcher. He died at the San Marcos River and was buried on its banks.

Colonel Cayetano Quintero delivered the prisoners to Arredondo, all the while subjecting them to the grossest of indignities. Arredondo awaited them on the plaza, surrounded by his henchmen and about a thousand spectators. He taunted the women, repeating a vulgar verse which had been sung in Béxar prior to his arrival and asking, "Whereabouts here is the woman who said she was going to eat my *huevos* roasted? They would do her more good raw! And the other, called Josefa Arocha, who offered five hundred pesos for the head of her husband [Pedro Treviño, an ex-rebel, who was among the royalist troops]?" He then dealt with the men as he had all rebels and sent the women to the *Quinta* to serve twenty days grinding corn and making *tortillas* while the children were driven into the streets to beg.[22]

By mid-September the rebellion had been crushed, and Texas lay desolate. Two thousand of the inhabitants and several tribes of Indians had fled across the Sabine. Arredondo had indeed snatched Texas from republicanism; he had effectively blocked the avenue for American aid to independence movements in the interior of Mexico; and he had reasserted the royal authority in the buffer province. Arredondo remained in San Fernando de Béxar until the spring of 1814, restoring, in his words, "complete quietude," before proceeding to his new headquarters in Monterrey.[23]

PART FOUR

Unknown, Unhonored, Unsung

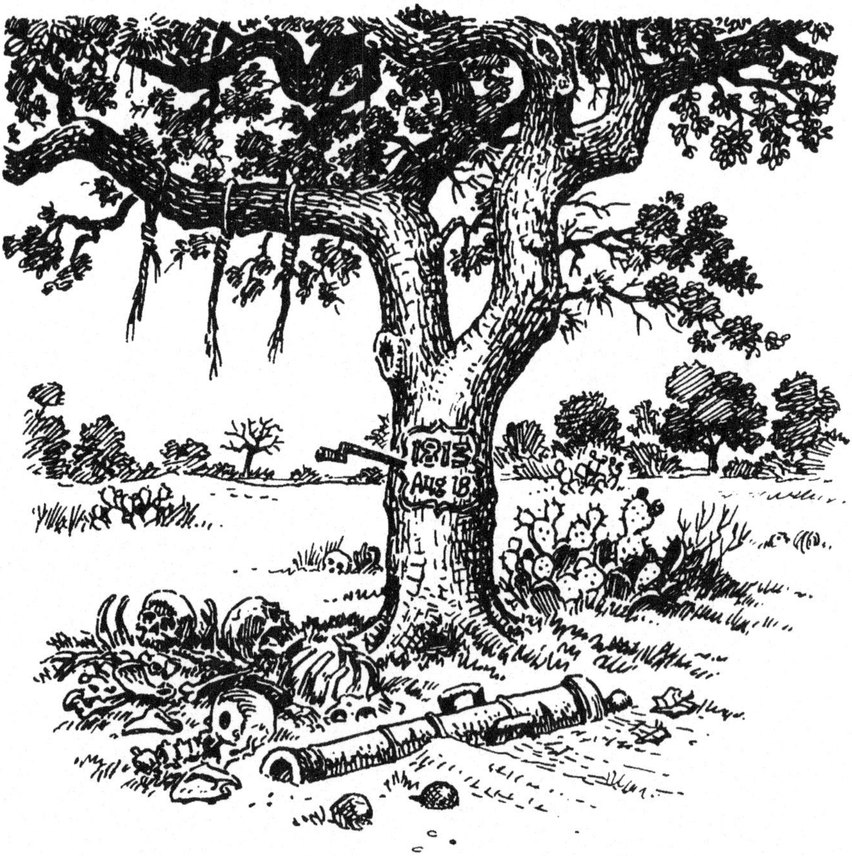
1813
Aug 18

11 *The Epilogue*

THE FIRST WAR OF INDEPENDENCE IN Texas had ended. The green flag of liberty — which had floated over the first republic of Texas from April 1 to August 18, 1813 — vanished so completely from the historical scene that it is not even counted today as one of the flags to wave over the State.

When freedom from the European yoke was finally achieved by Spanish Texas, it came through no effort on its part but as a windfall on July 18, 1821, when Governor Antonio Martinez declared for the *Plan de Iguala* and ordered his subjects to take the oath of allegiance to Agustiń de Iturbide.

Being chased across the Sabine with their tails between their legs was not the deterrent to the filibusters that might have been expected. Almost at once, Toledo, Gutiérrez, Perry, and others were busy with plans to invade Texas again, but America's preoccupation with the War of 1812 seemed to have dampened its citizens' zest for the venture. Taking time out to help Andy Jackson whip the British at New Orleans, the plotters were soon back to their old obsession.

Villars wrote that when Bernardo Gutiérrez was ousted as

President-Protector of Texas and Commander-in-Chief of the Republican Army of the North (it is noteworthy that Toledo succeeded only to the latter title), he left his family in Béxar. Gutiérrez himself wrote that the Government had refused permission for his family to accompany him, but this was not true, for the Junta expressly gave permission and made arrangements for his family to accompany him to Natchitoches. By April 1814, Gutiérrez was in New Orleans, where he attempted a new liberation movement. He fought in the Battle of New Orleans and, while in Louisiana, refused a proposal that he lead troops against Pensacola. Late in 1816, he was again in Natchitoches as an agent of Louis-Michel Aury — then resident commissioner of the rebel port on Galveston Island. Gutiérrez cooperated with the Mina expedition in 1817, accompanied James Long (the husband of General Wilkinson's niece, Jane Long) on expeditions into Texas in 1819 and 1820, and in 1820 was vice-president of the Supreme Council of the Long Expedition at Bolivar Point.

Iturbide, Emperor of Mexico in 1822–1823, recognized the independence efforts of the Gutiérrez de Lara brothers. In 1824, after an absence of thirteen years, Bernardo returned to Revilla and was elected Governor of Tamaulipas in July 1824, and made commandant-general of the state in March 1825. He resigned the governorship, but in December he became commandant-general of the *Provincias Internas de Oriente* (Arredondo's old job under the Spaniards), which post he held until late in 1826. Both brothers attended sessions of the Congress, which on July 18, 1824, decreed the death of Iturbide. José Bernardo was unyielding in his stand and cast his vote for execution, but José Antonio, who served as president of the Congress, withheld his vote. (Iturbide was shot the next day.) In 1839, Bernardo energetically opposed efforts of Antonio Canales, aided by a number of Texians, to set up the Republic of the Rio Grande. He died May 13, 1841, while on a trip to Santiago and was buried in the parish church near the altar of San José.[1]

After lingering around the Neutral Ground for a while and trying to organize another expedition, first with Dr. Robinson's help and then in competition with him for leadership, José Álvarez de Toledo drifted on to New Orleans, where he served as an aide to Louisiana Governor Claiborne during the British invasion. Misfortune in Mexico, while delivering a cargo of munitions sent by New Orleans merchants to the insurgents, stripped Toledo of his resources. In June 1816, along with his longtime associate, Juan Mariano Picornel, he made his peace with Spain, working with the venerable New Orleans priest, "Pere Antoine" Sedella, and the Spanish minister Onís for the faltering cause. Returning to Europe the following year, he embarked on a long diplomatic career, dying in Paris in 1858.[2]

On March 14, 1815, Toledo submitted to the insurgent government in Mexico a list of "foreign officers in the service of the Mexican Republic who had distinguished themselves in the Province of Texas." It listed Captain William Slocum and several others as having died in the battle of August 18, 1813, and Colonel Samuel Kemper as having died from measles in New Orleans in November 1814. Among those still "in actual service," he mentioned Colonel Henry Perry, Major Reuben Ross, Captain Josiah Taylor, Captain William B. Murray, and Adjutant Godwin B. Cotton.[3] Curiously, the list omitted the names of such notables as Magee, Forsythe, Bullard, and Wilkinson.

After the Medina defeat, Perry is said to have served in the U. S. Army for a brief period, participating in the Battle of New Orleans, then returning to filibuster again on the Texas frontier. As a colonel in the "Republican" army, he was to gather troops, sail for Matagorda, and capture La Bahía. There Gutiérrez de Lara was to join him with a second army to attack Béxar — a replay, it was hoped, of the Gutiérrez–Magee misadventure. Plans were discussed so openly that President Madison on September 1, 1815, issued a proclamation designed to end such schemes. Perry then gathered 150 men on the Sabine, and in November moved his camp to Bolivar Point, opposite Galveston Island. By September 1816, he had joined with Louis-Michel Aury, and in April 1817, he sailed with Mina for an invasion of Mexico. Breaking with Mina, he tried to seize La Bahía with some fifty men, but failed. Fleeing toward Nacogdoches, Perry committed suicide to avoid capture by Colonel Ygnacio Pérez, against whom he had fought both at Alazán and at Medina.[4]

Reuben Ross was one who apparently got his fill of filibustering. He had been a sheriff of Washington County, Virginia, and he returned to his home state. Some years later, while en route to Mexico in quest of remuneration for his services, he was killed either by robbers or by his Mexican servant. Villars said that Ross returned to Béxar before the battle of Medina, but there is no confirmation of this — nor of his service with Toledo in 1815. A nephew of the same name served in the

Texas Army from 1836 to 1839, and was in service under Canales on the Rio Grande.[5]

Another on whom filibustering palled was Henry Adams Bullard, distant cousin of the Presidents Adams, Harvard graduate, a lawyer, and fluent in five languages. Bullard soon gave up the Texas adventure for Louisiana politics. District Judge, member of the Louisiana Legislature, Whig member of the Twenty-second and Twenty-third Congresses, he was appointed to the Louisiana Supreme Court in January 1834. He also served as law professor at Louisiana State University and as the first president of the Louisiana State Historical Society.[6]

When he was dismissed as Indian Agent in 1814, possibly as a result of his involvement with the Magee–Gutiérrez Expedition, Dr. John Sibley also entered politics, eventually becoming a member of the Louisiana Senate. Along with Gutiérrez, he joined the short-lived James Long expedition to Texas in 1819, but soon he returned to his home near Natchitoches, where he died in 1837.[7] His co-conspirator, William Shaler, accompanied Toledo to Nashville late in 1813, and then to Washington City. Shaler participated in peace conferences in Europe in 1814, and in Algiers in 1815. From 1818 to 1830, he was consul general in Algiers, and he was again stationed in Havana, when he died in March 1833, during a cholera epidemic.[8]

Dr. Sibley's Spanish counterpart, Samuel Davenport, a wealthy man who had served the Spanish government loyally for many years in both Louisiana and Texas, moved his possessions safely to Natchitoches after abandoning the Gutiérrez–Magee Expedition while it was under siege at La Bahía. After the rebels were defeated at Medina, Arredondo offered 250 *pesos* for Davenport's head. In 1815, Davenport was living in Natchitoches, experimenting with sugarcane on his plantation, where he died in 1824.[9]

Other American reporters of affairs at La Bahía and Béxar lived on for many years. William McLane, one of the last survivors of the expedition, amassed a sizable fortune in Indiana and Kentucky before moving to San Antonio in 1854, where he died in May 1873, on his ranch — which later became that city's Alamo Heights.[10] John Villars was one of the prisoners taken by Arredondo to Monterrey and released. Villars settled in San Fernando, Coahuila, where he married the widow of Peter Boone, who had been wounded in the Medina battle and also was taken to Monterrey as a prisoner, and succeeded him as armorer to the Mexican army.[11] Warren D. C. Hall returned to Galveston with Perry in 1815, with Louis-Michel Aury in 1817, and again as a settler in 1835. President David G. Burnet appointed him adjutant general of the Provisional Government in 1836, and later he served the Second Republic of Texas as Secretary of War. In 1842, he joined the forces which expelled the Adrian Woll invasion of San Antonio. Hall practiced law for many years before his death in Galveston in 1867.[12] James Gaines was active in Texas affairs from 1823 or 1824, when he was elected *alcalde* of the newly organized Sabine District. Having served on the committee which drafted it, Gaines signed the Texas Declaration of Independence in 1836. He served three terms in the Senate of the Second Texas Republic. In 1849, he joined the California gold rush, and he died in Quartzberg, California, in November 1856.[13]

For those who would still dismiss the Battle of Medina as a flash-in-the-pan — a shattered ego trip, as it were — that was of no special significance to the eventual North-Americanization of the State, it would be well to note the respect paid to the lessons to be learned from that engagement by those two adversaries of 1836, Santa Anna and Sam Houston.

Don Antonio López de Santa Anna was a young lieutenant — not yet twenty, but with five years as a soldier behind him — when he accompanied Arredondo on his march north and became a participant in the battle of Medina. Others with Arredondo at Medina who were later to figure prominently in Texas affairs were Cristóbal Domínguez, interim governor 1813; Juan José Elguezábal, Mexican governor 1834–1835; Antonio Elosúa, *ayudante inspector* of Coahuila and Texas 1826–1833; Luciana García, interim Mexican governor 1823; Ygnacio Pérez. interim governor 1816–1817; and Domingo Ugartechea, a well-liked Mexican commander during most of the Second Texas Revolution. Santa Anna's contribution to the Medina fight could not have been particularly noteworthy since Arredondo, in his report to the viceroy, merely cited him for "great bravery" along with several other officers. But what Santa Anna learned that day must have been uppermost in his mind twenty-two years later when, at San Luís Potosí, on December 7, 1835, he issued a field order to Brigadier General Ramírez y Sesma, then en route to Béxar. The order included eight rules of conduct that Sesma was to observe — the last five of which reflected Santa Anna's preoccupation with his experiences at Medina:

> 4th. You are to observe the strictest military rule while on the road from Laredo to Béjar, taking the greatest possible precaution to avoid an ambush or nocturnal attack upon your camp.
>
> 5th. Should the enemy . . . [be in position] so much to his advantage that you consider it unlikely that you can defeat him, then you will avoid attacking him and manage your maneuvers to entice him to fight on different ground, . . . by undertaking a false retreat for a league or two.
>
> 6th. . . . Your own well-located artillery should deliver the first destructive blows. The cavalry in two columns will attract the enemy's attention to the flanks at the rear, taking advantage of any weakness or negligence . . . Upon noticing the slightest disorder or indecision within the enemy's ranks, a bayonet charge will be rapidly unleashed, . . . Once the action has begun, any vacillation is dangerous; victory is gained by the one who, without doubting his success for even a second, attacks or resists with the greatest order, promptitude and courage.
>
> 7th. . . . The slightest disorder is to be avoided, including that which is sometimes caused by the overenthusiasm of the soldiers.
>
> 8th. . . . Any calamitous event of any sort in these regions so far from aid would be irreparable, hence for that reason, nothing will be left to chance.[14]

It is interesting to speculate whether Santa Anna would have gone on to become the "Napoleon of the West" if he had not had the experience in *el encinal de Medina* which led to the crystalization of the foregoing rules for aggressive warfare.

Hard-drinking, irascible, closemouthed old Sam Houston, who finally out-retreated Santa Anna and licked him at San Jacinto, got his military baptism in the War of 1812. Fighting Creek Indians in Alabama, where he was gravely wounded, Houston could hardly have had much concern with, nor knowledge of, a battle fought in the far reaches of Spanish Texas, but the lengthened shadow of that grim fight apparently did make impact on him. More of a diplomat and politician than a fighter, he seems to have drawn much the same lesson from the Medina battle as did Santa Anna. Shortly after Houston became President of the second Republic of Texas, on February

7, 1837, he wrote the following to Albert Sidney Johnston,*
then commanding the Texian Army:

> In the event [at any time] of an engagement with the enemy one thing must be borne in mind, and cannot be too strongly impressed upon our troops *which is*: that the enemy may yield at first so as to draw our army into an ambuscade as they did at the battle of *Madena* when the Americans owing to their impetuosity and want of order were all destroyed.[15]

Texans like the story that General Houston caught the Mexican dictator "out of uniform" and dallying in his tent with the "Yellow Rose of Texas." Santa Anna's reputation as a womanizer highlights his military career. Be that as it may, had Santa Anna heeded his own advice to Sesma, the tables might have been turned at San Jacinto, and Texas might not have joined the bicentennial observance of the United States of America, nor would it comemmorate the approaching sesquicentennial of its own separation from the Mexican States.

While there are meticulously researched and carefully documented lists of the North American, European, and Mexican combatants at the Alamo, San Jacinto, Goliad, and in many lesser encounters and skirmishes, the names of but a handful of the Medina Survivors are recorded. Of those who fell in the action or on the retreat, even fewer names are known. Ninety-odd Americans were supposed to have made it across the Sabine, but no more than twenty can be positively identified. Some of them again fought for or served freedom either against Hispanic oppressors in Texas, against the British in the Battle of New Orleans, or both. Toledo, Wilkinson, Bullard, Kemper, Perry, McLane, Picornel, Aylette C. Buckner, Godwin B. Cotton, and George Orr are known to have fought at Medina. Add Gutiérrez, Dr. Samual Forsythe, Warren D. C. Hall, Reuben Ross, John Ash, Samuel Noah, and James Gaines — who were at La Bahía and Rosillo, but left Béxar before the Medina fight, and the list of known survivors is still slim. Of the dozen or more prisoners taken to Monterrey, only Villars and Boone are recorded.

Never in the history of this country, has there been a major battle with such a disproportionate number of unknown dead, and so many unhonored survivors! Except for an abbreviated

---

* Two of General Johnston's brothers were said to have been participants in the Medina battle.

list of "foreign" officers which Toledo drafted in 1815, no roster of American participants in the Gutiérrez–Magee Expedition has ever come to light. Considering that the expedition was spawned in the Neutral Ground, where many banditti and fugitives were recruited, and that after the execution of the Spanish officers in April 1813, there was a mass exodus of the earlier volunteers and their replacement with fresh adventurers, it is no wonder that the names of so few are known. Except for the leaders, the balance of the fragmentary list is made up of names encountered in contemporary writings. Walker appended such a list to his piece on the McLane narrative.[16]

One name on the list that defies precise identification — although his role is well-documented — is that of Wilkinson. Several writers have straddled the issue by referring to him only as "the son of General Wilkinson." Shaler did this in his letters to James Monroe, but Shaler may have had a reason for keeping Wilkinson's identity obscure. Both James Biddle Wilkinson and Joseph Biddle Wilkinson have been listed as names of the man who accompanied Bullard to Béxar to depose Gutiérrez and who later served as Toledo's aide in the battle of Medina. Whichever brother he was, he signed his name "Jas., (or Jos.) B. Wilkinson", and examination of the signature is inconclusive. After considering the options, this author believes that it was James, the elder of the two, who gave us the first eyewitness account of the Medina defeat. He died within a few days after his return to Natchitoches, which probably accounts for the fact that there were no further Wilkinson reports concerning his Texas misadventure.[17]

Walker also attempted to list the Hispanic republicans, many of whom descended from the first settlers of Texas. Again the list is scanty, although their numbers must have totaled well into the hundreds. We have Francisco Arocha, Vicente Travieso, Francisco Ruíz, and Pedro Prado, all of whom were exempted from Arredondo's amnesty of October 10, 1813, as was the "foreigner" Bernardo Dortolan. Juan Martín Veramendi and José Antonio Navarro were others who fled to the United States, later returning to take their places alongside the Anglo-Texian patriots. Tomás Arocha and Fernando Veramendi were two honored patriots who were marched barefoot and shackled from the Trinity to Béxar to face Arredondo's judgment. Of those whose lifeblood ebbed out on the sands of Medina, we can only account for Miguél Menchaca and José María Guadiana, and, possibly, the Frenchman Despallier.

Músquiz, the turncoat, enjoys a category alone. Of the hundreds executed by Arredondo and Elizondo, the names of only a few are known, including Antonio Delgado, his two brothers, and their Leal cousins. For obvious reasons, many *Tejanos* later found it the better part of valor to soft pedal their roles in the 1811–1813 independence movements and no records of their participation exist. Others changed sides, and found it expedient to expunge their prior allegiances. The republican soldiers who had slunk into the woods at Medina and later helped butcher the retreating survivors and hang up their quartered carcasses as trophies of their loyalty, would have been among that number. It is significant of the ebb and flow of *Tejano* loyalties that, of the thirty men who had put their signatures to two republican proclamations from Béxar in April 1813, at least four were among the royalist officers recommended for promotion by Arredondo following the Medina battle! A fifth, Pedro Treviño, was known to have been with the royalists; his rebel wife, Josefa Arocha, posted a bounty of 500 *pesos* for his head.[18]

Of particular interest is the double deserter Juan Galván. A soldier of the presidial company at Béxar, he deserted early and served Gutiérrez as a courier in carrying propaganda materials to Revilla. At La Bahía, where he was the officer in charge of the horse herd, he deserted again, taking the *caballada* with him to the royalists. Whether he fought at Medina is not known, but we do know he was with Elizondo in his advance to Béxar in mid-June. Elizondo referred to him as the "famous Corporal *Juan Galbán*," who co-commanded with brevet *Alférez* Tomás Saucedo the successful raid on *Puesto de Salado*, where three Americans were killed and 300 horses and twenty prisoners were taken. For his fine performance in this midnight surprise attack, Elizondo promoted Galván two ranks to the grade of *Alférez* — which Arredondo promptly cut back to sergeant, reproving Elizondo for committing him to the double promotion "which the Most Excellent Señor Viceroy has not granted me at one time."[19] Galván's name appears again several years later as a sergeant of the Béxar company, which would suggest that he had escaped capture at the Alazán, and remained with Elizondo. One might also speculate whether Galvan Creek bears his name. Perhaps Arredondo rewarded him with a tract of land in the vicinity for his perfidy at La Bahía and his achievements at *Puesto del Salado*. It must be noted here that there was also an American named John

Galvan. He appears as a lieutenant colonel and as Toledo's aide on the latter's list of foreign officers. This Galvan understood no Spanish! [20]

On the Spanish side, Arredondo scrupulously recommended each of his officers for a one-grade promotion in his report to the Viceroy Calleja. The promotions were not made, and three years later he sent another list to the new Viceroy, Juan Ruíz de Apodaca, with the same request for those officers still within his command. So we have what is probably a complete roster of the royalist officers. However, Arredondo mentioned only two of his noncoms, for both had been instrumental in saving his life in the battle. One was Corporal Mateo Sotelo of the Nuevo Santander Militia.[21] Sotelo is a singular name, and it is of interest that there was a Sotelo homestead grant on the Atascosa just below Pleasanton. In an old cemetery on the property there are two ancient red rock tombs. Could it be that Corporal Sotelo rests in one of these? One wonders what the outcome might have been that day had the corporal not been so quick to warn Arredondo of the American rifle aimed at him — an eventuality which would have left Elizondo in command of the royalist army at Medina.

Several writers have said that both Elizondo and Arredondo were accompanied by several hundred *rancheros,* many of them Béxar fugitives. Except for Colonel Ygnacio Pérez and the militia officers, these also go unrecorded. Colonel Pérez, the father-in-law of Governor Cordero of Coahuila, had been awarded title to a ranch on the Medina in 1808.

Therefore, if we add together the unidentified *Tejano* "republicans" and the unidentified *Tejano* "royalists", we have upward of *two thousand native born participants in the Medina battle who remain unknown.* This fact might not have been historically significant except that, during Arredondo's occupation of the city of Béxar, royalist Medina veterans largely displaced the *Tejano* population of the city, preempting first their properties and, in due turn, their positions as leading citizens. Following Arredondo's general pardon in October 1813, the way was opened for the turncoat rebel soldiers to reenter the mainstream of activity in Texas. Many settled permanently in the San Antonio area, and, in time, some achieved social and economic status of their own.

Considering the political tensions and divided loyalties holding over from the independence movements which Arredondo had just put down, plus those soon to arise as Mexico moved toward final independence in 1821, it is not surprising that many a San Antonio resident later found it wise to be vague about his own role in the 1813 madness.

Besides the mass burial by Trespalacios of the battlefield skeletons and of the skulls at the Medina River — and those bones left to bleach on the Brazos and the Trinity by Elizondo — the graves of Medina survivors are scattered from Virginia to California. None, however, challenges the imagination as does a lone grave found several years ago when Bexar County road workers stumbled onto a skeleton near Buena Vista, once an old Mexican settlement known as *Chamacuero,* some two miles north of the Medina River on the Laredo road. The grave showed evidence of the hasty interment of its occupant, and, in the course of events, the skeleton wound up in the custodianship of San Antonio's Witte Memorial Museum. There, Mrs. Anne Fox, the Museum's anthropologist, made extensive studies toward identifying the skeleton. A prime candidate would be Colonel Miguél Menchaca. When the skeleton was cleaned, a large lead shot — a grapeshot — was found embedded in the neck! Antonio Menchaca had written that the Colonel "was struck by a ball on the neck." He was brought with the retreating Mexicans, "died on the way and was buried on the Seguin road at the place called Menchaca Creek or Cañada de Menchaca." [22]

Neither Menchaca Creek nor the Seguin Road identify with the Buena Vista area today. However, in those days there was a road to the *las Yslitas* ranches which crossed the Medina at *paso de Borregos,* below the Laredo ford. The road led to ranches later granted to Erasmo Seguin in present Wilson and Karnes counties. Thus, in escaping from Arredondo's vengeance, Menchaca's friends might have taken this secondary road, and when their wounded leader expired, they hurriedly buried him on the spot.[23]

If these bones were Miguél Menchaca's, they attest to his apparent youthfulness at the time of his death. The skull still holds thirty-two perfect teeth, in exact alignment, except for one canine which projects slightly. Contemplating the skull, one is struck by the fact that this must have been a handsome man — with a dazzling smile. He could have been such a charismatic leader.

And his age? It was a moment that called for young men — for their vigor, their courage, and their freedom to travel hundreds of miles from home to tilt with the windmills and the dragons of their idealisms. Magee was only twenty-four when he mobilized the Republican Army of the North on the Sabine. Bullard was also twenty-four when he toppled the thirty-eight-year-old patriarch Gutiérrez and replaced him with thirty-four-year-old Toledo. Peter Boone, said to be a nephew of Daniel Boone, was just twelve when he was wounded in the thigh and taken prisoner in the Medina battle. Even the older adventurers were not in their golden years. Ross was thirty, Kemper thirty-four, and Shaler was thirty-nine when his intrigues almost brought down an empire. Arredondo was the graybeard of the lot. He was forty-five.

By these criteria, there is no reason to hold that the youthful skeleton that has found repose in a file drawer at the Witte Museum might not have been Menchaca.

Some of the most respected writers of Texas history have advanced the premise that the Gutiérrez–Magee Expedition was not an isolated filibustering foray into Spanish Texas, but a step in the continuous struggle for Texas independence, being part of that larger Mexican Revolution beginning with Hidalgo in 1810, and culminating with Mexican independence under Iturbide in 1821. To a limited extent that is true. The mandate Gutiérrez received, or thought he received from Hidalgo at Saltillo in March 1811, spiritually sustained him to the eve of the Medina debacle. However, the salient facts are that Gutiérrez and his fellow revolution-makers were encouraged, sponsored, and underwritten by the young government of the United States and many of its citizens, and that this assistance came with the full knowledge and tacit assent of its highest officials, including Secretary of State James Monroe, and perhaps even President Madison himself! Fear of possible Napoleonic or British intervention in Mexico was excuse enough. Dreams of expansion, greed, and the need to define the boundary of newly purchased Louisiana provided further incentive for this arrogant violation of Spanish sovereignty.

True, there must have been *Tejanos* in Béxar, Nacogdoches, and La Bahía who held fast to their belief in the doctrines and principles of the American and French revolutions — come what may — and whose hearts must have leapt with renewed hopes with the revolutionary philosophy aimed at them by Gutiérrez's propaganda blasts from the Louisiana frontier. The fact that men of Béxar such as Juan Galván and Miguél Men-

Epilogue 131

chaca journeyed to the Sabine to cast their lots with the republicans proves that such passions did exist among the native population. However, considering that the three towns were vastly isolated, even from each other, that the respective populations were small — everyone must have known most everyone else — and that the very struggle for survival in that cruel wilderness dictated a modicum of harmony among the inhabitants, it would seem that the *vecinos* would have found it expedient to support overtly whatever government or faction was in power. The dissidents — those not jailed or executed — usually found they had urgent business at their ranches or across the Sabine.

While revolutionary fires may have smoldered in many *Tejano* breasts, the fact is that when Magee and Gutiérrez arrived at La Bahía, they failed to receive the outpouring of help from Béxar that they had expected, which underscores the truth that their expedition was not welcomed by Texas republicans as a renewal of their own revolution. One needs only to recall Shaler's assault on Gutiérrez from Natchitoches and Bullard's tactics in overthrowing the very leader the *Tejanos* of Béxar had installed as president-protector of their new Republican State, to understand that the summer of 1813, in Béxar, was revolution brought to and imposed on the native population of Spanish Texas by an outright American-inspired filibuster.

12 Battleground Revisited

HISTORY, NAPOLEON ONCE SAID, IS A fable agreed upon. Nothing better illustrates this axiom than the collective opinion that has developed around the location of the Medina battleground. Historians, almost to a man, have given the impression that the engagement took place on the Medina River. *The Handbook of Texas* — that bible of Texas information — lists it as the "Battle of the Medina River."[1]

However, the reader who has avoided woolgathering during the previous chapters will know that North American republicans met Spanish royalists in a duel to the death some ten miles, *más ó menos,* [more or less] south of the river. Also, the reader will recall that the rebels reached this place only after a grueling march through blackjack sand so deep that it not only broke down many of the foot soldiers pulling the cannons but also forced the abandonment of perhaps five of their seven fieldpieces, leaving them stuck in the sandy ground.

Unlike mapmaker Stephen F. Austin — who on many of his maps placed crossed swords with the caption, "Genl Toledo Defeated Here" — the reader cannot yet point to a spot on a map and say, "This is where the battle of Medina took place."[2] Nor would the reader find at the site any hard evidence of the slaughter of 700 or more brave men. There had been no earthen entrenchments for today's battlefield buffs to ferret out — only a temporary breastwork which probably disappeared when the royalists gathered up their pack loads after the fight. There would be little in the way of relics remaining to lure the treasure hunter with his metal detector — frugal Arredondo had his men gather up everything of possible value after the rebels fled. All that might still be left to identify the site would be the musket and rifle balls that missed their targets and fell to the ground, along with some cannonballs and grapeshot. Arredondo wrote:

> ... in the four hours that the action lasted nine hundred and fifty [cannon] shots were fired, which had been listed, just in case, therefore the number was known. These were fired from seven cannon; for, although [at first] our number was eleven, two had been taken by the enemy and two that we had [were] dismounted.[3]

The cannons left stuck in the sand may have reduced the republican artillery pieces to two, but these — and possibly some others brought up later — were fired during the battle and contributed to the total firings. Not all the cannon shots were ball; most were probably grape and shell and some might even have been rounded stones. Rounded stones of cannonball size have been found in the area. Such battle artifacts as do remain might well be buried several feet under today's surface, due to shifting of the sands by the wind. There are fence rows in the area today that are marked by sand drifts as high as a man on a tractor.

So where then is the lost battlefield? And, if there are no physical remains to mark its location, what evidence does exist to point up its whereabouts?

Older residents of Losoya, in southern Bexar County, point to the tongue of land at the confluence of the Medina River and Losoya Creek — which was probably the site where Arredondo camped the night after the battle. Records of Our Lady of Mount Carmel Church, at El Carmen a mile up the river, trace the church's origin to the burial in 1817 — in a crypt under a small chapel — of the "neglected dead of the 1813 Battle of the Medina."[4] Discounting the discrepancy of the burial dates, this tradition might possibly stem from the later interment of the skulls by Governor Trespalacios in 1822; however, it is a matter of record that some months after the battle, Arredondo gave credit for his victory to the intercession of *la Santísima Virgen Nuestra Señora del Carmen* — thus fielding the possibility that the original burial at El Carmen indeed may have been in 1817, or earlier, and that the interred were royalist dead.[5]

The present church at El Carmen, its fourth, is located to the north of the presumed crypt location which today is enclosed by a chain link fence and lies behind a stone bell tower, which was preserved as a votary chapel when a church built in 1877, over the crypt site, was taken down. An earlier *capilla*, built before December 1855, when the first marriage was recorded, stood where the present building is. The town-site dates from 1875, when Bishop Pellicer laid out *Villa de Carmen* on a strip of land 100 *varas* wide by 5000 *varas* long, extending from the church to the Laredo Road ford of the Medina. Cattle drives from the south halted here for the night before the final day's drive to the railroad at San Antonio.[6]

At the intersection of Highway 281 and Farm Road 2537, there stands a forlorn historical marker which proclaims,

THE BATTLE OF THE MEDINA WAS FOUGHT HERE

at least ten miles from the battle site. However, this is the third location for the marker since it was first erected during the Texas Centennial observances in 1936 — not counting several years that it disappeared altogether, presumably in a Highway Department storage yard.

The researcher interested in locating the site of the Medina battle needs to sift and correlate many obscure clues over and beyond those found in the history books or in evidence at the site. Important among these would be the locations of two old roads: the Laredo Road and that older road with three names, the *camino real,* the Lower Presidio Road, or the Lower Rio Grande Road. In this area the old Spanish roads long since have been abandoned, but a careful search of the terrain will reveal their ruts as slight swales or depressions snaking across fields and through thickets, easily confused with natural gullies. Erosion control and soil conservation work during the past four decades have removed many of these traces. When the author first became interested in locating the Medina battlefield fifty years ago, the meanderings of the old roads were still fairly easy to follow.

Unfortunately, there is no assurance that evidence of a road visible today, or even fifty years ago, would reveal the route in use in 1813. There are indications throughout this region of deep boggy sands that the routes shifted from time to time to permit easier passage of the treacherous area. Unlike the Medina River, the Gallinas and Galvan creeks were easily forded, and the traveler did not have to follow the established trail if an alternative route better served his purpose. Also, there is documentary evidence that each of the roads at different times led to the three main fords of the Medina River.

The most reliable source of data concerning the old roads of this area are the deed and probate records of Bexar and Atascosa Counties. Incorporated in these records are field notes that define headright, bounty, and donations grants by both the Republic and the State of Texas, as well as concessions by the Mexican governors and grants by the Spanish kings — some going back well before 1813 — which make occasional references to the ancient roads and fords. In some instances the notes are precise: "West 1340 *varas* crossing Atascosa Creek, 1508 *varas* crossing Laredo Road, 1990 varas to a stake," making it possible to plot the road as it crossed survey boundaries and to trace its course on a modern map as well as on the site. In this example, the south line of the Antonio Amador Survey, Atascosa Creek has changed its course westward and now flows where the road once ran. Since lands along the traveled roads were claimed first, many of the surveys of record were run in the late Mexican and early Republic of Texas days, and the field notes might reflect conditions that existed some two or more decades after the Medina fight. Some of the older ranches, however, date from the Spanish period, so there are deed and probate recordings which refer to landmarks as they existed at an earlier time. One, for example, refers to four leagues granted on March 27, 1808, by the government of Spain to Captain Ygnacio Pérez on the south side of the Medina River, "beginning at a bluff at a pass in the river called *Paso Tranquitas*." Later, his son José Ygnacio Pérez, brother-in-law of Governor Antonio Cordero of Coahuila and acting Governor of Texas, did not succeed in defending his right and perfecting his title to this particular tract under the second Texas republic, but *Paso Tranquitas* has survived as the Perez Crossing of the Medina. Captain Ygnacio Pérez held title, also, to another league of land across the river and astride the *camino real*, which has remained in the hands of descendants.[7]

Another bit of evidence, almost completely ignored by those who have written about the Battle of Medina, is an anonymous account found in the Bolton Collection at the Bancroft Library, *Memoria de las Cosas mas notables que acaeciron en Béxar el Año de 13 mandando el Tirano Arredondo*. The author no doubt had been a resident of Béxar, and quite possibly a participant in the battle — as well as a rabid partisan! In translation, the account runs thirteen typewritten pages, but it is the first two that are of interest in locating the battle site. The writer described the royalist troops who advanced to the *Encinal*, thusly:

> ... the independent troops [the Mexicans and *Tejanos*], burning with love of country ... determined, against the military orders [of Toledo], to go to meet their enemies and fall upon them on the march; but, ... hurried on by a false lead which Elizondo gave them, they penetrated the thick forest of the *Encinal* [italics supplied]. The horses were mired up to their knees in sand which covers more than fifteen leagues, and they were met in the midst of it by the opposing army, who waited them on firm land ... rested, in good order, and in an advantageous position; while the brave fellows [the rebels] arrived with their cavalry so fatigued that they could scarcely maneuver them.[8]

Further on, he refers back to the "defeat of *El Encinal de Medina.*" — a persuading argument that the battle took its name, not from the Medina River as we have been led to believe, but from the dense oak woods in which it was so bitterly fought — then known as *el encinal de Medina!* [9]

Fray Morfi described these woods in his diary entry of December 30, 1777, calling them "the beautiful woods of Atascoso ... so dense that it scarcely afforded a path for the horses, and it was necessary to travel with great care in order not to be injured by the branches and trunks across the road." The next day, his party continued through these woods, and, after crossing the Gallinas, he noted "the nature of the country changes. The sand, *roble* and *encinos* cease, [and] woods of mesquite and cactus continue ... to the river." The passage of two centuries has not greatly altered the aspect of the countryside. The loamy soils and the mesquites leave off as one travels south and the sand, the live oaks, and the blackjacks commence abruptly several miles below the Medina.[10]

This demarkation in soil types appears clearly on county

soil maps prepared by the Soil Conservation Service. The large sweep of boggy blackjack sands — thought to have been the shoreline of a Tertiary sea — is called the Eufaula-Patilo-Nueces association, while the somewhat heavier soils northward toward the Medina River [which favor mesquite and cacti] are identified as the Poth-Wilco-Floresville association.[11]

Besides harboring the site of a great battle, the blackjack sands area — thousands of acres of which even today remain in virgin thicket — has had a colorful history as a hideout area for outlaws and, during Prohibition, was a prime locale for bootleg whiskey-making. The First and Last Chance Saloon at the county line was a mecca for both the thirsty traveler from the south and the weary motorist navigating the deep sandy ruts of the unpaved road. Young men of that period were known as "tub handle fighters" because, instead of using brass knucks, they clobbered their adversaries with the handles of galvanized washtubs. The deep friable sands are also fine peanut growing country, but the peanut farms, along with abandoned homesteads, are giving way to cattle ranches, and, along the southern perimeter, large areas of oaks [including the battle site] have been uprooted and replaced with coastal bermuda grass. For decades, sand pit operations have defaced sections of the *encinal* where access to highways and railroads made the undertaking commercially feasible.

Campo de Batalla de la inmediación de Medina. — 18 de Ag.⁰ de 1813.

— Joaquín de Arredondo

Thus did the victorious Commandant General conclude his letter from the battlefield to Lieutenant Colonel Don Juan Fermín de Juanicotena, provisional governor of Nuevo Santander and Arredondo's substitute at Aguayo.[12] His report to the Viceroy Calleja several weeks later, as published in *Gaceta del Gobierno de México*, was prefaced with:

> *El sr. brigadier D. Joaquín de Arredondo, commandante general interino de las provincias internas orientales, ha remitido al Exmo. sr. vir[r]ey el detall[e] de la gloriosa é importante victoria conseguido por su exército en las inmediaciones de Texas, y es como segue.*[13]

The title page of his report to the new Viceroy Apodaca in 1817, found in *Provincias Internas de Oriente* [from which the Hatcher translation was made] reads:

El Señor Comandante General remite el Detalle de la acción que sostuve el 18 de Agosto de 1813 en los Campos de Medina contra el exército Anglo Americano acaudillado por el revelde José Álvarez Toledo...[14]

The most profound inference that the reader might make from these three archival excerpts is that *nowhere* is there any mention whatsoever of the Medina River! This can hardly be attributed to oversight or to sloppy reporting, as Spanish writers of the period were most circumspect in such details and invariably used *"el río de"* or *"el arroyo de"* when referring to a water course. Indeed, in these same reports, Arredondo at least four times wrote *"el río de Medina,"* when reporting on maneuvers which related to that stream.

An eager, young historian, Mattie Austin Hatcher, seems to have been the culprit who led off in the propagation of the erroneous assumption that the battle had been fought on the Medina River. In her 1907 translation of Arredondo's report, she took translator's license and rendered the phrase *"en los Campos de Medina"* once as "'n the country near the Medina," and then, four times, she translated the identical Spanish words as "on the Medina." Moreover, she rendered as "on the Medina," such unrelated phrases as *"en el arenal* [sandy terrain] *de Medina"* and *"en el Encinal de Medina."* [15]

Although her published translation contained other inexcusable errors, such as rendering the Spanish *"Infantería"* as "cavalry," *"en columna"* as "in line," and introducing a footnote to the 1817 Mina expedition as an explanation for something Arredondo had first written in 1813, it would not be apt to fault Doctor Hatcher for botching the Medina references. In her youthful zeal she simply was unaware of the existence of the great blackjack oak woods commonly known a century earlier as *el encinal de Medina*; nor did she seem to have had more than a foggy concept of the terrain at and below the Medina River, so she latched onto the only landmark familiar to her, the Medina River, and contorted her translation to fit.

In the months after the battle, Arredondo had several occasions to write officially of his victory, and on each, save one, he located it *en los campos de Medina*. The exception was in a letter to Felix Trudeau, Spanish Vice Consul in Natchitoches, Louisiana, in which he parenthetically located the battle site for Trudeau as *"que fué á las inmediaciones del Rio de Medina."* Trudeau, who could be expected to find the Medina River on the rude maps on the period, would not have been familiar with the parochial *encinal*.[16]

On that day when Lieutenant Colonel Ygnacio Elizondo was mortally wounded on the banks of the Brazos by one of his officers, those Texas refugees who had gathered in Natchitoches commissioned "the citizen General D. José Álvarez de Toledo to organize a new expedition against the royal army, which robs, pursues and assinates [assassinates] us," to liberate their native soil from "the yoke of the European Spaniards." [17] On the following July 4th, Toledo issued a ringing proclamation to his troops, challenging them to avenge "the many victims sacrificed *en los campos de Medina y de la Trinidad*." Thus, both victor and vanquished seemed to be in agreement that the battle was fought, not on the Medina, but in *el encinal*, the sandy post oak thicket well south of the River.[18]

Support of this premise may be found in newspaper references during the past century. While those accounts are of little help in pinpointing the battleground, they do underscore the fact that the battle was not fought at or near the Medina River, but much farther south in what is now Atascosa County.

In 1873, when memories of living persons still recalled the battle and the Laredo Road remained the main traveled route through the area, *The Western Stock Journal*, published at Pleasanton, under the heading "Atascosa County," stated:

> It was in the Northern part of this county where the battle was fought between the Generals Arredondo and Toledo, in August, I think, 1813, which resulted in the defeat of the latter, who commanded the Mexican forces; the former commanded the Spanish troops.[19]

Noting the eighty-seventh anniversary of the "Battle of the Medina" in 1900, the *Galveston Daily News* remarked that it was the

> ... bloodiest battle ever fought in Texas ... More lives were lost than in all the battles and sieges of the war of the second republic on both sides put together. The field lies in what is now the western part of Atascosa County.[20]

Thus it appears that the confusion over the location of the Medina battleground is a twentieth century development that was "bellwethered" by an erroneous assumption drawn from the Hatcher translation — an impression that avalanched with the 1936 Texas Centennial observances when a great many people of patriotic and political bent made decisions regarding

Battleground Revisited 141

historical matters about which they had altogether too little knowledge. At least, throughout the nineteenth century, the battleground remained in the *encinal* and was not associated with the river!

The search for the Medina battleground thus narrows down to the fact that the engagement took place on the south bank of Galvan Creek — within a mile above the present-day county road that meanders westward from the old Pleasanton highway above the Las Gallinas settlement. All the viable clues that have surfaced point to this area, and, hopefully, a full-scale archeological investigation will be performed someday to substantiate this historical examination.

The location of Arredondo's encampment on the night before the battle can be pinpointed with equal certainty. As was pointed out in chapter six, Arredondo's camp was made at the place where today several shallow ponds flank the county road just as it crosses the ruts of the old *camino real*. Toledo's campsite at *Rodeo de la Espada* eludes precise location on today's maps, but the movement of his forces to the ambush site on the morning of the battle can be plotted. Because the Gallinas flows directly south after making a sharp turn where the old Pleasanton road now crosses it, Toledo would have had to have crossed the creek at or near that point. Today the area is the site of an artificially created fishing lake. He would have formed his ambuscade somewhat to the south of the creek. Both Arredondo's encampment and Toledo's ambuscade locations fit easily into the various maneuvers claimed for the two commanders by contemporary writers.

The ruts of the Lower Presidio Road [the *camino real*] can be found today less than 2500 yards to the west of the Galvan site. The Laredo Road ran about the same distance to the east. However, both armies approached the battle site on the diagonal: Arredondo from his campsite about two miles to the southwest and Toledo from his line below the Gallinas four miles to the northeast. These distances correspond exactly with the six miles reported between the two positions, and with accounts left by various reporters of Toledo's forced march through the sands and thickets in pursuit of Elizondo. Arredondo's maneuvers, though less explicit, fit within the two-mile distance, also. He could not have covered much ground while changing his marching order from column to line and then halting to set up his defensive position.

Traces of a road — probably the *camino que cortaba* — still can be found on both sides of the Galvan, and, if extended on the map, they lead from an intersection with the Laredo Road near or above present-day Stuart Lake to a juncture with the Lower Presidio Road where it crossed a small creek about one-half mile above Arredondo's campsite. The commanding hill, mentioned by several reporters as being behind Arredondo's line, exists as a ridge some 600 yards southwest of Galvan Creek.

If we overlay Arredondo's own account of his movements on the terrain between his overnight camp and the Galvan, it becomes quite clear that he maneuvered his army that morning on the *camino que cortaba*. How else could he have expected Elizondo to return to him *on that road* unless he intended to be on it himself later in the day? Sambrano, moving forward with reinforcements for Elizondo, met Lieutenant Cespedes, returning to report to Arredondo, *on that road*. Arredondo's stated purpose of crossing the Medina "by a different pass than the direct one" also falls into perspective. The direct one would have been *Paso Tranquitas,* or the Pérez Crossing [now part of Applewhite Road], which, as he said, posed the possibility of an enemy ambuscade. If, however, by utilizing the *camino que cortaba,* Arredondo could sneak across the Medina at the Garza ranch crossing, he would have accomplished two highly desirable objectives: he would have eliminated the need for moving his troops and cumbersome train across both the Medina River [where he expected an ambush] and Leon Creek [also a formidable canyon on the upper road], and he would have outflanked Toledo and placed his army squarely between the rebels and the city, controlling all approaches from the south.

What Arredondo obviously did not know, at daybreak on August 18, was that Toledo's army had taken the western leg of the Laredo Road and was waiting in ambush at the Gallinas. The road from Laredo split into two routes just north of the Galvan. The eastern route crossed Gallinas Creek almost immediately — merged with the old Laredo Trail, which had forded the Atascosa east of Pleasanton — and continued north to the El Carmen (or Losoya) crossing of the Medina River. The western leg swung out in a shallow arc and crossed the Gallinas several miles upstream — from which point a traveler could continue either north to the Garza ranch ford or northeast to the crossing at El Carmen. Arredondo expected Toledo to march out on the eastern road, which, for Toledo, was the more direct one if he expected to find Arredondo on the Laredo Road. Both generals appear to have based their plans on control of the Medina crossings. Toledo, however, seems to have had the better intelligence, for he knew where the royalists had made camp the night before.

The battlefield area has been cleared of trees and sprigged to coastal bermuda grass, but aerial photos made some years ago show it to have been wooded, with both live oaks and blackjacks, to correspond with contemporary reports. The lack of physical evidence that a great battle had been fought at the Galvan site is disappointing. However, the author has been able to make only the most cursory search, and he has little doubt but that an assiduous scanning of the area by competent operators with electronic metal detectors will turn up artifacts such as rifle and musket shot, grapeshot and even cannonballs, to verify the battle site. Permission of the property owners must be obtained before such a search is undertaken, and, under its antiquities law, the State of Texas may well claim any finds. Also, somewhere in some unpublished writings or in the musty stacks of some archive or public depository, there may be untapped clues which will document with even greater certainty the location of the battle fought in *el encinal de Medina*. Pending their discovery, let us get on with the business still before us — that of rescuing this forgotten battlefield of the First Texas Revolution from oblivion and according it the recognition it deserves.

Annotator and Editor's Postscript

THE PASSAGE OF MORE THAN 170 YEARS OF time has caused the site of *la batalla del encinal de Medina* (The Battle of the Encinal of Medina) to become more obscure than ever. In this year of 1985, very little physical evidence remains of the fateful battle that took place on August 18, 1813. The geographical, topographical, cartographical, and historical record, however, all indicate with certainty that the socalled "Battle of Medina" was fought near Galvan Creek in northern Atascosa County, and not on the Medina River some twelve miles distant in Bexar County. Author Ted Schwarz spent a good part of his lifetime deducing this, and after much study, deliberation, and on-site examination, I stand in substantial agreement with him.

In working on the *Forgotten Battlefield* project for over two years, I have immersed myself in Ted's notes, references, and his two separate manuscripts. I have spent many a weekend and other days with friends and helpers at the battlefield site, correlating it with all kinds of maps and diaries, and searching for battlefield artifacts. Although the search for cannonballs, musketballs, and other battlefield paraphernalia has been disappointing in results thus far, all other evidence found to date ascertains that the site described by Ted Schwarz is, indeed, the battlefield site.

The most obvious considerations that would prove this are the notations of the Stephen F. Austin maps of 1822, 1829, 1833, 1835, and the posthumous map of 1840. Austin, who had travelled the Laredo Road several times, shows the place of battle with the words "Depota de los Republicanos por Arredondo en 1813" on the Spanish maps, and the words "General Toledo Defeated 1813" on the English maps. The notation on the maps is about halfway between the Medina River and the Atascosa River on the Laredo Road. Some maps have the word "Encinal" printed close by. Galvan Creek is in this locale.

Another very easy check as to the location is the twenty mile measurement from San Antonio. The consensus of most witnesses who left a record, was that the Medina battle occurred about twenty miles south of San Antonio. The Galvan site fits this distance exactly.

The best piece of evidence that has come to light since I became actively engaged in this historical site identification project, is the diary of Jean Louis Berlandier, a Swiss naturalist who travelled the Laredo Road in February and March of 1828. The distances, directions, and descriptions noted by the astute Berlandier on his journey from Laredo to San Antonio, pinpoint the Medina battle as happening precisely at the place figured by Ted Schwarz. Consider the Berlandier diary as follows: [Italics supplied.]

> *February 26* [27]. It was half past nine when we left the camp at San Miguel. We made six leagues that day [one league = 2.63 miles] toward the north-northeast ... Close to five leagues from San Miguel is the *paraje* [place] called El Guajolote ...
>
> ... At La Parita ... everything is close at hand: It is one of the prettiest resting places on the road from Laredo to Béxar. We camped on the northern bank of the stream (for it is the general custom to cross any kind of torrent or river on the day of arrival, because often in a single night it can swell enough to no longer allow passage).
>
> *February 28*. Four leagues north-northeast of the camp we had just quitted is found a stream of limpid water called El Atascoso, where travellers sometime stop. ... It was still early when, after seven leagues of travel [from El Guajolote] to the north-northeast, we made a halt in a locality named Ranchería. A small stream which rises not far from there [the Galvan] joins the Medina [should be Atascosa].

Editor's Postscript

About three hundred meters from the camp, on the right bank of the stream and towards the south-southeast, rises a small hill about one hundred feet high known as La Loma de San Cristóbal. We all went to explore it, because being the only elevation on these plains it especially attracted our attention. It is some twenty meters in width by close to two hundred in length from the north-northwest to the southeast. It is made of a ferruginous sandstone, on top of which are found numerous bits of clayey iron ore which does not form layers at all, but which seem to be scattered in the greatest disorder as the consequence of some violent movement in the locality. On descending the hill and going towards the stream bed, one realizes that the hill rests on variegated sandstone (*arenisca abigarrada*), which lies exposed there.

February 28 [probably the 29th, for 1828 was a leap year]. Very early in the morning we started off to reach the Medina River, lying seven leagues from there. The route was level and almost always laid out through a lovely forest of oaks and nut trees. The ground is alternately sandy or covered with organic clay soil. The physical aspect of the countryside was in every way similar to fertile localities in temperate Europe in April or May; nontheless, we were still only in the month of February. The fruit of the nut trees which we encountered has a smooth shell so hard that it cannot be cracked without difficulty. That kind of nut seemed to me to be unsuitable for cultivation, in view of the smallness of the kernel compared with the thickness of the endocarp.

About four leagues from Ranchería, in the midst of the forest of oaks of which we have spoken, we arrived at the field of the battle of Medina, celebrated for the victory which the Spaniards won over the insurgents under the command of Gutiérrez and Toledo. On the fourteenth of August, 1814 [the actual date was August 18, 1813], the independent and Royalist armies — the first composed of about two thousand well-organized troops, the second of close to eight hundred ill-disciplined men — clashed in that locality. The first shock was cruel, but the insurgents (among whom were numbered Lipans, Texas creoles, and many American adventurers), commanded by Toledo, did not wish to follow his advice because he was a Spaniard. Trusting in their courage and unaware of the ruses of war, they had routed the right wing of the enemy when, believing victory assured, they disbanded and without order launched themselves on a troop which had made a feigned retreat. They were greeted by fresh reserves composed partly of cavalry, which drove them back, cutting them to pieces. The reserves followed them with sabers in the small of their backs as far as the other side of the Medina, covering the route with dead and wounded. The Spanish general don Joaquín Arredondo owed the victory of that unlucky day — which was so fatal for the inhabitants of Texas — to the ignorance and the insubordination of his adversaries, who battled with courage and up to the last moment bore the fire and the charges of the cavalry. The independents had a great deal of infantry and could have held out for a long time in the forest. But they tired in the sand, and, with everyone wanting to command, it was impossible to regroup to maintain the retreat with order and quiet discipline. A creole named Elizondo was charged with pursuing the fugitives and hounded them to the Trinity River, more than ——— leagues from there, executing all those who fell into his hands. After the battle the triumphant Arredondo had all the corpses of his army buried — perhaps one hundred in number. The more than four hundred insurgents killed in combat, however, were abandoned to the wild beasts as heretics by those alleged Christians, who were themselves perhaps less humane than their opponents.

The history of the Mexican wars of independence is glutted with reprehensible actions on the part of Royalist commanders. Ignorance — and, perhaps even more, prejudices instilled from childhood — often lead a man to commit certain actions which are not found except among nomadic tribes. In 1828 when we passed over the places where the battle was unleashed, the bones of those warriors were still to be found everywhere. Colonel Trespalacios in 1822 was more humane than the Spaniards. He gave burial to almost all the dead which were found. At the foot of an old oak, respected by the years, a grave was dug, and the remains of those adventurers who arrived to proclaim independence were buried. A cross carved in the trunk of that live oak indicates the site of the grave. Placed at the height of a man's head, renewed from time to time by the soldiers of the presidio who carve it as deep as the wood, it seems to be freshly engraved.

On the other side of the forest we traversed is the Medina River...*

Another piece of evidence that corroborates the Berlandier description is a diary account by José Mariá Sánchez.** Sánchez accompanied the Miér y Terán expedition of 1828 as the mapmaker. Berlandier was the naturalist. The diary account of Sánchez is in substantial agreement with the Berlandier account. Both identify *la loma del San Cristóbal* and *Rancherías*,

---

* Jean Louis Berlandier, *Journey to Mexico During the Years 1826 to 1834*, translated by Sheila M. Ohlendorf, I, 282–284 (Two volumes, Texas State Historical Association, Austin, 1981).

** José María Sánchez, "A Trip to Texas in 1828," *The Southwestern Historical Quarterly*, XXIX, 253–257, (Translated by Carlos E. Castañeda).

the deep sands, the forest of oaks and the hickory trees, the battle site, and all the bones that could still be found.

By way of comment, it should be said that the place names of San Miguel, Guajolote (now Turkey Creek), La Parita, and El Atascoso, are all well-known to Atascosa county residents. The place called Ranchería was undoubtedly a headquarters for the Rancho del Atascoso that belonged to Mission San José in the eighteenth century. La Loma del San Cristóbal can be identified as the hill near the present home of Alfred Sotelo on Tessman Road in Pleasanton, Texas. From this locale came much of the red sandstone that was used over the years to build the old Atascosa County Courthouse and many other buildings in and around Pleasanton.

From Ranchería, the actual distance to the Galvan battle site is about three- and one-half leagues (Berlandier figured it "about four leagues"). Although much of the battlefield area has been cleared to make fields, there are still sizeable groves of live oaks, post oaks, blackjack oaks, and hickory trees (the tree which provided the nut that Berlandier described as having "a smooth shell so hard it cannot be cracked without difficulty." (Dr. George B. Jaggy introduced this editor to the hickory tree, and what Berlandier said about the hickory nut was found to be true.)

The most tantalizing part of Berlandier's diary is his mention of the live oak tree that marked the mass grave that Governor Trespalacios provided for the victims in 1822. One wonders where it might have been. My friend Jerome Korus has located a large live oak, an especially handsome one with scars on it that form the shape of a cross, and at about the height of a man. This particular live oak is located on the farm that belongs to Mrs. Gerturde Korus. It stands within thirty yards of the track that old-time residents of the area called the *camino real*. My investigation shows that in reality this is the track of *el camino que cortaba*, the shortcut between the Lower Presidio Road and the Laredo Road which crosses the Galvan about two hundred yards south of the tree. Jerome and I have done quite a bit of probing for the hundreds of men that might be buried there, but so far no bones have been found. The sand in the locale is called "sugar sand" by local farmers, and it is about eight feet deep. Verification of this extraordinarily beautiful oak tree as being the one mentioned by Berlandier awaits further digging. In the meantime, it will have to be called the *¿Quién sabe?* tree.

José Antonio Navarro,* noble patriot of Texas and founding father of Atascosa County, had some interesting notations about the Medina battle in his memoirs. Following is a quote regarding the skeletons buried under an oak tree:

> After the independence of Mexico was gained, Governor Trespalacios crossed the Medina river towards San Antonio and upon viewing the prairies sprinkled with human skeletons, he had them collected and buried with full military honors.
>
> I distinctly remember the following inscription written on a square of wood which was on the trunk of an oak tree:
>
> *Aquí yacen los bravos mexicanos*
> *Que imitando el ejemplo de Leonidas,*
> *Sacrificaron su fortuna y vidas*
> *Luchando sin cesar contra tiranos.*
>
> [English Translation]
> Here lie the Mexican heroes
> Who followed the example of Leonidas,
> They sacrificed their wealth and lives
> Ceaselessly fighting against tyrants.

Should this oak tree ever be found, it would be the most significant part of the battlefield, and it would be worthy of designation as a national historic landmark.

The deep sand of the area, noted by Spanish diarists as *terra arenosa summate* (enormously deep sand), ranges in depth from eight to twenty feet. This deep sand has stymied much of my search for the remnants of the battlefield, whether they be bullets or bones. Longtime residents of the area advise me that objects such as bullets, arrowheads, and even bones tend to work themselves downward into the deep sand until they come to rest at the clay bottom. This, I believe, is the chief reason why my metal-detecting friends and I have been unable, so far, to find any musketballs or cannonballs. After lying in the sand for 170 years, they have had plenty of time to penetrate deeply into the sand, out of range for metal detectors.

Although no cannonballs or musketballs have yet been found to verify the battlefield site, the circumstantial evidence has been tantalizing. Jerome Korus, his brother Alfred, and their sister Virginia, for instance, have told me how they as

---

* José Antonio Navarro, *Apuntes Historicos Interesantes de San Antonio de Béxar* (publicados por varios de sus amigos, San Antonio de Béxar, 1869), pp. 18–19, which was translated into English in the *San Antonio Ledger*, June 5, 1869.

children would play in the field behind their house and would pick up bucketsful of rounded objects, which they do not remember as being of stone or metal — or either. The buckets of objects have long since disappeared. Alfred remembers digging around under the exposed roots of an oak tree in the vicinity of the ruts of *el camino que cortaba*, where he found the butts of four guns that he thinks were muskets. Here again, the butts have since disappeared, and only the memory remains.

Arthur Weynand, who was raised on a nearby farm, remembers his father telling him when he was but a little boy over sixty years ago, "Son, come here — I want to show you some hailstones that didn't melt." Mr. Weynand doesn't remember exactly which field they were in at the time or seeing them since, but the memory of the "hailstones that didn't melt" has remained indelible in his mind for many years. Mr. Weynand also remembers his father finding a small cannon lying in one of the sandy fields. It had no particular meaning to him, and his father used it to brace a broken fence post. Presumably, the cannon is still buried in the ground somewhere. When Mr. Weynand was a young boy, he himself found a tattered, half-rotten coat that was buried in sand. He remembers the coat as being red and having braid and brass buttons.

Another instance of finding battlefield artifacts in the area of this study was related to the editor by Curtis M. Mahula, who was raised on a farm that occupied the western portion of the Jacob Pinker survey near Galvan Creek. Mr. Mahula remembers his Grandpa Tom Mahula, many years ago, carrying around in his pocket three or four small cannonballs that he found on the Mahula farm. Grandpa Mahula liked to show them to other people as he also liked to show two old ramrods that he found on the place. As a boy, Curtis himself found some old gun breeches, probably muskets, near the same place where Alfred Korus, who lived on the eastern side of the Jacob Pinker survey, found some old gun breeches in some tree roots.

Ted Schwarz would be glad to know that the place of "Cañada de Caballos," the meeting place of Elizondo with Arredondo, can be identified. Elizondo, it will be remembered, set out from the Presidio of the Rio Grande to join forces with Arredondo, who set out from Laredo. They were to meet at Cañada de Caballos, which was thirty-five leagues from San Antonio. The measure of thirty-five leagues figures very close to the Laredo Road crossing of the Nueces River. Diary accounts by the *padres* Solís and Morfi tell of a "Cañada de Caballos" and a

"Cañada Verde" in that near vicinity. The Austin Map of 1829 shows a "Cañada Verde" place name on the north bank of the Nueces River at its Laredo Road crossing. Elizondo reached the place by a cut-off road that went from the Lower Presidio Road at Peña Crossing down the Nueces River to the Laredo Road. Early Spanish travellers could use the same road in going directly from Presidio San Juan Bautista to Presidio La Bahiá.

After the Battle of El Encinal de Medina, General Arredondo tarried long enough to take care of his wounded and dead. The records indicate (especially the Berlandier diary) that Arredondo buried his own dead soon after the battle, probably the next day. This writer believes that the bones lying in the crypt at El Carmen Church may well be those of the Spanish dead — while the bones of the insurgents were left bleaching in the sand of the encinal for about nine years. Hopefully, a thorough archeological dig will provide the answer to this problem in the not too distant future.

Right after the battle, Arredondo ordered his men to scour the battlefield and pick up everything that could possibly be used again. Presumably, many of the cannonballs that had not been buried in the sand were recovered — but certainly not all of them — for Arredondo himself reported firing 950 cannon shots. Musketballs must have been fired by the thousands, and it is not likely that many of them would be retrieved for reuse. One does find rounded stones in the area yet, which possibly could have been used as cannister or grapeshot.

My chief disappointment is the fact that to this date in 1985, I have been unable to find any clear-cut "hard evidence" of the battlefield. It is there, somewhere, in the *terra arenosa summate* — the enormously deep sands of the *encinal de Medina* — and it awaits being found. When more evidence is found, it will be reported, hopefully, in subsequent printings of this book.

My only variance with the conclusions drawn by Ted Schwarz — and it is only a relatively minor difference — is the location of the *camino que cortaba*. My examinations show it to have been about three-fourths of a mile to the southeast of the track figured by Ted. Roads of yesteryear, however, had a way of moving around, depending on seasonal and weather differences, and the cut-off road could easily, in 1813, have been where Ted thought it was. The ruts and traces I found could have been a later road, one that had use till more recent times.

In conclusion, this writer believes that *la batalla del en-*

cinal de Medina took place just where Ted Schwarz figured it did: on the banks on Galvan Creek about four miles northwest of present Leming, in Atascosa County, Texas. Historically, the site of the battle can be identified. Archeologically, much investigation needs to be done. Then the puzzle will be completed.

Robert H. Thonhoff

Fashing, Texas
June 1, 1985

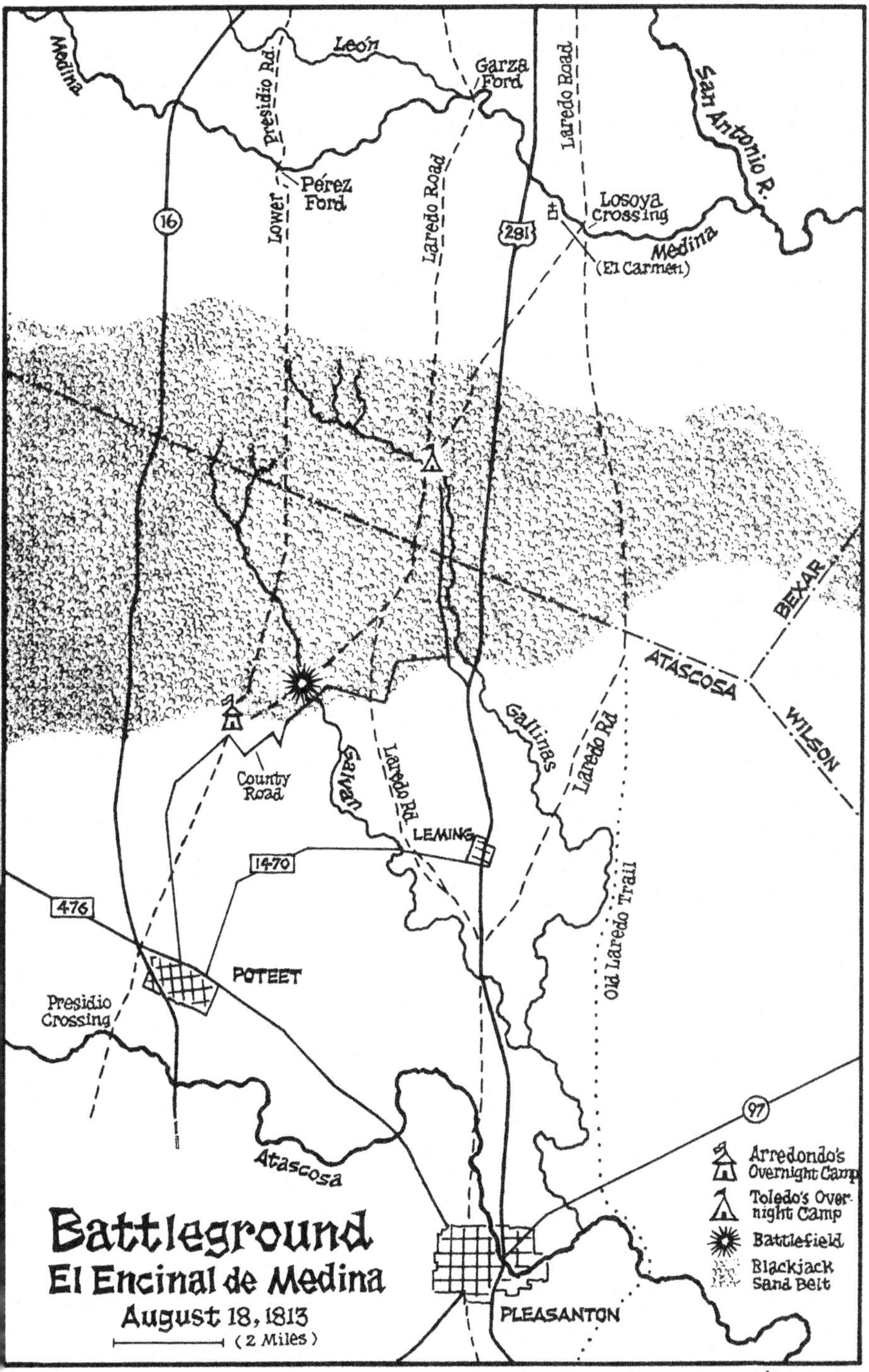

Medina
León
Presidio Rd.
Garza Ford
Laredo Road
San Antonio R.
Lower
Pérez Ford
Laredo Road
16
281
Losoya crossing
Medina
(El Carmen)
BEXAR
ATASCOSA
WILSON
Gallinas
Laredo Rd
Galvan
Laredo Rd
County Road
LEMING
1470
476
Old Laredo Trail
POTEET
Presidio Crossing
97
Atascosa
Arredondo's Overnight Camp
Toledo's Over-night Camp
Battlefield
Blackjack Sand Belt
Battleground
El Encinal de Medina
August 18, 1813
(2 Miles)
PLEASANTON

jaxon · 83

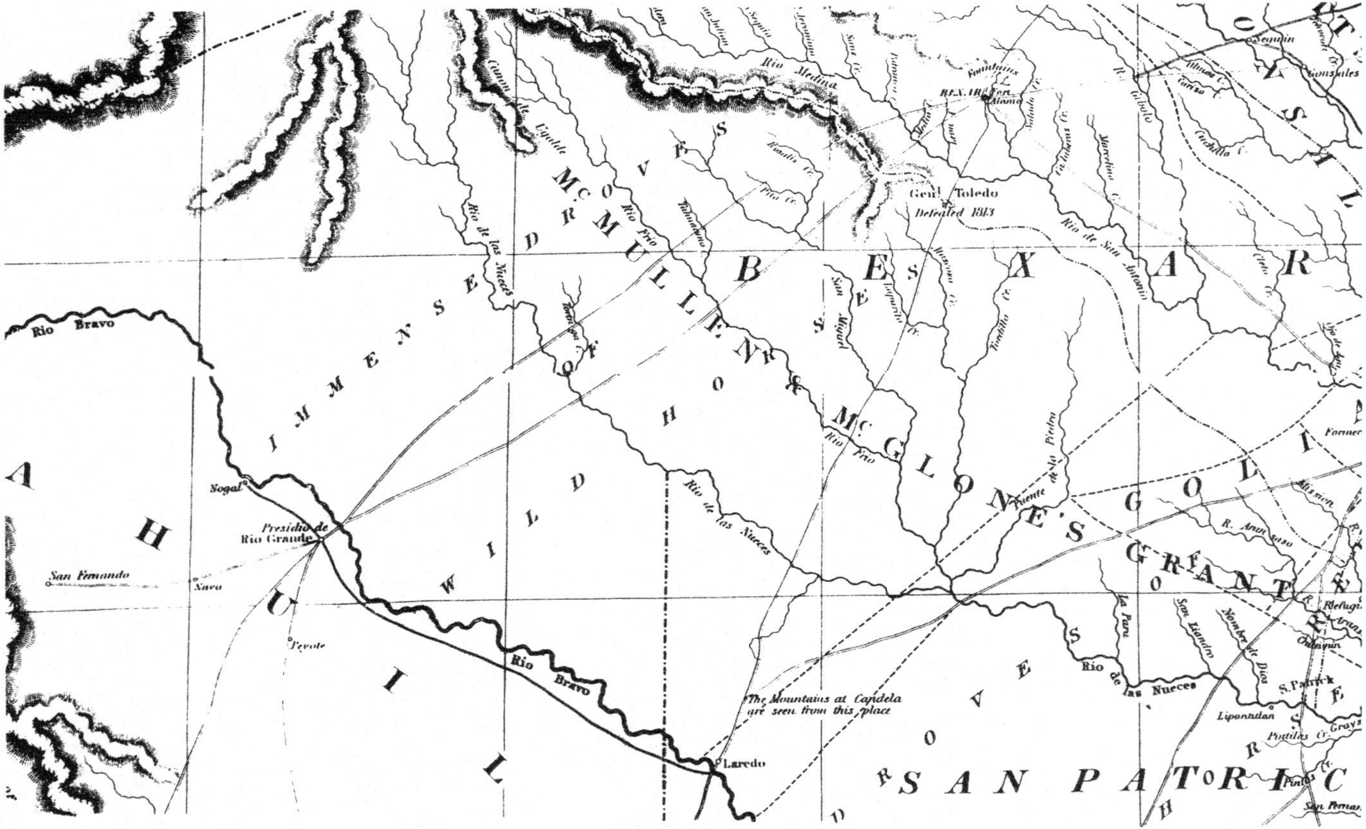

Rio Bravo
Nogal
Presidio de Rio Grande
San Fernando
Nava
Pevote
Laredo
Rio Bravo
The Mountains at Candela are seen from this place
IMMENSE DROVES OF WILD HORSES
Mc MULLEN & Mc GLONE'S GRANT
BEXAR
GOLIAD
SAN PATRICIO
Rio de las Nueces
Rio Frio
Rio Medina
Rio de San Antonio
Genl Toledo Defeated 1813
BEXAR
Fort Alamo
San Miguel
Seguin
Gonsales
Cuchillo C.
R. Cibolo
Marcelino C.
La Para
San Lleandro
Nombre de Dios
S. Patrick
Lipantitlan
Refugio
Mission
R. Aransaso
Rio de las Nueces

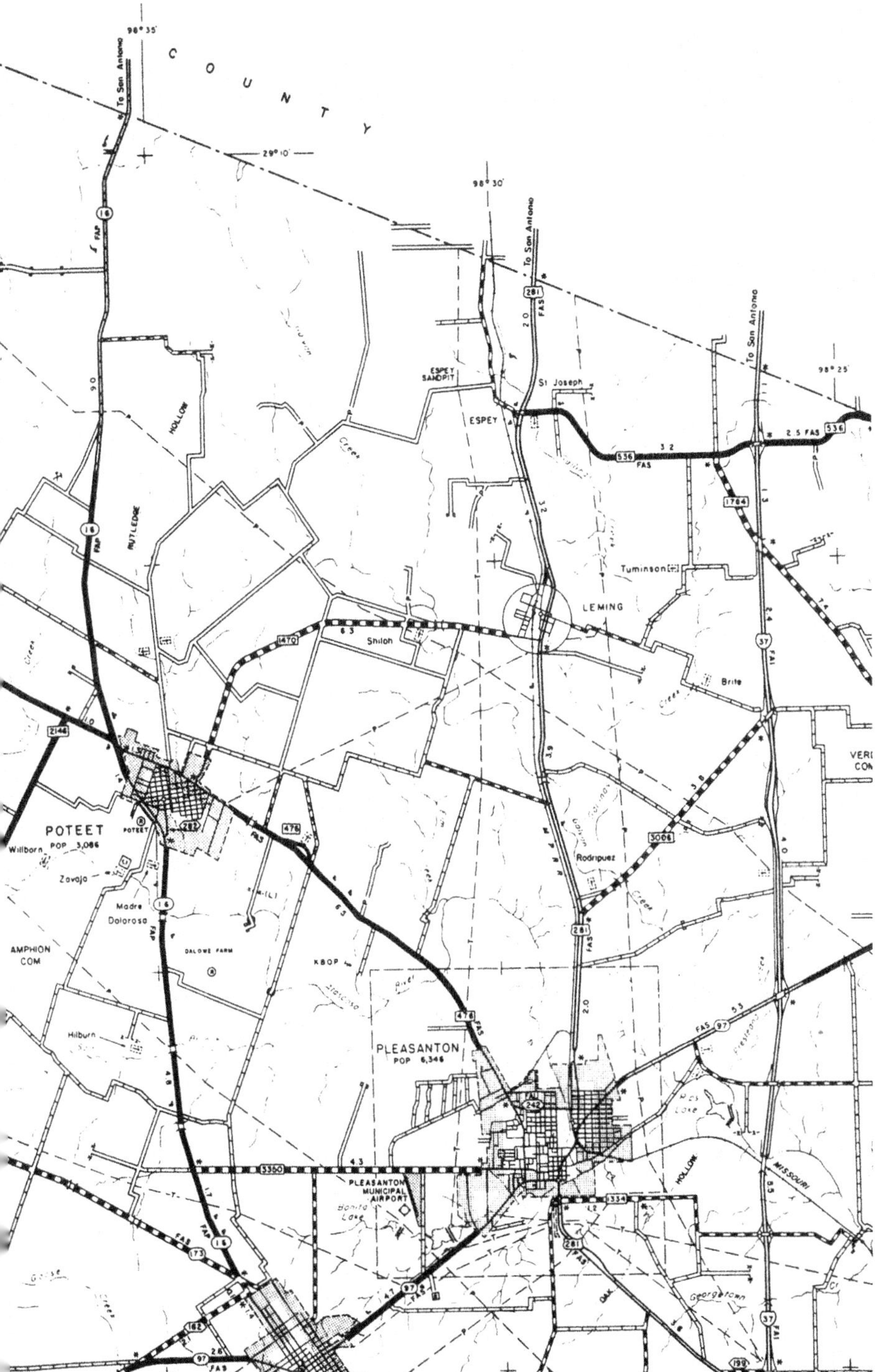
COUNTY
To San Antonio
To San Antonio
To San Antonio
ESPEY SANDPIT
St Joseph
ESPEY
RUTLEDGE
HOLLOW
Tuminson
LEMING
Shiloh
Brite
POTEET
POP 3,086
Willborn
Zavala
Madre Dolorosa
AMPHION COM
DALOWE FARM
Rodriguez
KBOP
PLEASANTON
POP 6,346
Hilburn
PLEASANTON MUNICIPAL AIRPORT
MISSOURI
HOLLOW
Georgetown
FAS
FAP
FAI

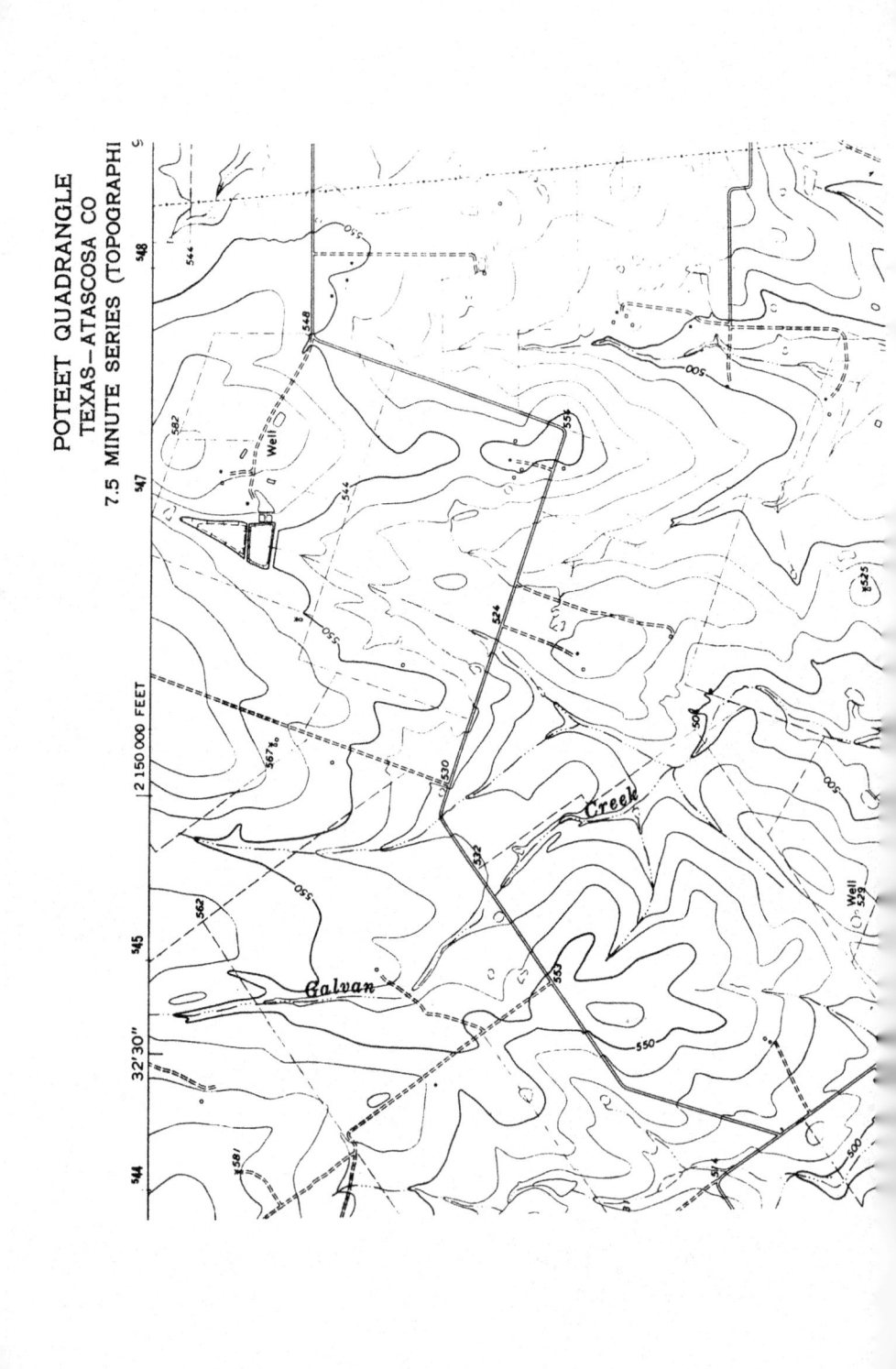

POTEET QUADRANGLE
TEXAS—ATASCOSA CO
7.5 MINUTE SERIES (TOPOGRAPHI

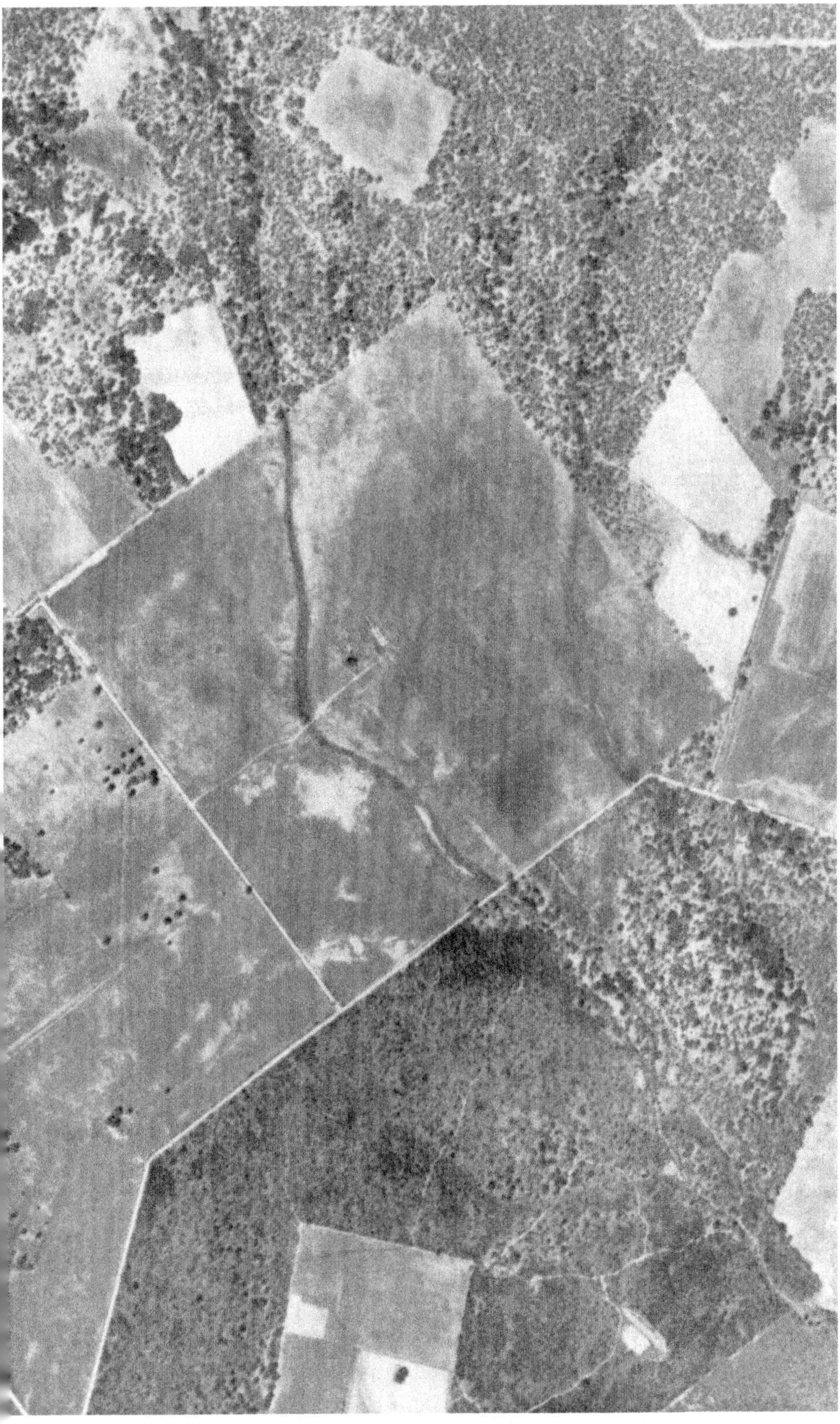

ATASCOSA
COP: OF GENERAL LAND OFFICE, AUSTIN, TEXAS.

SCALE IN VARAS

Jerome Korus and Robert H. Thonhoff standing in rut of the
Camino que Cortaba *on farm of Mrs. Gertrude Korus.*
January 27, 1985.

Panoramic view of cleared portion of battlefield site on James Engleman farm about four miles northwest of Leming, Texas. Galvan Creek flows through coastal bermuda pasture.
January 27, 1985.

Editor Robert H. Thonhoff stands next to Medina battle monument at intersection of US 281 and FM 2537, approximately ten miles from actual battle site. Photographed January 27, 1985. Inscription:

THE BATTLE OF
THE MEDINA

WAS FOUGHT HERE ON AUGUST 18, 1813 BY AN ARMY OF SPANISH ROYALISTS COMMANDED BY GENERAL JOSÉ JOAQUÍN ARREDONDO, WHICH DEFEATED WITH TERRIFIC SLAUGHTER THE REPUBLICAN ARMY OF THE NORTH COMPOSED OF ANGLO-AMERICANS, MEXICANS, AND INDIANS COMMANDED BY JOSÉ ALVAREZ DE TOLEDO — THUS ENDED AN ATTEMPT TO FREE TEXAS AND MEXICO FROM SPANISH RULE.

Erected by the State of Texas
1936

Front view of crypt site at El Carmen Church, where bodies of Arredondo's soldiers may be buried. January 27, 1985.

Back view of crypt site at El Carmen Church. Now enclosed by a chainlink fence, a church building formerly covered this site. January 27, 1985.

Editor Robert H. Thonhoff kneels next to Camino Real marker on Old Pleasanton Road between Thelma and Lehr in south Bexar County.   *January 27, 1985.*

Editor Robert H. Thonhoff kneels next to Camino Real marker on Old Pleasanton Road at Bexar–Atascosa County Line.
January 27, 1985.

Editor Robert H. Thonhoff shows a third Camino Real marker on the Old Pleasanton Road near the entrance to Maurice Weynand farm in northern Atascosa County.   March 30, 1985.

Copy of Arredondo's Report, Numero 1, on the arms, ammunition, and equipment taken from the enemy in the Battle on the 18th of August en el Arenal [sandy terrain] de Medina, and this city.

Número 2.

Estado que manifiesta los Muertos Heridos y Dispersos que tubo este Exército de Oriente en la acción sostenida contra la canalla que ocupara la Ciudad de Bexar el 18 de Agosto último en el Encinal de Medina

1.er Batallón Inf.ª de Veracruz	Muertos				Heridos				Dispersos			
	S	T	C	S	S	T	C	S	S	T	C	S
1ª Compañía	1	"	1	2	2	"	"	13	"	"	"	"
2ª	"	"	"	5	1	"	"	16	"	"	"	"
3ª	"	"	1	3	1	"	1	15	"	"	"	"
4ª	"	"	"	1	"	"	"	9	"	"	"	2
5ª	"	"	1	1	2	1	1	10	"	"	"	"
6ª	"	"	"	2	"	"	"	11	"	"	"	"
7ª	1	"	"	5	"	"	3	14	"	"	"	"
8ª	"	"	"	4	"	"	2	10	"	"	"	"
Total de Infant.ª	2	"	3	23	6	1	7	98	"	"	"	2
Cuerpo de Reserva de Caballería	"	"	"	3	"	"	2	8	"	"	"	"
1.er Esquadrón	"	"	1	7	"	"	2	21	"	"	"	"
2.° Id.	"	"	2	4	"	"	1	14	"	"	"	"
3.°	"	"	"	4	"	"	"	12	"	"	"	"
4.°	1	"	2	3	"	"	"	6	"	"	"	"
Total de caballería	1	"	5	21	"	"	5	61	"	"	"	"

Resumen General	Muertos	Heridos	Dispersos
Infantería	28	112	2
Caballería	27	66	"
Total	55	178	2

Nota.

No se incluyen en este estado al Señor Coronel Don Cayetano Quintero, Ten.te Coron.l D. Manuel Zambrano, Capitán D. Luciano García, D. Miguel Paredes, D. Antonio Zárate, Ten.te D. Pedro García, Alf.z D. Tomas de Oquillas, Sub. Ten.te Graduados Don Fran.co de la Hoz, D. Manuel Castro y Cadete D.n Severo Ruys, ni menos siento secenta y sinco Sargentos Tambores cavos y Soldados contusos, amás perecieron ciento sienta y tres Caballos, y heridos e inutilisados siento dies y nuebe.= Quartel General de San Antonio de Bexar 13 de Septiembre de 1813.= Es copia Monterrey 6 de Abril de 1817.= Por enfermedad del Sr.io.= Visente Arreola.= Rúbrica.)
Joaq.n de Arredondo
(Rúbrica)

Copy of Arredondo's Report, Numero 2, on the dead, wounded, and missing of the eastern army in the action sustained against the rabble that occupied the City of Bexar, the 18th of August last en el Encinal [oak forest] de Medina.

Jerome Korus and Robert H. Thonhoff standing under the ¿Quien Sabe? Tree, which may be the tree described by Berlandier that marked the burial place of Toledo's soldiers.
January 27, 1985.

Jerome Korus and Robert H. Thonhoff point to markings on the ¿Quien Sabe? Tree, where bones of Republican warriors may be buried. *January 27, 1985.*

Endnotes

In citing works in the notes, short titles have generally been used. Works frequently cited have been identified by the following abbreviations:

AGI	Archivo General de Indias
AGNM	Archivo General de la Nación, México
AHDN	Archivo Histórico de Defensa Nacional
LHQ	*Louisiana Historical Quarterly*
QTSHA	*The Quarterly of the Texas State Historical Association*
SWHQ	*Southwestern Historical Quarterly*

Chapter 1 — The Prologue

1. Montero to Salcedo, June 8, 1812, AGNM, Historia, transcripts C-B 840 and C-B 861.

2. Julia Kathryn Garrett, *Green Flag over Texas: A Story of the Last Years of Spain in Texas,* viii (hereafter cited as *Green Flag over Texas*).

3. José María Miquel i Vergés, *Diccionario de Insurgentes,* pp. 276-287.

4. *Diccionario Porrúa de Historia Biografia de México,* Tercero Edición, p. 958 (hereafter cited as *Diccionario Porrua*). Also, the 1952 edition, Walter Prescott Webb and H. Bailey Carroll, Eds., *The Handbook of Texas,* I, 749-750.

5. *Ibid.*; L. Gutiérrez de Lara, "Story of a Political Refugee," *The Pacific Monthly,* XXV, 2; Rie Jarrett, *Gutiérrez de Lara, Mexican Texan: The Story of a Creole Hero,* pp. 46-67.

6. Hubert H. Bancroft, *History of the North Mexican States and Texas,* II, 17-19; Frederick C. Chabot, *Texas in 1811: The Las Casas and Sambrano Revolutions,* pp. 23-25 (hereafter cited as *Texas in 1811*); J. Villasana Haggard, "The Counter-Revolution of Bexar, 1811," *SWHQ,* LXXI, 496-516; Webb and Carroll, Eds.; *The Handbook of Texas,* I, 305 and II, 950.

7. Frederick C. Chabot, *San Antonio in the 17th, 18th, and 19th Centuries*, p. 78 ; Richard G. Santos, "The Quartel of San Fernando de Béxar," *Texana*, V, 187-202.

8. James Gaines, "Information Obtained in 1835 from Captain Gaines (Sabine River)," in Charles Adams Gulick, Jr., and others, Eds., *The Papers of Mirabeau Buonaparte Lamar*, I, 285 (hereafter cited as *Lamar Papers*); Julia Kathryn Garrett, The War of Independence in Texas, 1811-1813, Ph.D. dissertation, p. 150 (hereafter cited as dissertation).

9. Julia Kathryn Garrett, "Dr. John Sibley of Natchitoches, 1757-1837," *LHQ*, XX, 399-431; Julia Kathryn Garrett, "Dr. John Sibley and the Louisiana-Texas Frontier, 1803-1814," *SWHQ*, XLIX, 399-431 and 599-609.

10. Gaines, *Lamar Papers*, I, 285.

11. Shaler to Monroe, May 2, 1812, Letters and Enclosures, in Special Agents, Vol. 2, folio 20, State Department Manuscripts, Microfilm Publication M-37, reel 2, National Archives, Washington, D.C. (hereafter cited as Shaler Papers).

12. Elizabeth West, Ed. and Trans., "Diary of José Bernardo Gutiérrez de Lara, 1811-1812," *The American Historical Review*, XXXIV, 55-75 and 281-294.

13. *Ibid.*

14. *Ibid.*; Webb and Carroll, Eds., *The Handbook of Texas*, II, 785.

15. Webb and Carroll, Eds., *The Handbook of Texas*, II, 595.

16. Garrett, *Green Flag over Texas*, pp. 104-107.

17. Salcedo to Viceroy, June 25, 1812, AGNM, Historia, transcripts C-B 840 and C-B 861.

18. Webb and Carroll, Eds., *The Handbook of Texas*, I, 467; J. Villasana Haggard, "The Houses of Barr and Davenport," *SWHQ*, XLIX 66-88.

19. Shaler to Monroe, May 2, 1812, in Shaler Papers.

20. Lorenzo de la Garza, *Dos Hermanos Héroes*, pp. 23-25.

21. Shaler to Monroe, May 2, 1812, in Shaler Papers.

22. Mattie Austin Hatcher, *The Opening of Texas to Foreign Settlement, 1801-1821*, p. 226; Carlos E. Castañeda, *Our Catholic Heritage in Texas*, V, 315 and VI, 73.

23. Shaler to Monroe, May 2, 1812, in Shaler Papers.

24. Montero to Salcedo, June 27, 1812, and Salcedo to the Viceroy, July 8, 1812, AHDN, transcripts C-B 840 and C-B 660.

25. Shaler to Monroe, May 2, 1812, in Shaler Papers.

26. *Ibid.*

27. Francis B. Heitman, *Historical Register and Dictionary of the United States Army, 1785-1903*, I, Pt. ii, 683.

28. Indian Office to Thomas Linnard, December 12, 1812, Letter Book C, June 1812 to April 1816, Indian Office, Department of the Interior, National Archives, Washington, D.C.

29. Webb and Carroll, Eds., *The Handbook of Texas*, II, 128-129.

30. Garrett, *Green Flag over Texas*, pp. 153-155; Webb and Carroll, Eds., *The Handbook of Texas*, II, 910; Thomas Maitland Marshall, *A History of the Western Boundary of the Louisiana Purchase*, pp. 1-8.

Chapter 2 — Revolution Sweeps Texas

1. Gaines, *Lamar Papers*, I, 285-286; John Villars, "Information Derived from John Villars, Native of Kentucky, San Buenaventura, Mexico," *Lamar Papers*, IV, Pt. 1, 278; Garrett, *Green Flag over Texas*, pp. 138-139 and 150-152.
2. Chabot, *Texas in 1811*, pp. 23-25; Haggard, "The Counter-Revolution of Bexar, 1811," *SWHQ*, XLIII, 222-235; Webb and Carroll, Eds., *The Handbook of Texas*, II, 951.
3. Webb and Carroll, Eds., *The Handbook of Texas*, I, 944.
4. Villars, *Lamar Papers*, VI, 146; Garrett, "Dr. John Sibley and the Louisiana-Texas Frontier, 1803-1814," *SWHQ*, XLIX, 415.
5. Villars, *Lamar Papers*, VI, 146.
6. *Ibid.*
7. *Ibid.*, *Niles Register*, October 17, 1812.
8. Documents Concerning American Encroachment into Texas, 1809-1812, AHDN, transcripts C-B 840 and C-B 660; Correspondence on Militiary Affairs of Texas, 1810-1812, AGNM, transcripts C-B 840 and C-B 661; *Niles Register*, October 17, 1812.
9. Manuel de Salcedo to Nemesio Salcedo, September 22, 1812, and José Bernardo Gutiérrez de Lara to Luís Grande, September 4, 1812, AHDN, transcripts C-B 840 and C-B 660.
10. Villars, *Lamar Papers*, VI, 145-155.
11. Shaler to Monroe, January 10, 1813, Shaler Papers.
12. Isaac Joslin Cox, "Monroe and the Early Mexican Revolutionary Agents," *The American Historical Association Annual Report, 1911*, I, 197-215.
13. Dr. John Hamilton Robinson, "Report of His Mission to Spanish Provinces in New Spain, to the Honorable James Monroe, Secretary of State, Washington, D.C., July 26, 1813," in Mexico: Filibustering Expeditions Against the Government of Spain, 1811-1816, State Department Manuscripts, National Archives, Washington, D.C. (hereafter cited as "Report of ... July 26, 1813.")
14. Garrett, dissertation, p. 289.
15. Shaler to Monroe, December 25, 1812, in Shaler Papers; Henry P. Walker, Ed., "William McLane's Narrative of the Magee-Gutierrez Expedition, 1812-1813," *SWHQ*, LXVI, 234-251 (hereafter cited as "McLane's Narrative"); Villars, *Lamar Papers*, VI, 147; J. B. Gutiérrez de Lara to the Mexican Congress, August 1, 1815, *Lamar Papers*, I, 12; Warren D. C. Hall, "The Mexican War of Independence in Texas, 1812-1813," *Lamar Papers*, IV, Pt. I, 280.
16. Villars, *Lamar Papers*, VI, 147; *Texas Almanac, 1861*, p. 459; Walker, "McLane's Narrative," *SWHQ*, LXVI, 574-575; Davenport to Shaler, included with Shaler to Monroe, December 25, 1812, and Shaler to Monroe, January 10, 1813, in Shaler Papers.
17. Gutiérrez to Shaler, November 25, 1812, and Magee to Shaler, November 25, 1812, in Shaler Papers.
18. Shaler to Monroe, December 25, 1812, in Shaler Papers.
19. "Extract of a Letter, dated Nachitoes [sic], March 13, 1813," *The Boston Patriot*, May 1, 1813; Walker, "McLane's Narrative,"

SWHQ, LXVI, 459; Villars, *Lamar Papers,* VI, 150; Hall, *Lamar Papers,* IV, Pt. 1, 280.
20. Robinson, "Report of... July 26, 1813," in Mexico: Filibustering Expeditions against the Government of Spain, 1811-1816.
21. Gutiérrez, *Lamar Papers,* I, 4; Gaines, *Lamar Papers,* I, 286; Garrett, "Dr. John Sibley and the Louisiana-Texas Frontier, 1803-1814," *SWHQ,* XLIX, 423; Walker, "McLane's Narrative," *SWHQ,* LXVI, 250.
22. *Ibid.*
23. *Ibid.*
24. Villars, *Lamar Papers,* VI, 150; Hall, *Lamar Papers,* IV, Pt. 1, 281; Walker, "McLane's Narrative," *SWHQ,* LXVI, 242-245 and 460-463.
25. Henderson R. Yoakum, *History of Texas from Its First Settlement in 1685 to Its Annexation to the United States in 1846,* I, 168 (hereafter cited as *History of Texas);* Félix D. Almaráz, Jr., *Tragic Cavalier: Governor Manuel Salcedo of Texas, 1808-1813,* pp. 169-170 (hereafter cited as *Tragic Cavalier).*
26. Communiques of Herrera, Salcedo, Gutiérrez, and Kemper, all dated April 1, 1813, in Shaler Papers; Depositions taken in the Villa de Laredo by Alférez Don José Antonio Venavides from Guillermo Saldaña, Veteran Soldier Guillermo Nabarro, Bachiller Don Feliciano Francisco Vela, and others on April 6, 8, and 15, 1813, AGNM, Historia, Tom. 3, transcripts 2Q193, No. 422.
27. *Ibid.*
28. Almaráz, *Tragic Cavalier,* pp. 124-129.
29. Zebulon Montgomery Pike, *Exploratory Travels through Western Territories of North America,* pp. 365-370.
30. Walker, "McLane's Narrative," *SWHQ,* LXVI, 463-465; Depositions in the Villa de Laredo by Venavides and others, April 6, 8, and 15, 1813, AGNM, Historia, Tom. 3, transcripts 2Q193, No. 422.
31. Walker, "McLane's Narrative," *SWHQ,* LXVI, 465n.
32. Shaler to Monroe, November 10, 1812, in Shaler Papers; Garrett, dissertation, p. 285n.

Chapter 3 — Texas an Independent State

1. Translations of the declaration appeared in the *Niles Register,* July 17, 1813; *The National Intelligencer,* July 13, 1813; and the *London Morning Chronicle,* August 19, 1813; see, also Garrett, dissertation, p. 329n.
2. Bachiller Feliciano Francisco Vela and others, Deposition Concerning the Execution of the Spanish Officers and the Installation of a Junta in Béxar, April 15, 1813, AGNM, Historia, Tom. 3, transcripts 2Q193, No. 422; Almaráz, *Tragic Cavalier,* p. 171.
3. Garrett, dissertation, p. 329n; Mattie Alice Austin, "The Municipal Government of San Fernando de Bexar, 1730-1800," *QTSHA,* VIII, 297-328.
4. Walker, "McLane's Narrative," *SWHQ,* LXVI, 466.
5. Garrett, *Green Flag over Texas,* pp. 194-195.

Endnotes

6. Onís to Salcedo,, Bexar Archives, reel 53, frame 142.
7. Shaler to Monroe, May 7, 1813, in Shaler Papers.
8. Sibley to Armstrong, May 7, 1813, in Garrett, "Dr. John Sibley and the Louisiana-Texas Frontier, 1803-1814," *SWHQ*, XLIX, 424-426.
9. Rowland Dunbar, Ed., W. C. C. Claiborne, *Official Letter Books*, 1801-1816, VI, 228.
10. *Ibid.*, V, 319 and VI, 122.
11. Robinson to Monroe, August 21, 1813, in Mexico: Filibustering Expeditions against the Government of Spain, 1811-1816; Garrett, dissertation, 344n.
12. Henry Adams Bullard, Book Review, *North American Review*, XLIII, 239.
13. Garrett, *Green Flag over Texas*, pp. 193-194; Hatcher, *The Opening of Texas to Foreign Settlement, 1801-1821*, Appendix, Document No. 22; Depositions of Aaron Mower, H. A. Bullard, and Samuel Alden, May 28, 1813, in Shaler Papers.
14. Shaler to Gutiérrez, May 28, 1813, in Shaler Papers.
15. *El Mexicano,*, June 19, 1813, in Shaler Papers; Shaler to Monroe, June 9, 1813, in Shaler Papers.
16. Robinson, "Report of. . . July 26, 1813," in Mexico: Filibustering Expeditions against the Government of Spain, 1811-1816.
17. *El Mexicano*, June 19, 1813, in Shaler Papers.
18. Shaler to Monroe, June 20, 1813, in Shaler Papers.

Chapter 4 — Spain Strikes Back

1. Arredondo to Elizondo, June 19, 1813, AGNM, Historia, Tom. 3, transcripts 2Q194, No. 423: Webb and Carroll, Eds., *The Handbook of Texas*, I, 71.
2. Webb and Carroll, Eds., *The Handbook of Texas*, II, 416-417.
3. Robert S. Weddle, *San Juan Bautista: Gateway to Spanish Texas*, pp. 365-369.
4. Garrett, *Green Flag over Texas*, p. 73.
5. *Ibid.*, pp. 185-186.
6. Elizondo to Arredondo, June 18, 1813, AGNM, Historia, Tom. 4, transcripts 2Q194, No. 423; Walker, "McLane's Narrative," *SWHQ*, LXVI, 468.
7. Arredondo to Elizondo, June 19, 21, and 28, 1813, AGNM, Historia, Tom. 4, transcripts 2Q194, No. 423.
8. Villars, *Lamar Papers*, I, 152.
9. Walker, "McLane's Narrative," *SWHQ*, LXVI, 466-468.
10. *Ibid.*
11. *Ibid.*, LXVI, 469-470.
12. *Ibid.*
13. *Ibid.*, LXVI, 471; Garrett, dissertation, 393-403; Garrett, "Dr. John Sibley and the Louisiana-Texas Frontier, 1803-1814," *SWHQ*, LXIX, 427-429; Luís de Onís to Salcedo, Endorsement, Bexar Archives, reel 3, frame 130; *Niles Register*, October 2, 1813; Arredondo to Elizondo, June 19, 21, and 28, 1813, AGNM, Historia, Tom. 4, transcripts 2Q194, No. 423.

14. Arredondo to Elizondo, June 19, 21, and 28, 1813, AGNM, Historia, Tom. 4, transcripts 2Q194, No. 423.
15. Walker, "McLane's Narrative," *SWHQ*, LXVI, 472.
16. Arredondo to Elizondo, June 19, 21, and 28, 1813, AGNM, Historia, Tom. 4, transcripts 2Q194, No. 423.
17. Garrett, "Dr. John Sibley and the Louisiana-Texas Frontier, 1803-1814," *SWHQ*, XLIX, 427-429.
18. *Niles Register*, October 2, 1813.
19. Garrett, dissertation, p. 399n; Garza, *Dos Hermanos Héroes*, pp. 59-60.

Chapter 5 — Shaler Switches Commanders

1. Commission Issued to General D. José Álvarez Toledo, Cádiz, July 14, 1811, included in Copias de los Papeles dirigidor por el Traidor Toledo desde la Nueva Orleans a las Cabecillas que componen la Junta de Rebeldes de N. España, AGI, Indiferente General de Nueva España, 136-7-9, transcripts 2Q162, No. 170; Bullard, Book Review, *North American Review*, XLIII, 238.
2. Garrett, *Green Flag over Texas*, p. 218.
3. *Ibid.*
4. Bullard to Shaler, June 27, 1813, and Jas. B. Wilkinson to Shaler, June 27, 1813, in Shaler Papers.
5. Walker, "McLane's Narrative," *SWHQ*, LXVI, 463.
6. Shaler to Monroe, July 10, 1813, Shaler Papers.
7. *Ibid.*
8. Interim Commission from the Provisional Government of Béxar, August 4, 1813, AGI, Indiferente General de Nueva España, 136-7-9, transcripts 2Q162, No. 170.
9. Anonymous, "Señor Edictor," Spanish translation of a letter appearing in the *Lexington* [Kentucky] *Reporter*, AGI, Indiferente General de Nueva España, 136-7-9, transcripts 2Q162, No. 170.
10. Harry McCorry Henderson, "The Magee-Gutierrez Expedition," *SWHQ*, LV, 55.
11. John Henry Brown, *History of Texas from 1685 to 1892*, I, 61.
12. Yoakum, *History of Texas*, I, 174.
13. Bancroft, *History of the North Mexican States and Texas*, II, 27.
14. Arredondo to Viceroy Calleja, September 13, 1813, AGNM, Historia, Tom. 4, transcripts 2Q194, No. 423.
15. Bullard, Book Review, *North American Review*, XLIII, 240.
16. Jas. B. Wilkinson, "Defeat of the Revolutionary Army Commanded by Toledo, Account of Battle," included with Shaler to Monroe, September 5, 1813, in Shaler Papers (hereafter cited as "Account of Battle, September 5, 1813").
17. Garrett, "Dr. John Sibley and the Louisiana-Texas Frontier, 1803-1814," *SWHQ*, LXIX, 599.
18. *Niles Register*, October 2, 1813; Bullard, Book Review, *North American Review*, XLIII, 240; Walker, "McLane's Narrative," *SWHQ*, LXVI, 474 and 577.

19. José M. Guadiana, Proclamations and Orders to March, AGNM, Historia, Tom. 4, transcripts 2Q194, No. 423.
20. Henry Stuart Foote, *Texas and Texans*, I, 192.

Chapter 6 — Arredondo Probes for Advantage

1. Arredondo to Viceroy Calleja, September 13, 1813, and addendum, September 14, 1813, AGNM, Historia, Tom. 4, transcripts 2Q194, No. 423; Arredondo to Viceroy Apodaca, April 6, 1817, AGNM, Provincia Internas de Oriente, Vol. 104, expediente 2, fojas 22, transcripts 2Q207, No. 492.
2. Anonymous, "Señor Edictor," in the *Lexington Reporter*, n.d., AGI, Indiferente General de Nueva España, transcripts 2Q162, No. 170.
3. George Howden, The Expedition of Father Gaspár de Solís into Texas, 1767–1768, Master's thesis, University of California, Berkeley, 1939, p. 102.
4. *Gaceta del Gobierno de México*, November 5, 1813, AGNM, Historia, Tom. 4, transcripts 2Q194, No. 478, p. 1248.
5. Antonio Menchaca, *Memoirs*, pp. 16–17.
6. Villars, *Lamar Papers*, VI, 152.
7. Gaines, *Lamar Papers*, I, 283–285.
8. Walker, "McLane's Narrative," *SWHQ*, LXVI, 474–475.
9. Arredondo to Viceroy Calleja, Campo del Atascoso, 17 de Agosto de 1813, AGNM, Historia, Tom. 4, transcripts 2Q194, No. 423, p. 105.
10. Howden, The Expedition of Father Gaspár de Solís into Texas, 1767–1768, p. 102.

Chapter 7 — Toledo Moves to Set a Trap

1. Walker, "McLane's Narrative," *SWHQ*, LXVI, 474.
2. Guadiana, Order of March, Quartel Gral. de Béxar, August 13, 1813, AGNM, Historia, Tom. 4, transcripts 2Q194, No. 423, pp. 100–101.
3. Anonymous, "Señor Edictor," in the *Lexington Reporter*, n.d., AGI, Indiferente General de Nueva España, transcripts 2Q162, No. 170.
4. *Ibid.*
5. *Ibid.*
6. *Ibid.*
7. Walker, "McLane's Narrative," *SWHQ*, LXVI, 474–476.
8. Bullard, Book Review, *North American Review*, XLIII, 241.
9. *Ibid.*
10. Menchaca, *Memoirs*, pp. 16–17.
11. Frederick C. Chabot, *Excerpts from the Memorias for the Province of Texas*, pp. 66–67.
12. Bullard, Book Review, *North American Review*, XLIII, 241.
13. Wilkinson, "Account of Battle, September 5, 1813," in Shaler Papers.

14. Bancroft, *History of the North Mexican States and Texas*, II, 27-28.
15. *Ibid.*
16. Hall, *Lamar Papers*, IV, Pt. 1, 280.

Chapter 8 — Discovery, Pursuit, Mutiny

1. Mattie Austin Hatcher, Trans., "Joaquin de Arredondo's Report of the Battle of the Medina, August 18, 1813," *QTSHA*, XI, 223 (hereafter cited as "Arredondo's Report").
2. Walker, "McLane's Narrative," *SWHQ*, LXVI, 475; Anonymous, "Account of an Eye Witness of the Operations since the Arrival of General Toledo at San Antonio . . ." in the *Lexington Reporter*, n.d., AGI, Indiferente General de Nueva España, 136-7-9, transcripts 2Q162, No. 170, pp. 10-11.
3. *Ibid.*
4. *Ibid.*
5. Wilkinson, "Account of Battle, September 5, 1813," in Shaler Papers.
6. Bullard, Book Review, *North American Review*, XLIII, 241.
7. Hatcher, Trans., "Arredondo's Report," *QTSHA*, XI, 223.
8. *Ibid.*, XI, 223-226; Wilkinson, "Account of the Battle, September 5, 1813," in Shaler Papers.
9. Hatcher, Trans., "Arredondo's Report," *QTSHA*, XI, 223-226.
10. Wilkinson, "Account of the Battle, September 5, 1813," in Shaler Papers.
11. *Ibid.*
12. Bullard, Book Review, *North American Review*, XLIII, 241-242.
13. *Tri-Weekly Alamo Express* (San Antonio, Texas), February 20, 1861.
14. Walker, "McLane's Narrative," *SWHQ*, LXVI, 234-235 and 580.
15. Anonymous, "Account of an Eyewitness of the Operations since the Arrival of General Toledo at San Antonio . . ." in the *Lexington Reporter*, n.d., AGI, Indiferente General de Nueva España, 136-7-9, transcripts 2Q162, No. 170, pp. 11-12.
16. Hatcher, Trans., "Arredondo's Report," *QTSHA*, XI, 223-224.
17. *Ibid.*
18. *Ibid.*
19. Walker, "McLane's Narrative," *SWHQ*, LXVI, 475-476.
20. Bullard, Book Review, *North American Review*, XLIII, 241.
21. Anonymous, "Account of an Eye Witness of the Operations since the Arrival of General Toledo at San Antonio . . ." in the *Lexington Reporter*, n.d., AGI, Indiferente General de Nueva España, 136-7-9, transcripts 2Q162, No. 170, pp. 9-10.
22. *Ibid.*
23. Walker, "McLane's Narrative," *SWHQ*, LXVI, 475-476; Guadiana, Orden del Ciudadano General José Álvarez de Toledo al Ciudadano Cor. Henrry [sic] Perez [Perry], Comandante en Gefe de los

Voluntarios..., Quartel Gral. de Béxar, 5 de Agosto de 1813, AGNM, Historia, Tom. 4, transcripts 2Q194, No. 423, pp. 193-195.
    24. Gaines, *Lamar Papers*, I, 283-284.
    25. Menchaca, *Memoirs*, pp. 16-17.

Chapter 9 — Disaster in the Encinal

    1. Yoakum, *History of Texas*, I, 174; Homer S. Thrall, *A Pictorial History of Texas*, p. 120; Bancroft, *History of the North Mexican States and Texas*, II, 29n.
    2. Wilkinson, "Account of the Battle, September 5, 1813," in Shaler Papers.
    3. *Niles Weekly Register*, October 9, 1813.
    4. Garrett, "Dr. John Sibley and the Louisiana-Texas Frontier, 1803-1814," *SWHQ*, XLIX, 599.
    5. Gaines, *Lamar Papers*, I, 283; Walker, "McLane's Narrative," *SWHQ*, LXVI, 476.
    6. Pauline A. Pinckney, *Painting in Texas: The Nineteenth Century*, p. 189.
    7. Lester R. Dillon, Jr., "American Artillery in the Mexican War, 1846-1847," *Military History of Texas and the Southwest*, XI, 25n.
    8. Walker, "McLane's Narrative," *SWHQ*, LXVI, 476-477.
    9. Bancroft, *History of the North Mexican States and Texas*, II, 29n.
    10. Wilkinson, "Account of the Battle, September 5, 1813," in Shaler Papers.
    11. Gaines, *Lamar Papers*, I, 283.
    12. Menchaca, *Memoirs*, pp. 10-11.
    13. John Warren Hunter, "The Battle of the Medina," *Frontier Times*, Vol. 3, No. 3, pp. 9-16. Hunter wrote a series of three articles in his *Frontier Times* publication in October, November, and December, 1925, that purported to be a translation of the "autobiography" on one Carlos Beltran, an American who resided in Béxar, and who participated in the battles of Alazán and Medina. Due to the many differences with other firsthand accounts, Mr. Hunter's articles must be discounted as historical fiction based on accounts by Yoakum and Hatcher. The author's research has found that there is no evidence that any such autobiography ever existed.
    14. Hatcher, Trans., "Arredondo's Report," *QTSHA*, XI, 223-225.
    15. Seb. S. Wilcox, Ed., "Arredondo's Report of the Battle of Medina, Written August 18, 1813, from the Battlefield," *SWHQ*, XLIII, 254-258; "Arredondo's Report to the Viceroy of His Victory in Texas," *Gaceta del Gobierno de México*, November 5, 1813, 1139-1145.
    16. Menchaca, *Memoirs*, p. 17.
    17. Wilkinson, "Account of Battle, September 5, 1813," in Shaler Papers.
    18. *Ibid.*
    19. *Ibid.*; Hatcher, Trans., "Arredondo's Report," *QTSHA*, XI, 223-226.

20. Bullard, Book Review, *North American Review*, XLIII, 242.
21. Walker, "McLane's Narrative," *SWHQ*, LXVI, 476–477.
22. *Ibid.*
23. Bullard, Book Review, *North American Review*, XLIII, 242.
24. Gaines, *Lamar Papers*, I, 283.
25. Chabot, *Texas in 1811*, pp. 28–30.
26. Hunter, "The Battle of the Medina," *Frontier Times*, Vol. 3, No. 3, p. 13.

Chapter 10 — Swift Vengeance

1. Arredondo to Viceroy Calleja, September 13, 1813, AGNM, Historia, Tom. 4, transcripts 2Q194, No. 423, pp. 143–162; Arredondo to Viceroy Apodaca, April 6, 1817, AGI, Provincias Internas de Oriente, Tom. 104, transcripts 207, No. 492, pp. 1–22.
2. Walker, "McLane's Narrative," *SWHQ*, LXVI, 478.
3. Villars, *Lamar Papers*, VI, 153.
4. Anonymous, "Señor Edictor," in the *Lexington Reporter*, n.d., AGI, Indiferente General de Nueva España, transcripts 2Q162, No. 170.
5. Menchaca, *Memoirs*, p. 17.
6. Hatcher, Trans., "Arredondo's Report," *QTSHA*, XI, 227.
7. Menchaca, *Memoirs*, p. 17.
8. Villars, *Lamar Papers*, VI, 153.
9. Hatcher, Trans., "Arredondo's Report," *QTSHA*, XI, 227–228.
10. Villars, *Lamar Papers*, VI, 153; Walker, "McLane's Narrative," *SWHQ*, LXVI, 478.
11. Garrett, *Green Flag over Texas*, pp. 225–226; Villars, *Lamar Papers*, VI, 153–154. See also *Memoirs For the History of the War in Texas*, by Vicente Filisola, Eakin Press, Austin, 1985. W. Woolsey, TR.
12. Almaráz, *Tragic Cavalier*, pp. 171–172.
13. Walker, "McLane's Narrative," *SWHQ*, LXVI, 478; Hatcher, Trans., "Arredondo's Report," *QTSHA*, XI, 227–228.
14. Walker, "McLane's Narrative," *SWHQ*, LXVI, 226; Villars, *Lamar Papers*, VI, 53; Anonymous, "Memoria de las Cosas mas notables que Acaeciron en Béxar el Año 13 mandando el Tirano Arredondo," translated transcript in the Herbert E. Bolton Collection.
15. Elizondo to Arredondo, September 2, 1813, AGNM, Historia, Tom. 4, transcripts 2Q194, No. 423, pp. 182–186.
16. *Ibid.*
17. Anonymous, "Memoria de las Cosas mas notables que Acaeciron en Béxar el Año 13 mandando el Tirano Arredondo," translated transcript in the Herbert E. Bolton Collection; Villars, *Lamar Papers*, VI, 154; John Warren Hunter, "The Battle of Alazan," *Frontier Times*, III, 47; Hatcher, Trans., "Arredondo's Report," *QTSHA*, XI, 231; Shaler to Monroe, September 19, 1813, in Shaler Papers.
18. Shaler to Monroe, September 19, 1813, in Shaler Papers.
19. *National Intelligencer*, August 14, 1819.
20. Shaler to Monroe, September 7, 1813, in Shaler Papers.
21. Elizondo to Arredondo, September 12, 1813, AGNM, Historia, Tom. 4, transcripts 2Q194, No. 423.

22. Anonymous, "Señor Edictor," in the *Lexington Reporter*, n.d., AGI, Indiferente General de Nueva España, transcripts 2Q162, No. 170.
23. Garrett, "Dr. John Sibley and the Louisiana–Texas Frontier, 1803–1814," *SWHQ*, XLIX, 601 and 608; Anonymous, "Memoria de las Cosas mas notables que Acaeciron en Béxar el Año 13 mandande el Tirano Arredondo," translated transcript in the Herbert E. Bolton Collection. For a newly discovered account of Arredondo's activities the reader is referred to a new book, General Vicente Filisola's *Memoirs for the History of the War in Texas*, translated by Wallace Woolsey, and published by Eakin Press, Austin, 1985.

Chapter 11 — The Epilogue

1. *Diccionario Porrúa*, p. 958; Webb and Carroll, Eds., *The Handbook of Texas*, I, 749–750; Gutiérrez de Lara, "Story of a Political Refugee," *The Pacific Monthly*, XXV, 2–3; Garza, *Dos Hermanos Héroes*, pp. 23–25; Jarrett, *Gutiérrez de Lara, Mexican-Texan: The Story of a Creole Hero*, pp. 46–67.
2. Harris Gaylord Warren, "José Álvarez de Toledo's Initiation as a Filibuster, 1811–1813," *Hispanic American Historical Review*, XX, 58–82; Harris Gaylord Warren, "José Álvarez de Toledo's Reconciliation with Spain and Projects for Suppressing Rebellion in the Spanish Colonies," *LHQ*, XXIII, 827–863; Webb and Carroll, Eds., *The Handbook of Texas*, II, 785–786.
3. Toledo to el sr. Presidente de los Estados Unidos de México, February 12, 1815, AGI, Indiferente General de Nueva España, 136-7-9, transcripts 2Q162, No. 170.
4. Henry Stuart Foote, *Texas and the Texans or Advance of the Anglo-Americans to the Southwest*, I, 191n; Warren, *The Sword Was Their Passport: History of American Filibustering in the Mexican Revolution*, pp. 66–68; Webb and Carroll, Eds., *The Handbook of Texas*, II, 364; Fane Downs, "Governor Antonio Martinez and the Defense of Texas from Foreign Invasion, 1817–1822," *Texas Military History*, VII, 27–43; Virginia H. Taylor, *The Letters of Antonio Martinez: Last Spanish Governor of Texas, 1817–1822*, pp. 44.
5. Foote, *Texas and the Texans or Advance of the Anglo-Americans to the Southwest*, I, 186n; Villars, *Lamar Papers*, VI, 145–155; Webb and Carroll, Eds., *The Handbook of Texas*, II, 507; Toledo, "Relación de los oficiales extrangeros ál servicio de la Republica Mexicana q. se han distinguido en las diferentes en la Provincia de Texas," March 14, 1815, AGI, Indiferente General de Nueva España, 136-7-9, transcripts 2Q162, No. 170.
6. Dora J. Bonquois, "The Career of Henry Adams Bullard, Louisiana Jurist, Legislator, and Educator," *LHQ*, XXIII, 999–1106; Everett S. Brown, Ed., "Letters from Louisiana, 1813–1814," *Mississippi Valley Historical Review*, XI, 573–579.
7. Garrett, "Dr. John Sibley of Natchitoches, 1757–1837," *LHQ*, XX, 399–431; Webb and Carroll, Eds., *The Handbook of Texas*, II, 608–609.

8. Webb and Carroll, Eds., *The Handbook of Texas*, II, 596.

9. Autos de Indulto Proclaimed October 10, 1813, at San Fernando de Béxar, *Gaceta del Gobierno de México*, AGNM, Historia, Tom. 4, transcripts 2Q194, No. 478, p. 1248; Webb and Carroll, Eds., *The Handbook of Texas*, I, 467; Haggard, "The Houses of Barr and Davenport," *SWHQ*, XLIX, 66-88; Haggard, "The Neutral Ground between Louisiana and Texas, 1806-1821," *LHQ*, XXVIII, 1001-1128.

10. Walker, "McLane's Narrative," *SWHQ*, LXVI, 234-237.

11. Noah Smithwick, *Evolution of a State*, p. 44.

12. Webb and Carroll, Eds., *The Handbook of Texas*, II, 757.

13. *Ibid.*, I, 659.

14. Richard G. Santos, *Santa Anna's Campaign against Texas, 1835-1836*, pp. 9-11.

15. Marilyn McAdams Sibley, Ed., "Letters from Sam Houston to Albert Sidney Johnston, 1836-1837," *SWHQ*, LXVI, 253-255; It is interesting to note that two of General Johnston's brothers were said to have been in the Medina battle.

16. Toledo, "Relación de los oficiales extrangeros ál servicio de la Republica Mexicana q. se han distinguido en las diferentes en la Provincia de Texas," March 14, 1815, AGI, Indiferente General de Nueva España, 136-7-9, transcripts 2Q162, No. 170; Walker, "McLane's Narrative," *SWHQ*, LXVI, 580-588.

17. Heitman, *Historical Register and Dictionary of the United States Army, 1789-1903*, I, Pt. ii, 683.

18. Anonymous, "Memoria de las Cosas mas notables que Acaeciron en Béxar el Año 13 mandando el Tirano Arredondo," translated transcript in the Herbert E. Bolton Collection; José María Guadiana and others, "Fidelisimos Criollos," Ciudad de San Fernando de Béxar, April 22, 1813, and "Escuchad amados Criollos," n.d., AGNM, Historia, Tom. 4, transcripts 2Q194, No. 423.

19. Arredondo to Elizondo, June 19, 20, and 28, 1813, AGNM, Historia, Tom. 4, transcripts 2Q194, No 423.

20. Toledo, "Relación de los oficiales extrangeros ál servicio de la Republica Mexicana q. se han distinguido en las diferentes en la Provincia de Texas," March 14, 1815, AGI, Indiferente General de Nueva España, 136-7-9, transcripts 2Q162, No. 170.

21. Hatcher, Trans., "Arredondo's Report," *QTSHA*, XI, 220-236.

22. Menchaca, *Memoirs*, p. 38.

23. Ygnacio Pérez to Governor Cristóbal Domínguez, September 10, 1813, Bexar Archives, reel 53, frame 166.

Chapter 12 — Battleground Revisited

1. Webb and Carroll, Eds., *The Handbook of Texas*, II, 169.

2. Eugene C. Barker, *The Life of Stephen F. Austin, Founder of Texas, 1793-1836*, p. 41; cf. Austin maps for 1822, 1829, 1833, and 1835. Austin passed by the battleground on his way to Mexico City in 1822. The author's first interest in the location of the Medina battle-

ground was triggered by an Austin map on display in the Alamo in the 1920s.

3. Hatcher, Trans., "Arredondo's Report," *QTSHA*, XI, 23.

4. "History of El Carmen," Typescript in the files of Our Lady of Mount Carmen Church, Losoya, Texas.

5. *Ibid.*; Order Appointing a War Council to Advise Him Concerning Defense against the Mina Expedition, April —, 1817, AGNM, Historia, transcripts 2Q194, No. 423.

6. "History of El Carmen," transcript.

7. Cf. Virginia H. Taylor, *The Spanish Archives of the General Land Office of Texas* for Spanish and Mexican land grants in Atascosa County; Bexar County Deed and Probate Filings, transcripts prepared by Judge Justin Bowen.

8. Anonymous, "Memoria de las Cosas notables que Acaeciron en Béxar el Año 13 mandando el Tirano Arredondo," translated transcript in the Herbert E. Bolton Collection.

9. *Ibid.*

10. Frederick C. Chabot, *San Antonio and Its Beginnings*, pp. 34, 40–41, and 117–118; Carlos E. Castañeda, Trans. and Ed., *Juan Agustín Morfi, History of Texas, 1673–1779*, p. 39; Fray Juan Agustín Morfi, "History of Texas, 1673–1779," excerpt in *Our Heritage*, publication of the San Antonio Genealogical Society, July 1960.

11. Cf. General Soil Map, Atascosa County, Texas, in *Soil Survey of Atascosa County, Texas,* page following p. 131.

12. Wilcox, Ed., "Report of the Battle of Medina, Written from the Battlefield, August 18, 1813," *SWHQ*, LXIII, 254–258.

13. Arredondo to Viceroy Calleja, forwarding papers left by the rebels, Béxar, September 13 and October 23, 1813, AGNM, Historia, Operaciones de Guerra, Arredondo, 1813–1820, Tom. 4, transcripts

14. Arredondo to Viceroy Apodaca, enclosing copy of September 13, 1813, report to Viceroy Calleja, April 6, 1817, AGNM, Provincia Internas de Oriente, Vol. 104, expediente 2, fojas 22, transcripts 2Q207, No. 492.

15. Cf. Hatcher, Trans., "Arredondo's Report," *QTSHA*, XI, 220–236; Arredondo to Viceroy Calleja, September 13, 1813, and addendum, September 14, 1813, AGNM, Historia, Tom. 4, transcripts 2Q194, No. 423.

16. Arredondo to Consul Felix Trudeau, September ——, 1813, AGNM, Historia, Tom. 4, transcripts 2Q194, No. 423.

17. Toledo, Commission from the Inhabitants of Texas to Organize a New Expedition against the European Spanish Royal Army, September 12, 1813, AGI, Indiferente General de Nueva España, 136–7–9, transcripts 2Q162, No. 170.

18. Toledo, Proclamation to the Troops, Quartel Gral. al Oeste del Río Sabinas, July 4, 1814, AGI, Indiferente General de Nueva España, 136–7–9, transcripts 2Q162, No. 170.

19. *The Western Stock Journal* (Pleasanton, Texas), May 6, 1873.

20. *The Galveston Daily News,* August 19, 1900.

Bibliography

I. PRIMARY SOURCES

A. Unpublished Material

Archival Information

[Anonymous]. "History of El Carmen," Typescript in the files of Our Lady of Mount Carmel Church, Losoya, Texas.

———. "Memoria de las Cosas mas notables que Acaeciron en Béxar el Año 13 mandando el Tirano Arredondo." Translated transcript in the Herbert E. Bolton Collection, Bancroft Library, The University of California, Berkeley.

———. "Señor Edictor." Translation into Spanish of a letter appearing in the *Lexington* [Kentucky] *Reporter*, n.d., forwarded by Toledo, New Orleans, n.d. Archivo General de Indias, Sevilla, Indiferente General de Nueva España, 136-7-9. Transcripts 2Q162, No. 170. The University of Texas Archives, Austin.

Arredondo, Joaquín de. Letters to Lieutenant Colonel Ygnacio Elizondo concerning Elizondo's advance on Béxar and defeat at Alazán, Laredo, June 19, 21, and 28, 1813. Archivo General de la Nación, México, Historia, Operaciones de Guerra, Arredondo, 1813–1820, Tom. 4. Transcripts 2Q194, No. 423. The University of Texas Archives, Austin.

———. Letter to Viceroy Félix Mariá Calleja, Campo del Atascoso, August 17, 1813. Archivo General de la Nación, México, Historia, Operaciones de Guerra, Arredondo, 1813–1820, Tom. 4. Transcripts 2Q194, No. 423. The University of Texas Archives, Austin.

———. Letters to Viceroy Calleja, forwarding papers left by the rebels, Béxar, September 13 and October 23, 1813. Archivo General de la Nación, México, Historia, Operaciones de Guerra, Arredondo, 1813–1820, Tom. 4. Transcripts 2Q194, No. 423. The University of Texas Archives, Austin.

———. Report to Viceroy Calleja, reporting his victory in the Battle of Medina, Béxar, September 13, 1813. Archivo General de la Nación, México, Historia, Operaciones de Guerra, Arredondo, 1813–1820, Tom. 4. Transcripts 2Q194, No. 423. The University of Texas Archives, Austin.

———. Addendum to his September 13, 1813 report to Viceroy Calleja, forwarding letters received from Elizondo, Béxar, September 14, 1813. Archivo General de la Nación, México, Historia, Operaciones de Guerra, Arredondo, 1813–1820, Tom. 4. Transcripts 2Q194, No. 423. The University of Texas Archives, Austin.

———. Letter to Vice Consul Félix Trudeau, Béxar, September ———, 1813. Archivo General de la Nación, México, Historia, Operaciones de Guerra, Arredondo, 1813–1820, Tom. 4. Transcripts 2Q194, No. 423. The University of Texas Archives, Austin.

———. Order appointing a War Council to advise him concerning defense against the Mina Expedition, Monterey, April ———, 1817. Archivo General de la Nación, México, Historia, Operaciones de Guerra, Arredondo, 1813–1820, Tom. 4. Transcripts 2Q194, No. 423. The University of Texas Archives, Austin.

———. Letter to Viceroy Juan Ruíz de Apodaca, enclosing copy of his September 13, 1813 report to Viceroy Calleja, Monterey, April 6, 1817. Archivo General de la Nación, México, Provincias internas de Oriente, Vol. 104, expediente No. 2, fojas 22. Transcripts 2Q207, No. 482. The University of Texas Archives, Austin.

Bexar County. Deed and Probate Filings. Transcripts prepared in 1905 by Judge Justin Bowen. 6 Vols. Privately owned.

Elizondo, Ygnacio. Report to Arredondo, giving an account of his advance to the outskirts of Béxar, Campo de Batella al frente de Béxar, June 18, 1813. Archivo General de la Nación, México, Historia, Operaciones de Guerra, Arredondo, 1813–1820, Tom. 4. Transcripts 2Q194, No. 423. The University of Texas Archives, Austin.

———. Letter to Arredondo, giving an account of his defeat in the battle of Alazán, Quartel Subalterno de Río Grande, June 23, 1813. Archivo General de la Nación, México, Historia, Operaciones de Guerra, Arredondo, 1813–1820, Tom. 4. Transcripts 2Q194, No. 423. The University of Texas Archives, Austin.

———. Report to Arredondo, giving account of his pursuit of the fleeing rebels, Campamento Español en el Puesto de Trinidad, September 2, 1813. Archivo General de la Nación, México, Historia, Operaciones de Guerra, Arredondo, 1813–1820, Tom. 4. Transcripts 2Q194, No. 423. The University of Texas Archives, Austin.

———. Letter to Arredondo, concluding with an account of his having been wounded, Campamento del Ojo de Agua de los Brazos, September 12, 1813. Archivo General de la Nación, México, Historia, Operaciones de Guerra, Arredondo, 1813–1820, Tom. 4. Transcripts 2Q194, No. 423. The University of Texas Archives, Austin.

Guadiana, José María, Ysidro de la Garza, José Manuel Prieto, and others. Proclamation, "Fidelisimos Criollos," Ciudad de San Fernando de Béxar, April 22, 1813. Archivo General de la Nación, México, Historia, Operaciones de Guerra, Arredondo, 1813–1820, Tom. 4. Transcripts 2Q194, No. 423. The University of Texas Archives, Austin.

———. Proclamation, "Escuchad amados Criollos," n.d. Archivo General de la Nación, México, Historia, Operaciones de Guerra, Arredondo, 1813–1820, Tom. 4. Transcripts 2Q194, No. 423. The University of Texas Archives, Austin.

———. Order of March, Quartel Gral. [de Béxar], August 13, 1813. Archivo General de la Nación, México, Historia, Operaciones de Guerra, Arredondo, 1813–1820, Tom. 4. Transcripts 2Q194, No. 423. The University of Texas Archives, Austin.

Indian Office. Letter to Thomas Linnard, December 12, 1812. Letter Book C, June 1812, to April 1816, Indian Office, Department of the Interior Manuscripts, National Archives, Washington, D.C.

Nabarro, Guillermo. Deposition concerning executions of the Governors Manuel Salcedo and Simón de Herrera and other Spanish Officers, Villa de Laredo, April 8, 1813. Archivo General de la Nación, México, Historia, Operaciones de Guerra, Arredondo, 1813–1820, Tom. 3. Transcripts 2Q193, No. 422. The University of Texas Archives, Austin.

Onís, Luís de. Endorsement to Nemesio Salcedo. Bexar Archives. Microfilm reel 53, frame 142. The University of Texas Archives, Austin.

Pérez, Ygnacio. Letters to Governor Cristóbal Domínguez, August 29 to September 10, 1813, from various ranchos. Bexar Archives. Microfilm reel 53, frames 166, 184, 186, and 194. The University of Texas Archives, Austin.

Robinson, Dr. John Hamilton. "Report of His Mission to Spanish Provinces in New Spain, to the Honorable James Monroe, Secretary of State, Washington, D.C., July 26, 1813," in Mexico: Filibustering Expeditions Against the Government of Spain, 1811–1816. State Department Manuscripts. Microfilm Publication T-286. National Archives, Washington, D.C.

Salcedo, Manuel de. Documents concerning American Encroachment into Texas, 1809–1812. Archivo Historico de Defensa Nacional, Mexico City. Transcripts C-B 840 and C-B 660. Herbert E. Bolton Collection, Bancroft Library, University of California, Berkeley.

———. Correspondence on Military Affairs of Texas, 1810–1812. Archivo General de la Nación, México, Historia, Operaciones de Guerra, Salcedo, Manuel. Herbert E. Bolton Collection. Transcripts C-B 840 and C-B 661. Bancroft Library, University of Califorina, Berkeley.

Saldaña, Guillermo. Deposition concerning the Capture of Béxar, Villa de Laredo, April 6, 1813. Archivo General de la Nación, México, Historia, Operaciones de Guerra, Arredondo, 1812–1813, Tom. 3. Transcripts 2Q193, No. 422. The University of Texas Archives, Austin.

Shaler, William. Letters and Enclosures. Special Agents, Vol. 2, folio

20. State Department Manuscripts. Microfilm Publication M-37, reel 2. National Archives, Washington, D.C.

Toledo, José Antonio Álvarez de. Commission from the American Deputies, Cádiz, July 14, 1811, included in "Copias de los Papeles por el Traidor Toledo desde la Nueva Orleans á los Cabecillos que Componen la Junta de Rebeldes de. N. España." Archivo General de Indias, Sevilla, Indiferente General de Nueva España, 136-7-9. Transcripts 2Q162, No. 170. The University of Texas Archives, Austin.

———. Interim Commission from the Provisional Government of Béxar, August 4, 1813, included in "Copias de los Papeles ... Toledo ..." Archivo General de Indias, Sevilla, Indiferente General de Nueva España, 136-7-9. Transcripts 2Q162, No. 170. The University of Texas Archives, Austin.

———. Commission from the Inhabitants of Texas to Organize a New Expedition against the European Spanish Royal Army, Natchitoches, September 12, 1813, included in "Copias de los Papeles ... Toledo ..." Archivo General de Indias, Sevilla, Indiferente General de Nueva España, 136-7-9. Transcripts 2Q162, No. 170. The University of Texas Archives, Austin.

———. Proclamation to the Troops, Quartel Gral. al Oeste del Río Sabinas, July 14, 1814, included in "Copias de los Papeles ... Toledo ..." Archivo General de Indias, Sevilla, Indiferente General de Nueva España, 136-7-9. Transcripts 2Q162, No. 170. The University of Texas Archives, Austin.

———. Relación de los Oficiales Extrangeros ál Servicio de la Republica Mexicana q. se han distinguido en las Diferentes en la Provincia de Texas, New Orleans, March 14, 1815, included in "Copias de los Papeles ... Toledo ..." Archivo General de Indias, Indiferente General de Nueva España, 136-7-9. Transcripts 2Q162, No. 170. The University of Texas Archives, Austin.

———. Letter to *el sr. Presid'te de los Estados Unidos de México*, New Orleans, February 12, 1815, included in "Copias de los Papeles ... Toledo ..." Archivo General de Indias, Sevilla, Indiferente General de Nueva España, 136-7-9. Transcripts 2Q162, No. 170. The University of Texas Archives, Austin.

———. General Order to the Citizen Colonel Henrry [sic] Pérez [Perry] Reorganizing the American Volunteers, Béxar, August 5, 1813. Archivo General de la Nación, México, Historia, Operaciones de Guerra, Arredondo, 1813-1820, Tom. 4. Transcripts 2Q194, No. 423. The University of Texas Archives, Austin.

Vela, Bachiller Feliciano Francisco, Antonio Fuentes, Guadalupe Caso, and others. Deposition concerning the Execution of the Spanish Officers and Installation of a Junta in Béxar, Laredo, April 15, 1813. Archivo General de la Nación, México, Historia, Operaciones de Guerra, Arredondo, 1812-1813, Tom. 3. Transcripts 2Q193, No. 422. The University of Texas Archives, Austin.

Veramendi, Fernando. Appraisal of Articles Confiscated from the

Enemy in the Battle of Alazán, San Fernando de Béxar, June 27, 1813. Bexar Archives. Microfilm reel 53, frame 130. The University of Texas Archives, Austin.

Wilkinson, James Biddle. "Defeat of the Revolutionary Army Commanded by Toledo, Account of Battle," included with Shaler to Monroe, Natchitoches, September 5, 1813. Special Agents, Vol. 2, folio 20. State Department Manuscripts. Microfilm publication M-37, reel 2. National Archives, Washington, D.C.

B. Published Material

Books and Articles

Arredondo, Joaquín de. "Report of the Battle of the Medina, Written August 18, 1813, from the Battlefield." Seb. S. Wilcox, Ed. *Southwestern Historical Quarterly*, XLIII, No. 2 (October 1939), 254–258.

———. "Report of the Battle of the Medina, August 18, 1813." Mattie Austin Hatcher, Trans. *The Quarterly of the Texas State Historical Association*, XI, No. 3 (January 1908), 220–236.

———. "El sr. brigadier D. . . ., comandante general interino de las provincias internas orientales, he remitido al Exmo. sr. virrey . . ." *Gaceta del Gobierno de México*, November 5, 1813, Archivo General de la Nación, México, Historia de Operaciones de Guerra, Arredondo, 1813–1820, Tom. 4, No. 478, 1139–1148.

———. Autos de indulto proclaimed October 10, 1813, at San Fernando de Béxar. *Gaceta del Gobierno de México*, Archivo General de la Nación, México, Historia de Operaciones de Guerra, Arredondo, 1813–1820, Tom. 4, No. 478, 1248.

Austin, Mattie Alice. "The Municipal Government of San Fernando de Bexar, 1730–1800," *The Quarterly of the Texas State Historical Association*, VIII, No. 4 (April 1905), 277–352.

Brown, Everett S., Ed. "Letters from Louisiana, 1813–1814," *Mississippi Valley Historical Review*, XI (January 1925), 573–579.

Bullard, Henry Adams. Book Review. *North American Review*, XLIII (July 1836), 226–243. Republished by AMS Press, Inc., New York, 1965.

Castañeda, Carlos E., Trans. and Ed. *Juan Agustín Morfi, History of Texas, 1673–1779*. 2 Vols. The Quivira Society, Albuquerque, 1935.

———. *Our Catholic Heritage in Texas, 1519–1936*. 7 Vols. Von Boeckmann-Jones Company, Austin, 1936–1958.

Chabot, Frederick C. *San Antonio of the 17th, 18th and 19th Centuries*. The Naylor Printing Company, San Antonio, 1929.

———. *Juan Agustín Morfi, Excerpts from Memorias for the History of the Province of Texas*. The Naylor Printing Company, San Antonio, 1932.

———. *Texas in 1811: The Las Casas and Sambrano Revolutions*. The Yanaguana Society, San Antonio, 1941.

Claiborne, William C. C., Rowland Dunbar, Ed. *Official Letter Books, 1801–1816*. 6 Vols. Jackson, Mississippi, 1917.

Dunbar, Rowland, Ed. *William C. C. Claiborne, Official Letter Books, 1801–1816*. 6 Vols. Jackson, Mississippi, 1917.

Foik, Paul J., Ed., and Peter J. Forrestal, Trans. "The Solís Diary of 1776." Texas Catholic Historical Society, *Preliminary Studies*, Vol. 1, Austin, 1931.

Forrestal, Peter J., Trans., and Paul J. Foik, Ed., "The Solís Diary of 1767." Texas Catholic Historical Society, *Preliminary Studies*, Vol. 1, Austin, 1931.

Gaines, James. "Information Obtained in 1835 from Capt. Gaines (Sabine River)." Charles A. Gulick, Jr. and others, Eds. *The Papers of Mirabeau Buonaparte Lamar*. 6 Vols. Texas State Library, Austin, 1921–1928.

Garrett, Julia Kathryn. "Dr. John Sibley of Natchitoches, 1757–1837," *Louisiana Historical Quarterly*, XX (1927).

———. "The First Constitution of Texas, April 17, 1813," *Southwestern Historical Quarterly*, XL, No. 4 (April 1937), 290–308.

———, Ed. "Dr. John Sibley and the Louisiana-Texas Frontier, 1803–1814," *Southwestern Historical Quarterly*, XLIX, Nos. 3 and 4 (January and April 1946), 399–431 and 599–609.

Gulick, Charles A., Jr., and others, Eds. *The Papers of Mirabeau Buonaparte Lamar*. 6 Vols. Texas State Library, Austin, 1921–1928.

Gutiérrez de Lara, José Bernardo. "Diary of José Bernardo Gutiérrez de Lara, 1811–1812." Elizabeth West, Ed. and Trans. *The American Historical Review*, XXXIV, No. 1 (October 1928), 55–76, and No. 2 (January 1929), 281–294.

———. "J. B. Gutiérrez de Lara to the Mexican Congress, August 1, 1815," Charles A. Gulick and others, Eds., *The Papers of Mirabeau Buonaparte Lamar*. 6 Vols. Texas State Library, Austin, 1921–1928.

Hall, Warren D. C. "The Mexican War of Independence in Texas, 1812–1813 (c. 1850?)." Charles A. Gulick and others, Eds., *The Papers of Mirabeau Buonaparte Lamar*. 6 Vols. Texas State Library, Austin, 1921–1928.

———. "Revolution in Texas, 1812." *Texas Almanac*, 1861, pp. 456–462. (An article prepared from notes furnished by Colonel W. D. C. Hall.)

Hatcher, Mattie Austin, Trans., "Joaquín de Arredondo's Report of the Battle of the Medina, August 18, 1813," *The Quarterly of the Texas State Historical Association*, XI, No. 3 (January 1908), 220–236.

———, Ed. "Diary of a Visit of Inspection of the Texas Missions Made by Fray Gaspar José de Solís, 1767–1768," translated by Margaret Kenney Kress, *Southwestern Historical Quarterly*, XXXV, No. 1 (July 1931), 28–76.

Heitman, Francis B. *Historical Register and Dictionary of the United States Army, 1789–1903*. Government Printing Office, Washington, D.C., 1903.

Lamar, Mirabeau B. *The Papers of Mirabeau Buonaparte Lamar*. Charles A. Gulick and others, Eds. 6 Vols. Texas State Library, Austin, 1921–1928.

Bibliography

Menchaca, Antonio. *Memoirs*. Yanaguana Society Publications, San Antonio, 1937.
Morfi, Fray Juan Agustín. *History of Texas, 1673-1779*. Carlos E. Castañeda, Trans. and Ed. 2 Vols. The Quivira Society, Albuquerque, 1935.
———. *Excerpts from Memorias for the History of the Province of Texas*. Frederick C. Chabot, compiler. The Naylor Printing Company, San Antonio, 1932.
———. "History of Texas, 1673-1779." Excerpt, translator not identified. *Our Heritage*. San Antonio Genealogical Society, San Antonio, July 1960.
Pike, Zebulon Montgomery. *Exploratory Travels through the Western Territories of North America*. Denver Edition, 1889.
Santos, Richard G. "The Quartel de San Fernando de Béxar," *Texana*, V, No. 3 (Fall 1967), 187-202.
———. *Santa Anna's Campaign against Texas, 1835-1836*. Texian Press, Waco, 1968.
Sibley, Marilyn McAdams, Ed. "Letters from Sam Houston to Albert Sidney Johnston, 1836-1837," *Southwestern Historical Quarterly*, LXVI, No. 2 (October 1962), 253-255.
Smithwick, Noah. *Evolution of a State*. Gammel Book Co., Austin, 1900.
Solís, Fray Gaspar José de. "The Solís Diary of 1767," Paul J. Foik, Ed., and Peter J. Forrestal, Trans. *Preliminary Studies*, Vol. 1. Texas Catholic Historical Society, Austin, 1931.
———. "Diary of a Visit of Inspection of the Texas Missions Made by Fray Gaspar José de Solís, 1767-1768." Mattie Austin Hatcher, Ed., and Margaret Kenney Kress, Trans. *Southwestern Historical Quarterly*, XXXV, No. 1 (July 1931), 28-76.
Taylor, Virginia H. *The Spanish Archives of the General Land Office of Texas*. Austin, 1955.
———. *The Letters of Antonio Martínez: Last Spanish Governor of Texas, 1817-1822*. Texas State Library, Austin, 1957.
Villars, John. "Information Derived from John Villars, Native of Kentucky, San Buenaventura, Mexico." Charles A. Gulick, Jr., and others, Eds. *The Papers of Mirabeau Buonaparte Lamar*. 6 Vols. The Texas State Library, Austin, 1921-1928.
Walker, Henry P., Ed., "William McLane's Narrative of the Magee-Gutierrez Expedition, 1812-1813," *Southwestern Historical Quarterly*, LXVI, Nos. 2, 3, and 4 (October 1962; January and April 1963), 234-251, 457-479, 569-588.
West, Elizabeth, Ed. and Trans., "Diary of José Bernardo Gutiérrez de Lara, 1811-1812," *The American Historical Review*, XXXIV, No. 1 (October 1928), 55-75, and No. 2 (January 1929), 281-294.

II. SECONDARY SOURCES

A. Published Material

Books

Almaráz, Félix D., Jr. *Tragic Cavalier: Governor Manuel Salcedo of Texas, 1808-1813.* University of Texas Press, Austin and London, 1971.

Bancroft, Hubert H. *History of the North Mexican States and Texas.* 2 Vols. San Francisco, 1889.

Brown, John Henry. *History of Texas from 1685 to 1892.* 2 Vols. L. E. Daniel, St. Louis, c. 1892. Republished by the Pemberton Press, Austin, 1970.

Carroll, H. Bailey, and Walter Prescott Webb, Eds. *The Handbook of Texas.* 2 Vols. The Texas State Historical Association, Austin, 1952.

Diccionario Porrúa de Historia, Biografía y Geografía de México. Tercero Edicion. Mexico City.

Faulk, Odie B. *The Last Years of Spanish Texas, 1778-1822.* Mouton & Company, The Hague, 1964.

Foote, Henry Stuart. *Texas and the Texans or Advance of the Anglo-Americans to the Southwest.* 2 Vols. Philadelphia, 1841. Republished in facsimile, The Steck Company, Austin, 1935.

Garrett, Julia Kathryn. *Green Flag over Texas: A Story of the Last Years of Spain in Texas.* The Cordova Press, Inc., New York and Dallas, 1939. Reprinted by the Pemberton Press, Austin, 1969.

Garza, Lorenzo de la. Dos Hermanos Héroes. Guerrero, Tamaulipas, México, 1913.

Hatcher, Mattie Austin. *The Opening of Texas to Foreign Settlement, 1801-1821.* University of Texas Press Bulletin No. 2714. University of Texas Press, Austin, 1927.

Jarrett, Rie. *Gutiérrez de Lara, Mexican-Texan: The Story of a Creole Hero.* Creole Texana, Austin, 1949.

Marshall, Thomas Maitland. *A History of the Western Boundary of the Louisiana Purchase.* University of California Press, Berkeley, 1914.

Miquel i Vergés, José Mariá. *Diccionario de Insurgentes.* Editorial Porruá, S.A., México, D.F., 1969.

Pinckney, Pauline A. *Painting in Texas: The Nineteenth Century.* University of Texas Press, Austin, 1967.

Texas Almanac [1858-1873]. Richardson and Company, Galveston, Texas.

Thrall, Homer S. *A Pictorial History of Texas.* N. D. Thompson, St. Louis, 1879.

Warren, Harris Gaylord. *The Sword Was Their Passport: History of American Filibustering in the Mexican Revolution.* Louisiana State University Press, Baton Rouge, 1943.

Webb, Walter Prescott, and H. Bailey Carroll. *The Handbook of Texas.* 2 Vols. The Texas State Historical Association, Austin, 1952.

Weddle, Robert S. *San Juan Bautista: Gateway to Spanish Texas.* University of Texas Press, Austin, 1968.

Yoakum, Henderson K. *History of Texas from Its First Settlement in 1685 to Its Annexation to the United States in 1846.* 2 Vols. J. S. Redfield, New York, 1855. Reprinted in one volume, The Steck Company, Austin, n.d.

Articles

Bonquois, Dora J. "The Career of Henry Adams Bullard, Louisiana Jurist, Legislator, and Educator," *Louisiana Historical Quarterly,* XXIII, No. 4 (October 1940), 999-1106.

Cox, Isaac Joslin. "Monroe and the Early Mexican Revolutionary Agents," *The American Historical Association Annual Report,* 1911, I, 197-215.

Dillon, Lester R., Jr. "American Artillery in the Mexican War, 1846-1847," *Military History of Texas and the Southwest,* XI, No. 1 (1973), 2-29.

Downs, Fane. "Governor Antonio Martinez and the Defense of Texas from Foreign Invasion, 1817-1822," *Texas Military History,* VII, No. 1 (Spring 1968), 27-43.

Gutiérrez de Lara, L. "Story of a Political Refugee," *The Pacific Monthly,* XXV (January 1911), 2.

Haggard, J. Villasana. "The Counter-Revolution of Bexar, 1811," *Southwestern Historical Quarterly,* XLIII, No. 2 (October 1939), 222-235.

———. "The Houses of Barr and Davenport," *Southwestern Historical Quarterly,* XLIX, No. 1 (July 1945), 66-88.

———. "The Neutral Ground between Louisiana and Texas, 1806-1821," *Louisiana Historical Quarterly,* XXVIII, No. 4 (October 1945), 1001-1128.

Henderson, Harry McCorry. "The Magee-Gutierrez Expedition," *Southwestern Historical Quarterly,* LV, No. 1 (July 1951), 43-51.

Hunter, John Warren. "San Antonio's First Great Tragedy," *Frontier Times,* III, No. 1 (October 1925), 41-48.

———. "The Battle of the Alazan," *Frontier Times,* III, No. 2 (November 1925), 41-48.

———. "The Battle of the Medina," *Frontier Times,* III, No. 3 (December 1925), 9-16.

Warren, Harris Gaylord. "José Álvarez de Toledo's Initiation as a Filibuster, 1811-1813," *Hispanic American Historical Review,* XX, No. 1 (February 1940), 58-82.

———. "José Álvarez Toledo's Reconciliation with Spain and Projects for Suppressing Rebellion in the Spanish Colonies," *Louisiana Historical Quarterly,* XXIII, No. 3 (July 1940), 827-863.

III. DISSERTATIONS AND THESES

Garrett, Julia Kathryn. The War of Independence in Texas, 1811–1813. Ph.D. dissertation, Bancroft Library, University of California, Berkeley, 1934.

Howden, George. The Expedition of Father Gaspar José de Solís into Texas, 1767–1768. Master's thesis, Bancroft Library, University of California, Berkeley, 1939.

IV. NEWSPAPERS

Boston Patriot, The. Boston, May 1, 1813. Original copy in the Author's possession.

Democratic Press, The. Philadelphia, June 11, 1813. Original copy in the author's possession.

El Mexicano. Natchitoches, June 19, 1813. Copy found in William Shaler Papers in Special Agents, Vol. 2, folio 20, State Department Manuscripts, National Archives, Washington, D.C.

Gaceta del Gobierno de México. México, D.F., November 5, 1813. Copies for 1811, 1812, and 1813 are found in Archivo General de la Nación, México, Historia, Operaciones de Guerra, Arredondo, 1813–1820, Tom. 4, No. 478.

Galveston Daily News, The. Galveston, August 19, 1900. Clipping in the DRT Alamo Library, San Antonio.

London Morning Chronicle. London, August 19, 1813.

National Intelligencer. Washington, D.C., August 14, 1819.

Niles, H., *The Weekly Register.* Baltimore, September 1812, through October 1813.

Tri-Weekly Alamo Express. San Antonio, February 4, 1861.

Western Stock Journal, The. Pleasanton, Texas, May 6, 1873. Vol. 1, No. 1. Original in The University of Texas Archives, Austin.

V. MAPS

General Land Office Maps. Atascosa, Bexar, and Wilson counties, 1860 to 1896. General Land Office, Austin.

General Soil Map, Atascosa County. Atascosa County Soil & Water Conservation District Office, Pleasanton, Texas.

Stephen F. Austin Maps for 1822, 1829, 1833, 1835, and 1840. Archives, Texas State Library, Austin.

United States Department of Agriculture-ASCS aerial photographs of northern Atascosa and southern Bexar counties. USDA-ASCS Aerial Photography Field Office, Salt Lake City, Utah.

United States Department of Interior, Geological Survey, 7.5 Minute Series (Topographic) Maps. Thelma, Losoya, Poteet, and Pleasanton Quadrangles, 1958.

INDEX

A
Acatita de Baján, 70
Acosta, Sergeant, 110
Adair, General, 14, 40
Adams, John, 5, 59
Adams, the Presidents, 122
Aguayo, 45, 47, 69, 138
Alamo, 125
Alamo Heights, 122
Alazán [See Battle of]
Alazán Creek, 49
Alden, Samuel, 57, 58
Allende, (insurgent chieftan), 48
Allende, Ignacio, 6, 7
Antonio Amador Survey, 136
Antonio, José, 120
Amador, Antonio, 136
Apodaca, Juan Ruiz de, 102, 128
Apodaca, Viceroy, 138
Arispe, Félix, 13
Arocha, [Family], 38, 108, 111
Arocha, Angela, 111
    Francisco, 109, 126
    Josefa, 115, 127
    Tomás de, 61, 81, 126
Arredondo, 34, 47, 48, 49, 53, 54, 62, 63, 64, 65, 70, 71, 72, 73, 74, 75, 77, 78, 80, 81, 83, 86, 87, 88, 89, 90, 91, 92, 95, 96, 97, 101, 102, 103, 104, 105, 107, 108, 109, 110, 113, 115, 120, 122, 123, 126, 127, 128, 130, 134, 135, 139, 140, 141, 142, 146, 148, 151, 152
Arredondo, Joaquín de, 45, 47, 69, 138, 147
Arroyo de La Piedra, 80, 81
Arroyo de Nuncio, 110
Ash, John, 125
Atascosa County, 136, 137, 140, 145, 149, 150, 153
Atascosa Creek, 136, 137, 142, 146, 149
Atascosa [River], 128, 137, 142, 146
Atascoso (Rancho), 70, 71, 74, 88
Aury, Louis-Michel, 120, 121, 123
Austin, Stephen F., 133, 146, 152
Ayish Bayou, 20

B
Baján, 48
Bancroft Library, 137
Bancroft, H. H., 63, 64, 80, 81, 99, 100
Banegas, José Francisco, 13
Barr (House of), 11
Bastrop, Baron de, 48
Battle of Alazán, 52, 53, 55, 77,

193

80, 92, 113, 121
Battle of Béxar, 13
Battle of Medina, [See chapters on battle], 34, 65, 80, 110, 119-153
Battle of New Orleans, 121, 125
Battle of Rosillo, 30, 34, 64
Battle of Salado, 30
Bayou Pierre, 8, 10
Bergara, Anselmo, 21, 22
Berlandier, Jean Louis, 146-147, 148, 149, 152
Béxar, [See also, San Fernando de], 9, 12, 15, 17, 21, 22, 24, 27, 29, 30, 31, 33, 34, 39, 40, 42, 47, 48, 50, 52, 54, 58, 60, 61, 62, 63, 74, 70, 71, 72, 78, 80, 81, 91, 92, 108, 109, 114, 115, 120, 121, 126, 127, 128, 130, 131, 136, 146
Béxar County, 129, 134, 145
Bolivar Point, 120, 121
Bolton Collection, [Bancroft Library], 137
Bolton, Herbert E., 5
Bonita Creek, 74
Boone, Daniel, 130
  Peter, 122, 125, 130
  Mrs., 122
Boston Patriot, 27
"Brannon, Sam," [See Sambrano]
Brazos River, 110, 114, 129, 140
Brown, John Henry, 63, 64
Buckner, Aylette C., 125
Buena Vista, 129
Bullard, 44, 58, 59, 60, 62, 63, 64, 69, 71, 78, 79, 80, 86, 90, 93, 99, 101, 103, 104, 105, 108, 121, 122, 125, 130, 131
Bullard, Henry Adams, 43, 44, 57, 59
Burnet, David G., 123
Burr, Aaron, 14, 16

C
Cádiz,
Calinette [See La Tour]
Calleja del Rey, Félix Maria, 69
Calleja, Félix María, 6, 47, 54
Calleja (the Viceroy), 63, 102, 128, 138
Camacho, Don Manuel, 113, 115
camino que cortaba, 88, 142, 149, 151, 152
Camino Real, 71, 74, 80, 88, 89, 111, 141, 149
Camino Real Crossing, 79
Campo del Atascoso, 70, 71, 74
Campomento Español en el Puesto de Trinidad, 113
Cañada de Caballos, 71
Cañada de Caballos, 151
Cañada Verde, 152
Canales, Antonio, 120, 122
Cañeda de Menchaca, 102, 129
Carondelet, Governor, 13
Casas, Captain, 48
  Juan Bautista de las, 7
Casas Uprising, 6, 88
Cespedes, José María, 72, 88, 142
Chamacuero, 129
Chapa, *Alférez* Manuel, 111, 113
Charcos de las Gallinas, 71
Chihuahua, 6, 23, 27, 40, 47
Claiborne, Governor, [Louisiana], 8, 10, 120
  William C. C., (U.S. Territorial Governor), 11, 41
Coahuila, 31, 48, 123, 128, 136
Cogswell, Nathaniel, 42, 57, 58
Colonie, (*chef de cuisine*), 57
Colorado River, 110, 111
Concepción Mission, 30
Cordero [family], 31
Cordero, Antonio, 4, 8
  Governor, 16, 128
  Mrs., (See Perez), 31

Manuel Antonio, 31, 136
Cortes, (Spanish), 10, 57
Cotton, Godwin B., 57, 121, 125
Coushatta Indians, 28, 29, 50, 63, 64
Creek Indians, 124

D

Darby, William, 114
Davenport (House of), 11
Davenport, Peter Samuel, 11, 16, 20, 24, 25, 122
"Dead Man's Tank,"
Delgado, 27, 33, 34
Delgado, [Family], 34, 38, 108, 111, 127
Delgado, Antonio, 29, 31, 111, 127
Gabino, 22
Despallier, Bernardo Martin, 13, 20, 21, 126
Blaz P., 13
Charles, 13
Domínguez, Cristóbal, 3, 4, 5, 123
Dortolan, Bernardo, 126

E

El Atascoso, 146, 149
El Atascoso Ranch, 71
el camino que cortaba, 88, 142, 149, 151, 152
El Camino Real, [See Camino]
El Carmen, 134, 135, 142
El Carmen Church, 152
El Carmen Crossing, 142
El encinal de Medina, 6, 63, 69, 97, 99, 105, 124, 137, 138, 139, 140, 141
El Guajolote, 146, 149
Elguezábal, Juan José, 123
El Mexicano, 43
El Puente de Calderón, 69
El Puesto de Salado, 49, 50
Elizondo, 48, 49, 50, 51, 53, 54, 55, 59, 64, 70, 71, 78, 81, 86, 88, 89, 91, 92, 99, 108, 109, 110, 111, 113, 114, 115, 127, 128, 129, 141, 142, 148, 151, 152
Elizondo, Ygnacio, 47, 72, 87, 114, 137
Elosua, Antonio, 102, 123
Encinal de Medina, [See particularly 119–153]
Escandón, José de, 6
Espada Mission, 88
Espada Mission Ranch, 82
Eufaula-Patilo-Nueces Association, 138
Eustis, (Secretary of War), 9

F

Flores, Antonio, 20
Flournoy, General, 41
Foote, ———, 64
Forsythe, 121
Forsythe, Samuel, 61, 125
Fort Claiborne, 11, 14, 16
Fox, Anne, 129
Frio River, [See Rio Frio]

G

Gachupiń Revolt, 45
Gaines, Edmund P., 28
James, 8, 9, 19, 22, 28, 33, 34, 64, 73, 80, 94, 99, 101, 104, 108, 123, 125
Gallinas Creek, 82, 89, 92, 136, 137, 141, 142
Galvan Creek, 90, 92, 101, 136, 141, 142, 143, 145, 146, 149, 151, 152, 153
Galvan, John, ["John Galbán"], 127, 128
Galván, Juan, 13, 24, 130
Galveston Daily News, 140
Galveston Island, 120, 121, 123
Garcia, Luciana, 123
Garrett, 24
Garrett, Dr., 39, 52
Julia Kathryn, 10, 48
Garza Ranch, 75, 79, 88, 89, 142
Garza Ranch Crossing, 88, 142
Garza Ranch Ford, 87, 142
Garza, Ysidro de la, 21, 114

Gerard, M., 42, 43
Goliad, 125
Goose Creek, 74
Graham, John, 9
Grande, Luis, 21, 22
　María Cándida, [Despallier], 13, 21
Guadiana's (order of march), 81
Guadiana, José María, 28, 77, 126
Guajolote (now Turkey Creek), 146, 149
Guillén, Cabo Ermenegildo, 3, 4, 5, 9, 13, 17
Gutiérrez-Magee Expedition, 6, 81, 121, 122, 126, 130
Gutiérrez de Lara Family, 12, 47, 55, 108
Gutiérrez de Lara, Bernardo, 4, 6, 7, 8, 9, 10, 11, 12, 13, 14, 15, 17, 20, 21, 23, 24, 25, 27, 28, 29, 30, 31, 34, 38, 39, 40, 42, 43, 47, 48, 49, 50, 53, 54, 55, 58, 59, 60, 61, 62, 70, 119, 120, 121, 122, 125, 126, 127, 130, 131, 147
　Don José, (the priest), 12, 13
　brothers, 120
Gutierrez, [Mrs. Bernardo], 55

H

Hall, Warren D. C., 25, 27, 34, 38, 81, 123, 125
Hatcher, Mattie Austin, 138, 139
Havana, 10, 122
Henderson, Harry McCorry, 63
Herrera, Colonel, 100
　Governor, 23, 25, 27, 29, 30, 31, 33, 47, 110
　Simón de, 4, 7, 30, 33, 47
Hidalgo, 6, 7, 10, 45, 48
Hidalgo, y Costilla, Miguél, 5
Hidalgo, Father, 61, 69, 130
Hildalgo Revolt, 45
Holmes, Captain, 27

House of Barr and Davenport, 11
Houston, Sam, 123, 124, 125
Huaxteca, 45
Hunter, (writer), 31, 109, 113

I

Iturbide, 5, 130
Iturbide, Agustiń de, 119, 120

J

Jackson, Andy, [President Andrew], 119
Jaggy, George, 149
Jaraname, [Aranama] Indians, 111
Jiménez, (insurgent chieftain), 48
Jiménez, Mariano, 6, 7
Johnston, Albert Sidney, 125
Johnston brothers, 125
Jourdanton, 74
Juanicotena, Juan Fermín de, 69, 102, 107, 138
Junto de Gobierno, 38

K

Karnes County, 129
Kemper, 34
Kemper, Nathan, 20
　Reuben, 20
　Samuel, 20, 28, 30, 33, 37, 38, 39, 40, 89, 92, 94, 103, 108, 121, 125, 130
Kennedy, Capt[ain], 52
Korus, Alfred, 150, 151
　Gertrude, 149
　Jerome, 149, 150
　Virginia, 150

L

La Bahía, 15, 21, 23, 24, 25, 27, 28, 31, 58, 71, 101, 110, 111, 121, 127, 131, 152
la Garita, 78, 81
Laguna de la Espada, 72, 80
La Laguna de las Animas, 19
La Loma del San Cristóbal, 147,

Index

148, 149
Lamar, Mirabeau B., 73, 113
La Parita, 74, 146, 149
La Peña, 53
Laredo, 69, 70, 71, 146, 151
Laredo Ford, [See Laredo Road]
Laredo Road, 72, 108, 136, 141, 142, 143, 146, 149, 151, 152
Laredo Trail, 142
las Yslitas Ranches, 129
La Tour, [Callinette], 57
Leal, [Family], 108, 113, 127
Leming, 153
Leon, 49
Leon Creek, 79, 142
Lexington Reporter, 78, 79, 85, 91, 93
Linares, 70
Linnard, Thomas, 15
Lipan Apaches, 64
Lipan Indians, 28, 29, 147
Long Expedition, 120
Long, James, 120, 122
 Jane, 120
López, *Alférez* Francisco, 83, 86, 87
Losoya, 134, 142
Losoya Creek, 108, 134
Louisiana Territory (purchase), 5, 9, 41
Louisiana-Texas Frontier, 12, 39, 114, 131
Louisiana State Historical Society, 122

M

Madison Battalion, 94
Madison, President James, 5, 6, 10, 121, 129
Magee, 39, 121, 130, 131
 Augustus William, 6, 12, 15, 16, 17, 22, 23, 25, 28
Magee-Gutiérrez Expedition, 6, 122
Maíz, 45
Mahula, Tom, 151

Curtis M., 151
Martinez, Antonio, 119
Massiot, Louis, 42, 52, 58
Matagorda Bay, 8, 43, 121
McArdle, Henry, 100
McFarland, Captain, 24, 29, 77
 John, 28, 49, 50
McKim, 53
McLane, 29, 31, 34, 38, 49, 50, 52, 53, 54, 60, 64, 71, 73, 77, 79, 83, 85, 87, 90, 92, 93, 99, 100, 101, 103, 104, 108, 109, 110, 125, 126
McLane, William, 23, 25, 28, 81, 122
McMullen County
Medina, 73, 119-153
Medina River, 65, 87, 88, 93, 97, 102, 108, 129, 133, 134, 135, 138, 139, 140, 142, 145, 146, 147, 148, 150
Menchaca Creek, 129, 143
Menchaca, 17, 27, 38, 60, 63, 70, 78, 80, 81, 89, 93, 96, 101, 102, 105, 108, 109
 Antonio, 72, 73, 79, 95, 96, 102, 129
 José Felix, 4, 8, 9, 21, 62
 Miguél, 21, 29, 30, 50, 51, 59, 62, 92, 94, 95, 126, 129, 130, 131
Mexican War, 100
Miér y Terán Expedition of 1828, 148
Miguél, Lieutenant, 8
Military Plaza, 31
Mina, 121
Mina Expedition, 120, 139
Mississippi District, 41
Monclova, 7
Monroe, Secretary of State James, 6, 9, 10, 12, 14, 15, 22, 23, 39, 40, 42, 43, 53, 60, 61, 114, 126
Monterrey, 63, 73, 109, 115, 122
Montero, Bernardo, 11, 19, 20, 21

Montura, Colonel, 29
Morelos, 5
Morfi, Fray Agustín, 80, 137, 151
Mower, Aaron, 57
Murray, William B., 121
Musquis [See Musquiz]
Musquiz, [Miguél, or Miguél Eca y], 104, 105, 126
Ramon, 104

N

Nacogdoches, 3, 4, 11, 15, 16, 19, 20, 24, 28, 40, 42, 57, 60, 108, 111, 113, 114, 121
Napoleon, 5, 15, 133
Nashville, 122
Natchez, 57
Natchitoches, 3, 8, 9, 11, 12, 13, 14, 15, 17, 25, 38, 40, 42, 54, 55, 57, 58, 59, 61, 99, 114, 120, 126, 131, 139
National Intelligencer, 34, 114
Navarro, José Antonio, 33, 34, 113, 126, 150
Sanchez, 47
Neutral Ground, 3, 6, 8, 12, 14, 15, 16, 17, 22, 28, 33, 62, 120, 125
New Orleans, 16, 119
Niles Register, 33, 38, 63, 99
Noah, Samuel, 125
Nolan, Philip, 16, 105
North American Review, 78
Nueces River, 151, 152
Nuevo Coahuila, 7
Nuevo Galicia, 47
Nuevo Leon, 7, 30, 33, 47
Nuevo Santander, 4, 6, 7, 13, 45, 47, 69
Nuevo Santander Militia, 128

O

Onis, Luis de, 40, 42, 121
Orleans Territory, 8
Orr, George, 125

Our Lady of Mount Carmel Church, 134
Overton, General, 9

P

Paillette, (French agent), 40, 43
Parita Creek, 74
Parita Hill, 74
paso de Borregas
Paso de las ormigas, 9
paso del Salto, 111
Paso Tranquitas, 136, 142
Pellicer, Bishop, 135
Peña Crossing, 152
Pérez Crossing, 75, 136
Pérez Ranch, 79
Pérez, Gertrudis, [See Cordero], 31
José Ygnacio, 123, 136
Ygnacio, 72, 121, 128, 136
Perry, Henry, 51, 52, 59, 62, 63, 70, 78, 81, 89, 103, 108, 119, 121, 123, 125
Oliver H., 51
Philadelphia Democratic Press, 34
Picornel, Juan Mariano, 57, 58, 121, 125
Pike, Zebulon, 22, 23, 33
Pinker, Jacob, 151
Plan de Iguala, 119
Plaza de las Armas, 7
Pleasanton, 128, 140, 141, 142, 149
Poth-Wilco-Floresville Association, 138
Poteet, 74
Prado, Pedro, 31, 126
Presidio del Rio Grande, 47, 49, 53, 151
Presidio La Bahiá, [See La Bahiá]
Presidio Road, [Lower], 135, 141, 142, 149, 152
Presidio San Juan Bautista, 152

Index

Provincias Internas de Oriente, 120
Puesto del Salado, 127

Q

Quartzberg, California, 123
¿Quién Sabe? tree, 149
Quinta, the, 110, 115
Quintero, Cayetano, 115
Quirk, Edmund, 20

R

Ranchería, 147, 149
Rancherías, 70, 71, 148
Rancho del Atascoso, 149
Rancho de Bemen, 113
Rayón, Ignacio López, 13
Red River Region, 8
Red River, 8
Revere, Paul, 5
Revilla, 4, 47, 55, 120
Río Frío, 48
Rio Grande, 4, 37, 105, 122
Rio Grande Road, [Lower], 135
Rio Grande Valley, 22
Rio de las Sabinas, 3
Robinson, John Hamilton, 22, 23, 24, 27, 34, 40, 41, 43, 47, 120
Rodeo de la Espada, 79, 80, 82, 89, 94, 141
Rodriguez, *Alférez* Fernando, 111
  Mariano, 61
Rollins, Charley, 28
Ross, Reuben, 20, 25, 27, 28, 29, 39, 43, 50, 51, 121, 125, 130
  Reuben (nephew of above), 121
Ruíz, Francisco, 31, 59, 126
Rutledge Hollow, 74

S

Sabine District, 123
Sabine River, 28, 115, 121, 130, 131
Salado Creek, 29
Salcedo, 23, 24, 25, 27, 31, 37
Salcedo, Governor, 11, 13, 15, 17, 23, 29, 30, 47, 110, 111
  Manuel Maria de, 7, 8, 33
  Nemesio Salcedo y, 9, 13, 22, 23, 25, 33, 40, 42, 43, 47
Salitre Prairie, 20
Salt Branch, 74
Sambrano, Don José Dario, 110
Sambrano, Juan Manuel, 7, 17, 19, 20, 21, 30, 88, 89, 90, 91, 92, 99, 110, 142
San Antonio, 64, 71, 78, 79, 108, 123, 128, 146, 150
San Antonio Ledger, 34, 150
San Antonio de Valero, 8
San Augustine, 20
Sanchez, José Mariá, 148
San Fernando, Cathedral, 110
San Fernando, Coahuila, 122
San Fernando de Béxar, 4, 6, 7, 19, 37, 38, 41, 49, 59, 77, 107, 115
San Ildefonso, (Treaty), 5
San Jacinto, 124, 125
San José Mission, 120, 149
San Juan Bautista, 49
San Luís Potosí, 45, 47, 123
San Marcos, 12
San Marcos River, 115
San Miguel, 146, 149
Santa Anna, Antonio López de, 100, 123, 124
Santiago, 120
Saucedo, Tomás, 111, 127
Sava, Juan, 27, 29
Schwarz, Ted, 145, 146, 151, 152, 153
Scott, Captain, 24
Sedella, "Pere Antoine," 121
Seguin Road, 129
Seguin, Erasmo, 129
Senobio, *Padre*, 113
Serrano, Miguél, 114
Sesma, Ramirez, 123
Shaler, 28, 31, 34, 37, 41, 42, 43,

44, 48, 54, 57, 58, 61, 62, 69, 100, 114, 130, 131
Shaler, William, 9, 10, 11, 12, 14, 15, 16, 22, 23, 25, 40, 53, 59, 60, 122
Sibley, Dr., 11, 12, 14, 15, 16, 34, 37, 40, 41, 52, 53, 54, 60, 62, 63
John, 8, 40, 99, 100, 121
Slocum, William, 59, 121
Solís, Fray, 71, 74
Padre, 151
Sotelo grant, 128
Sotelo, Alfred, 149
Mateo, 128
Spanish Cortes, 10
Stuart Lake, 142

T

Tamaulipas, 120
Tampico, 54
Taylor, 63, 85, 103, 108
Taylor, Josiah, 30, 78, 121
Tessman Road, 149
Texas Declaration of Independence, 123
Thrall, 97
Tilden, 71
Toledo, General, 59, 60, 61, 62, 72, 75, 77, 78, 79, 80, 81, 82, 83, 85, 86, 89, 92, 93, 94, 95, 99, 100, 101, 103, 108, 111, 114, 119
Toledo, José Alvarez de, 6, 10, 34, 39, 40, 42, 43, 54, 57, 58, 59, 63, 65, 69, 120, 121, 122, 125, 126, 129, 130, 133, 139, 140, 141, 142, 143, 146, 147
Tonkawa Indians, 28, 29, 64
Travieso, Vicente, 126
Treaty of San Ildefonso, 5
Trespalacios, Mexican Governor, 73, 129, 134, 148, 149, 150
Treviño, Pedro, 115, 127
Trinidad, 20, 21, 22, 23, 28, 111

Trinity River, 22, 110, 111, 114, 126, 129
Tri-Weekly Alamo Express, (San Antonio), 90, 91
Trudeau, Felix, 139
Turkey Creek, 74, 149

U

Ugartechea, Domingo

V

Veracruz, 45, 54
Veramendi, Fernando, 126
Juan Martin, 126
Villa de Carmen, 135
Villa de Laredo, 71
Villa of San Fernando, 108
Villa Trinidad, 13
Villars, 52, 53, 64
John, 19, 20, 24, 25, 27, 29, 73, 80, 93, 108, 109, 110, 111, 119, 121, 122, 125

W

Washington City, 122
Washington, George, 33, 59
Wells of Baján, 6
Western Stock Journal, 140
Weynand [Family], 151
Weynand, Arthur, 151
Wilkinson, 87, 89, 90, 93, 99, 101, 103, 108, 121, 125, 126
General, 33, 44, 59, 60, 63, 64, 78, 80, 85, 89, 90, 102, 105, 120, 125
James Biddle, 4, 16, 44, 58, 60, 126
Joseph Biddle, 126
Wilson County, 129
Witte Memorial Museum, 129, 130
Woll, Adrian, 123
Wollestonecraft, Captain, 16, 17

Y
Yoakum, 23, 24, 63, 73, 81, 97, 99, 100, 109, 113

Z
Zacatecas, 7
Zambrano, [See Sambrano]

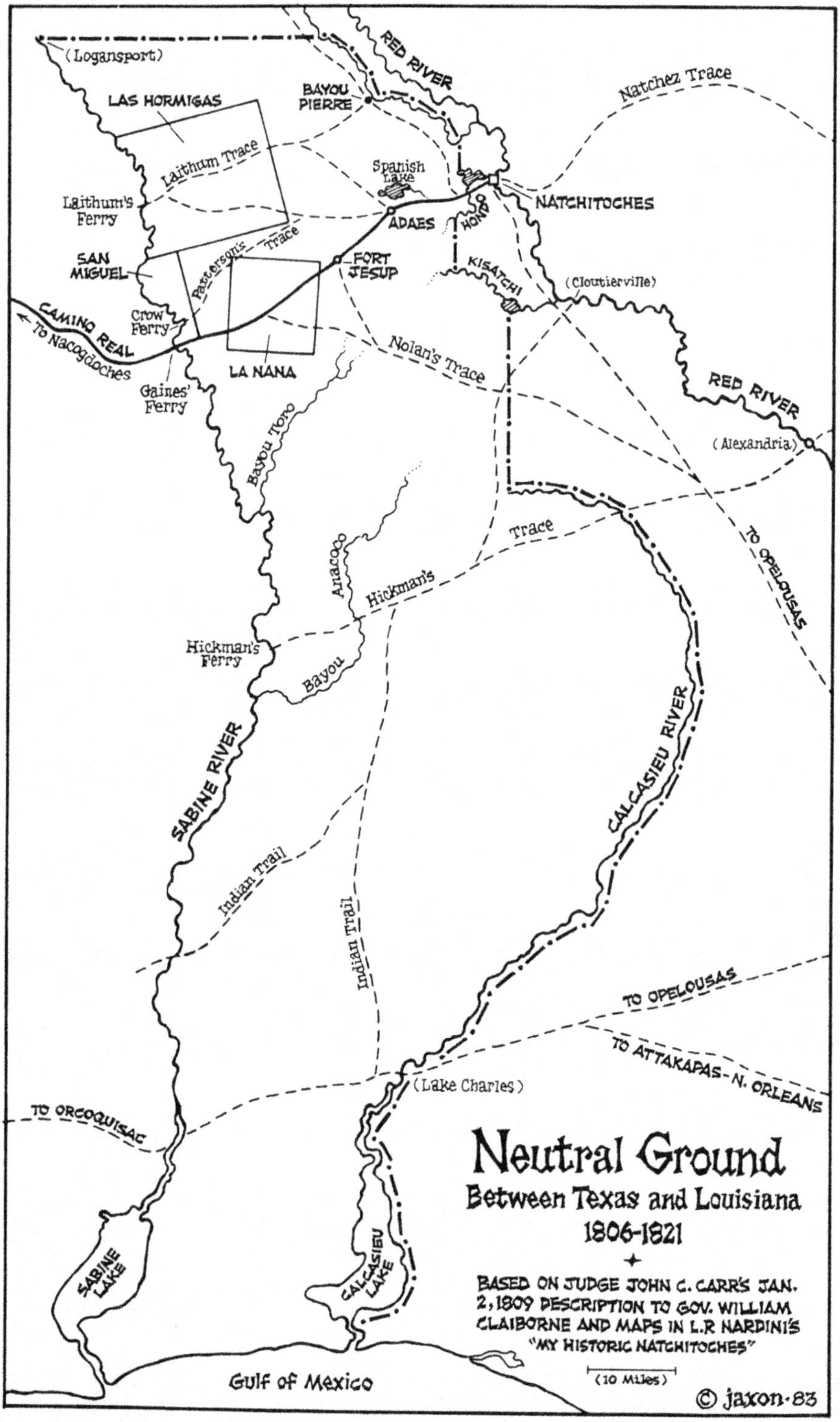

(Logansport)
RED RIVER
Natchez Trace
BAYOU PIERRE
LAS HORMIGAS
Laithum Trace
Spanish Lake
NATCHITOCHES
Laithum's Ferry
ADAES
HONDO
SAN MIGUEL
Patterson's Trace
FORT JESUP
KISATCHI
(Cloutierville)
CAMINO REAL
To Nacogdoches
Crow Ferry
Nolan's Trace
LA NANA
Gaines' Ferry
RED RIVER
(Alexandria)
Bayou Toro
Trace
Anacoco
Hickman's
TO OPELOUSAS
Hickman's Ferry
Bayou
CALCASIEU RIVER
SABINE RIVER
Indian Trail
Indian Trail
TO OPELOUSAS
TO ATTAKAPAS-N. ORLEANS
(Lake Charles)
TO ORCOQUISAC
Neutral Ground
Between Texas and Louisiana
1806-1821
BASED ON JUDGE JOHN C. CARR'S JAN. 2, 1809 DESCRIPTION TO GOV. WILLIAM CLAIBORNE AND MAPS IN L.R NARDINI'S "MY HISTORIC NATCHITOCHES"
SABINE LAKE
CALCASIEU LAKE
(10 Miles)
Gulf of Mexico
© jaxon-83